SOUTH INDIAN FEUDATORY DYNASTIES

SOUTH INDIAN FEUDATORY DYNASTIES

VENKATESHA

Foreword

K.V. RAMESH

SHARADA

Sharada Publishing House
DELHI-110 035
2000

First Published : 2000

ISBN : 81-85616-62-0

Published by :
B.L. Bansal
SHARADA PUBLISHING HOUSE
(Publishers on India's Past & Present)
40, Anand Nagar, Inderlok,
Delhi - 110035. Tel. : 5117390

Laser Typesetting by :
Sri Balaji Computers
4615/13, Tri Nagar, Delhi-35
Ph. : 7108270

Printed at :
Santosh Offset
Delhi-110 035

To

my beloved Professor

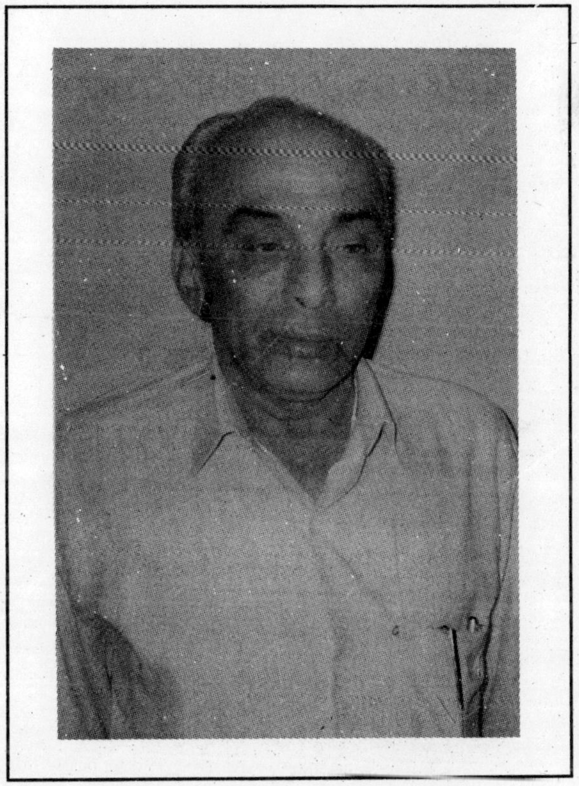

Dr. B.K. Gururaja Rao. M.A., Ph..D.

CONTENTS

FOREWORD

Dr. Venkatesha's *South Indian Feudatory Dynasties* (5th Century A.D. to 1336 A.D.) is a welcome addition to the growing research writings on the political history of the lesser Indian dynasties. In compiling this well-documented work the scholar has not spared any effort and has thoroughly studied and analysed the contents of nearly six hundred and fifty stone and copper plate inscriptions which form the bulk of the available historical source material for this period. Taking help and guidance from earlier research works on the subject and, more importantly, basing his conclusions on more recent epigraphical discoveries, Dr. Venkatesha has effected noticeable improvements in our understanding of the history of over a dozen minor ruling families of pre-Vijayanagara Karnataka in particular and South India in general.

This type of micro-study is an important prerequisite for the fuller understanding of Karnataka's political history. A large number of inscriptions bear witness to the fact that the imperial houses of Karnataka heavily depended upon their hereditary subordinates for their own stability both in times of war and peace. As the present author himself rightly observes "it may not be an exaggeration to say that these feudatory powers as the back bone for the easy and smooth running of the administration and also for the realisation of the cherished ambitions of their overlords."

While it is true that the history of the minor dynasties of Karnataka had been engaging the attention of researchers and historians right from the days of John Faithful Fleet, the present work by Dr. Venkatesha makes use of numerous new epigraphs discovered as recently as until about a decade and a half ago and has thus updated our knowledge on the rulers belonging to these minor ruling houses and their dealings with their imperial overlords.

I have, therefore, great pleasure in commending this work to the world of scholars and students alike.

K.V. Ramesh
Jt. Director General (Retd.) and
Formerly Director (Epigraphy)
Archaeological Survey of India.

Mysore
25-08-1998

PREFACE

The writers of Indian History, from the beginning, have been concentrating on the study of the major ruling dynasties of the country and the contributions of the smaller ruling families are either ignored or summarily disposed off. But this practice has resulted in the distortion or imbalance of the contributions of regional units to the socio-cultural milieu of the country, though this imbalance may not be so obvious in the case of political and administrative arrangements. Hence of late, the historians, having released this lacunae, have changed their approach from macro-to micro level studies. Each region has its way of looking at the daily life of the people, their religious customs, food habits, dress or ornamentation which can be vividly understood by the study of the records regionally. Taking the history of Karnataka itself, for instance we notice considerable variations in beliefs and customs, food habits, dress and ornamentation etc., in Southern Karnataka (Mysore Country or Kaveri basin) from that of Northern regions (Dharwad-Bijapur or the Krishna basin).

Having understood this important fact, recent historians have undertaken the detailed studies of minor or regional dynasties and their contributions for understanding the comprehensive history of Karnataka. Notable among these workers, mention may be made of Dinakara Desai (1951) Govinda swamy (1965), V. Balambal (1978) and B.R. Gopal (1982). While these writers have taken up in depth studies of some individual or local dynasties, B.R. Gopal has attempted to study some of the more important of the feudetory states in Karnataka in his work.But he has not covered all the dynasties in his study. Hence this attempt is made to provide a comprehensive picture as far as possible of all the minor dynasties of Karnatak, during the medieval period. It is important to note that the minor dynasties and their rulers have played a notable role in nation building activities, upliftment of the social institutions in general and, cultural development.

In this task of reconstructing the history of the country, sources, throwing light on the material culture, and socio-religious beliefs, and pratices form the contemporary sources are to be used in a scientific way. Among such sources, epigraphs plays a significant part. No doubt numismatics, archeological remains and literary works could also suppliments these reliable epigraphical accounts.

The present work is the revised version of my doctroal thesis submitted to the faculty of Ancient History and Archaeology of the Mysore University. Mysore Unviersity accepted the thesis and awarded the Degree of Doctor of Philosophy for the same.The Unviersity further permitted me to publish the same, for which act of kindness, I am greatful to the authorities of the Unviersity.

I conducted my research leading to the Ph.D., under the guidance of Dr. B.K. Gururaja Rao, formerly professor in the Department of Ancient History and Archaeology of Mysore University. He helped at every state of my research with great care.I am indebted to him.

In the initial stages of my research Dr. A.V. Narasimaha Murthy, the then professor of Ancient History and Archaeology in the Mysore Universiry supervised my research work for which I am thankful to him.

Dr. K.V. Ramesh now Retired Joint Director General of Archaeology, Archaeological survey of India, Government of India, was the Director of Epigraphy at that time, not only permitted me to consult the epigraphical collections in the Department and the library of the Directorate but also encouraged me throughout my research. Further he has been kind enough to contribute the foreword to this book. I thank him heartily for all his kindness.

I remember the help of Shri. M.N. Katti, Dr. C.R. Srinivasan, Dr. T.S.Ravishankar and Smt. G. Savatri, of the Driectorate, Archaeological Survey of India, Mysore.

I also sincerely acknowledge with thanks the help received from Dr. S.H. Ritti Professor of Ancient Hostory and Epigraphy of Karnataka University and G.S. Mailari Rao, Professor of English, Mysore University (both now retired). My senior college Dr. S. S. Subramonia Iyer, Retired Deputy Superintending Epigraphist, and Dr. K. M. Bhadri, Superintending Epigraphist, ASI, Mysore, those who have taken much pains to correct the proofs. I am indebted to them.

I will be failing in my duty if I do not duly record my grateful thanks to Dr. L. N. Swamy, Lecturer in JSS. Frist Grade College, Mysore, for preparing the manuscript for the press and the keen interest he has taken in seeing the book come out in the present form.

Venkatesha

ABBREVIATIONS

Book, Journals, etc.

ARIE.	Annual Report on Indian Epigraphy
ARSIE.	Annual Report on South Indian Epigraphy
CTA.	Chittoor Through the Ages
COK.	Coins of Karnataka
Coorg Ins.	Coorg Inscriptions
CII.	Corpus Inscriptionum Indicarum
Culture.	Some Contributions of South India to Indian Culture
DKD.	Dynasties of Kanarese Districts
E. C.	Epigraphia Carnatica
E. I. Or Ep. Ind.	Epigraphia Indica
FOSI.	Feudatories of South India
HAS.	Hyderabad Archaeological Series
HISI.	Historical Inscriptions of Southern India (Sewell's List)
HOSI	History of South India
IA.	Indian Antiquary
IHQ.	Indian Historical Quarterly
IMP.	Inscriptions from Madras Presidency
JBBRAS.	The Journal of the Bombay Branch of the Royal Asiatic Society
JESI.	The Journal of the Epigraphical Society of India
JIH.	Journal of Indian History

JOR.	Journal of Oriental Research
KI.	Karnataka Inscriptions
KTA	Karnataka Through the Ages
KUJ.	Karnataka University Journal
MAR.	Mysore Archaeological Reports
MDSIK.	Minor Dynasties of South India : Karnataka
MUCK.	Mahamandalesvaras under the Chalukyas of Kalyani
Mys. Ins.	Mysore Inscriptions
MCI.	Mysore and Coorg from Inscriptions
Mys. Gaz.	Mysore Gazetteer
QJMS.	Quarterly Journal of the Mythic Society
SII.	South Indian Inscriptions
Select Ins.	Select Inscriptions
SIHI	Studies in Indian History and Culture

Place Names

Ag.	Arkalgud
Ak.	Arsikere
Bg.	Bagepalli
Bl.	Belur
Bp.	Bowringpet
Cb.	Chik-Ballapur
Cd.	Chiteldroog
Cg.	Coorg
Ch.	Chamarajanagar
Ck.	Chikkanayakanahalli
Cl.	Chellakere
Ci.	Channagiri
Cm.	Chikmagalur
Cn.	Channarayapatna

Ct.	Cintamani
Dg.	Davanagere
Gb	Gubbi
Gd.	Goribidanur
Gu.	Gundlupet
Hg.	Heggadadevankote
Hk.	Holalkere
HN.	Hole Narsipur
Hn.	Hassan
Hs.	Hunsur
Jl.	Jegalur
Kd.	Kadur
Kg.	Kunigal
Kl.	Kolar
Kp.	Koppa
Kmi.	Kumsi
Kr. or Kp.	Krishnarajpet
Md.	Mandya
Mg.	Mudgere
Mb.	Mulbagal
Mj.	Manjarabad
Mk.	Molakalmuru
Ml.	Malavalli
Mr.	Malur
My.	Mysore
Ng.	Nagamangala
Nj.	Nanjangud
Nr.	Nagar
Pg.	Pavagada

Sa.	Sagara
Sb.	Sorab
SB.	Sravana Belgola
Sd.	Sidlaghatta
Sg.	Sringeri
Sh.	Shimoga
Si.	Sira
Sk.	Shikaripur
Sp.	Srinivaspur
Sr.	Srirangapattana
Tk	Tarikere
Tl	Tirthahalli
Tm.	Tumkur
TN.	Tirumakudal Narasipur
Tp.	Tiptur
Yd.	Yedatore
Yl	Yelandur

I
INTRODUCTION

Historical researches in Karnataka based on epigraphs began on a sound footing with the advent of great savant Fleet who as early as 1896 remarked "The history of an Imperial dynasty without a detailed notice of at least the important feudatory families will be incomplete."[1] His observation holds good even to this day if we consider the work done on the feudatory dynasties of India in general and of Karnataka in particular.

To begin with, Fleet was the first and foremost to write on the feudatory dynasties and he stressed the importance of the study of these families.[2] Dinakara Desai's work in this field based on the epigraphs is worthy of note.[3] Later, Mahalingam, Govindaswamy, Balambal, Srinivasan and other scholars worked on different feudatory dynasties of South India and have enriched our knowledge by their writings.[4] Some scholars[5] have quoted them occasionally, in the course of their researches. But on the whole, work on the history of the feudatory dynasties has remained incomplete and inadequate since enough attention has not been paid to it.

Recently, a laudable attempt has been made by B.R. Gopal to present a concise and connected history of some of the minor dynasties of Karnataka in the early and mediaeval periods, down to the sixteenth century from the available source materials. He himself claims that his work is not exhaustive in character.[6]

In this thesis, it is our endeavor to present a systematic and comprehensive history of some feudatory dynasties of Karnataka on the basis of the epigraphs which have come to light in recent years. The recent discoveries which shed much light on various problems concerning the feudatory families, are also incorporated in the work.

The thorough examination and study of the epigraphs belonging to the feudatory families have thrown much light on their history. Their highlights are furnished below in brief.

The earlier opinions of the scholars who worked on these feudatory families have been discussed and reviewed on the basis of the recent discoveries. The genealogy and the chronology of the Santaras has been reconstructed from the careful study of their epigraphs. They reveal the interesting fact that the Santaras forged matrimonial alliances with contemporary chiefs to strengthen and consolidate their power thus enabling them to rule over the Santelige-1000 province for more than four hundred years. The study of the epigraphs of the Sindas of Erambarage, on the contrary, shows that the matrimonial alliances failed to bring about the desired results sometimes as in the case of Kalachuri Bijjala and Chavunda II who continued to be on inimical terms even after striking marital alliance.

Some of the contemporary chiefs have been properly identified. For example, Polasinda, the chief of the Sindas of Bagadage married Bijjal adevi, whose father is described as *Khandave-mandalesvara*. The *Khandave-mandelsvara* referred to in this record has been identified with Vira Gomka (I) *alias* Banavadityadeva of the Bana family of *Khandavamandala*[7]. Further, the origin of the Pandya lineage doubtfully ascribed earlier[8] to Virapandya mentioned in a record[9] belonging to Gutts Vikramaditya I has been rectified by identifying Virapandya of the record[10] of 1162 A.D. with the lineage of the Uchchangi which had been earlier ascribed to the Pandyas of the Hayve family[11] on the basis of an inscription of Kamadeva dated 1113 A.D., has been discarded in this thesis on the basis of a comparative study of the records belonging to both the families. Further, the beginning of the rule of Palattapandya, a chief of a family bearing the appellation 'Pandya', has been fixed as 1185 A.D., after a careful study of the external evidences.[12]

Source Material

The present work is mainly based on the study of more than 600 lithic and copper plate inscriptions. Most of the inscriptions and copper plate charters referred to herein belong to the sovereigns of Karnataka beginning with the Imperial Rashtrakutas down to the Yadavas of Devagiri. Further, the records which are used here range in date from early times and more precisely from the 5th century A.D. to the 14th century. A.D.

The following table provides an inventory of inscriptions both on stone and copper plates that are available for each dynasty.

Dynasty	**Stone Epigraphs**	**Copper-plate Grants**
The Early chiefs	15	1
The Banas	111	3
The Silaharas	34	26
The Santaras	90	-
The Sindas	99	1
The Ratts	22	-
The Changalvas	33	-
The Kongalvas	32	-
The Kadambas of Karadikal and Nurumbade	9	-
The Haihayas of Aralu and Morata	23	-
The Nidugal Cholas	64	-
The Pandyas of Uchchangi	56	-
The Guttas	29	-
	617	+ 31
Total		**648**

From the above, it can be deduced that the largest number of epigraphs belongs to the Banas and only a few to the Kadambas of Karadikal and Nirumbada. This table includes the relevant stone epigraphs and copper plate grants available from the neighbouring states also. .

Besides, the evidence of the lead and potin coins discovered in the excavation at Chandravalli and attributed to the Satavahanas and their feudatories have been taken into consideration in dealing with the Chutas under the early chiefs.

Further, the literary sources have also been made use of to corroborate the facts gleaned from inscriptions.

The feudatory dynasties played an important role in the history of

Karnataka. The stability of the major powers was dependent upon the political support they got from the feudatory dynasties. It may not be an exaggeration to say that these feudatory powers shaped and moulded the political destinies of their imperial masters and served as the backbone for the easy and smooth running of administration and also for the realisation of the cherished ambitions of their overlords. The rule of Chalukya Vikramaditya VI (1076-1126 A.D.) can be cited here as an instance; he appointed many subordinates all over his kingdom so that he could have the vast empire under his effective control.

The crucial role of the feudatories in regional administration and in war and their support to the sovereign cannot be underestimated. The study interestingly reveals two facts viz., loyalty and divergence.

The feudatories often changed their allegiance from one imperial house to another either due to the changing circumstances or of their own volition. Some of them seem to have never totally severed their connection with their original masters even when they were sinking into oblivion. They continued to cherish their affiliation with their forgotten or forsaken masters in their records.[13]

The prominent role of Achugi II, a chief belonging to the Sinda family of Erambarage, in the conquests of his suzerain Chalukya Vikramadity VI stands as an example of the loyalty of the feudatories.[14] The local military force under the control of a subordinate was fully dedicated to the welfare of the empire as well as its imperial ruler.

On the contrary, it is also observed from the study of the epigraphs that the feudatory chiefs who, at times, tried to throw off the yoke of their suzerains, enjoyed independent rule only for short durations before they were again brought under subjugation. This was mainly due to their poor military resources and stamina and the enormous power of the contemporary imperial dynasties to whom, by sheer force of circumstances, they had to subordinate their interest.

Indian historians have not made a serious differenciation between feudatories and minor dynasties; while dealing with South India including Andhra Pradesh and Karnataka. In fact, most of the writers take the two terms as synomymous. The word feudatory in South Indian history particularly with regard to pre -Vijayanagara period; cannot note any significance or connotation of the word 'feudal' as found in Europian history. In South Indian context the word has been used by K.A. Nilkanta Sastri in the *Cholas*, T.V. Mahalingam in *South Indian Polity*, A.S. Altekar in *Rashtrakutas and their times*; S.H. Ritti in the *Sevunas* and A.V. Narsimha Murthy in the *Sevunas of Devagiri* in the sense of a subordinate dynasty to an imperial powers like the Chalukya, the Hoysala, the

Sevuna etc. In other words, these scholars have established a tradition of equating the minor dynasties with feudatories. B. R. Gopal prefers to call them minor dynasties but he feels that they were not always feudatories and some times they tried to establish themselves as indipendent. This is fallacious argument because these minor dynasties were never independent in the real sense of the term. They were in the habit of changing the sides depending upon exigencies of the political situation. They tried invariably to become independent but they were never successful. A few inscriptions of these dynasties might have failed to mention the name of the imperial power and that does not mean that they were independent; but they were feudatories. Even the term minor dynasty suffers from serious difficulties. It is a term of comparative significance. The question is which dynasty minor with regard to what other dynasty? Dynasties cannot be grouped as major or minor without any proper criterian. The Banavasi Kadambas can be considered a major dynasty from their cultural achievements. But they became minor from the political aspects. Kadamba Mayura Sarma can not be called a king of a minor dynasty because of his great political service to Karnataka in inaugurating a new dynasty. The Kadambas of Goa also can not be termed minor in the history of their coinage which is richer than that of the Hoysalas and Sevunas. Thus the term minor dynasty suffers from serious defects. Following the long tradition of the historical works of Fleet, Nilakanta Sastri, Mahalingam, Ritti and Narasimha Murthy, the term feudatory family is used in this volume. It is stated earlier in this work that it has no overtones of European feudal dynasties. That term is used in the sense of subordinate dynasties of the imperial powers like the Rashtrakutas, The Hoysalas, The Cholas etc. Imperial powers are those who did not recognise any overlord or superior power for a long time and continuously too. Even when they started as feudatories they threw off the yoke of subordination permanently and hence are entitled to be called imperial or major dynasties. Thus there is no finality with regard to the use of these terms and the preference for one term depends upon the view point of the author. Since this study is more oriented towards the political history, the term feudatory dynasties is justifiably preferred. Many interesting facts of this kind have been discussed in detail in the respective chapters.

The present study brings to light the history of some feudatory dynasties of Karnataka in twelve chapters. The terms "feudatory dynasties" used in this monograph denotes only subordinate families of the then imperial powers. It may be remembered here that the same connotation was implied by various scholars in their respective works. This nomenclature was widely used as early as 1896.

From the second to the thirteenth chapters, important feudatory dynasties of Karnataka as shown above in a table are dealt with.

REFERENCES

1. Fleet : DKD., p. 535.
2. *Ibid.*
3. Desai : *MUCK.*
4. (a) Mahalingam, T.V. : *Banas In South Indian History*
   (b) Govindaswamy, M.S. : *The Role of Feudatories in Pallava History*
   (c) Balambal, V. : *Feudatories of South India*
   (d) Srinivasan, C.R. : *Kanchipuram Through the Ages*
   (e) Sampath, M.D. : *CTA.*
5. (a) Hiriyannaiah, K.N. : *Report on Minor Dynasties of Karnataka* (1000-1300 A.D.).
   (b) Radha, M. : *Report on Life and Times of Hoysala Narasimha III* (1254-91A.D.).
6. Gopal, B.R. : *MDSIK.*, p.6.
7. *Ep. Ind.*Vol. XXXVIII, p. 236 ff.
8. *SII.*Vol. XVIII, Introduction, p. xxii.
9. *Ibid.*No. 296.
10. *Ibid.*Vol. IX,Pt. I, No. 293.
11. KTA., p. 410.
12. Cf. Desai : *MUCK.*, p. 260; Rice : *EC.*, XI (1903), Introduction, p, 18.
13. *SII.*, VI, No. 557; *CII.*, VI, p. 25.
14. *EI.vol.* XX, p. 118.

II

THE BANAS

A bird's eye-view of the political history of the Banas reveals that they governed some isolated pockets of different regions and often they were eclipsed by the imperial powers in the different phases of South Indian history. One can notice their struggle for survival or re-emergence depending upon the fluctuations of their fortune. In consonance with the tradition of the day, they never lagged behind in laying claims to mythological ancestry. The early Banas claim to have descended from the demon-king Bali, son of Virochana, who is stated to have granted the earth in a sacrifice to Vamana,[1] one of the incarnations of Vishnu. They also claim to be the lords of Nandagiri, Nandidurga in Chikkaballapur Taluk, Kolar District and Parivipura[2] i.e., Parigi, of Hindupur Taluk, Anantapur District. Bana, son of Bali is said to have been an ardent devotee of Siva and was His doorkeeper[3]. The Puranic connection of Bali or Mahabali with Vishnu is narrated in the Udayendiram grant of Bana Vikramaditya II[4] (c. 909-12 A.D.).

Sampath has done much spade work relating to the history of the Banas.[5] He has formulated the chronology of the individual Bana feudatories and has arrived at the most acceptable dates with precision and accuracy after having examined the various theories of earlier scholars. Therefore, I have generally adopted the date suggested by him throughout this chapter. Sampath is of the opinion that the earliest reference to the existence of the Bana family can be traced back to as early as about the second century A.D. on the basis of literary evidence. However, in the absence of corroborative epigraphical evidence, this view becomes questionable.

The Talagunda pillar inscription[6] of Kadamba Kakusthavarman (c. 422-77 A.D.) furnishes the earliest reference to the Banas wherein the ruler

Mayurasarman (c. 337-57 A.D.) is stated to have levied tribute from the Brihad - Banas,[7] who were at the head of a feudal confederacy. Brihad-Banas of this record, according to Kielhorn, correspond to Perumbana of Tamil inscriptions. Next, the Halmidi inscription[8] (assignable to the middle of the 5th century A.D.) refers to the heroes of the Banas. According to the Gudimallam copper-plate,[9] the early members of the Bana family ruled over the country to the west of the road leading to Andhra (*Andhrat-pathah Paschimatah kshitih*). The Tamil and the Kannada records also express the same view with some regional variations.[10]. Authentic records of the earlier rulers of this dynasty are not available. However, the statement given in Ganga Kongunivarman's record, that "he was anointed to conquer the Bana-mandala"[11] gives a pointed verbal expression to the inherent hostility that existed mutually between the Gangas and the Banas [12]. The genealogy of the early Bana rulers is made available by the following records.

1. Udayendiram copper-plates of Vikramaditya II[13]

2. Gudimallam copper-plates of the same ruler[14] and

3. Mudiyanur copper-plates of Malladeva [15].

All these three records uniformly refer to Jayanandivarman (also known as Nandivarman) and Vijayaditya as the first two kings of the family. The Kudalur grant [16] of the Ganga ruler Marasimha II, the genuineness of which is doubted, would have us believe that the Gangas overpowered the Banas and they (the Gangas) are extolled therein as lords of the Kolalapura (viz., modern Kolar) etc.

Jayanandivarman (Nandivarman) (c. 782-83-793 A.D.).

All the three records mentioned above admit that he was the first member of this dynasty. He is also mentioned as Banadhiraja-Nandivarman. [17] Jayanandivarman of the Udayendiram grant[18] "who ruled the land west of the road to the Andhra country" is identified with Nandivarman of the Gudimallam charter.[19] The donor of the Gudimallam plates, named Nandi, who granted the village called Viprapitha to some Brahmanas, is the same as Nandivarman mentioned in another verse of the same grant.[20] Mahavalivanarayar of the Tiruvallam inscription[21] is also identified with Jayanandivarman. If this surmise holds good, we have to believe that his rule extended upto 793 A.D. to which year the last mentioned inscription belongs.[22] The Belkere inscription[23] assignable to about the 8th century A.D. on paleographical grounds also refers itself to the 3rd year of the reign of Nandivarman where he is called as Vriddharaja *alias* Mahabali Banarasa.

Vijayaditya I (c. 793-845 A.D.):

Vijayaditya who succeeded his father Jayanandivarman is described as a great warrior, brave man,[24] skillful and diligent in the discharge of his royal duties[25] and as a man of great valour.[26] After the defeat of Pallava Dantivarman by the Rashtrakuta king Govinda III[27] (793-814 A.D.) the Banas accepted the overlordship of the latter. The Nandi plates of Govinda III[28] (806 A.D.) record the grant made at the request of Kshatriya Mahabali Banaraja named Sriparumar, of the village of Kandamangala, to Isvaradeva, a pontifical head of the *sthana (matha)* in the temple on the hill. Sriparumar of this grant is identified as Vijayaditya I.[29] Bana Vidyadhara of the Chikkaballapur copper-plates[30] (810 A.D.) is also identified with Vijayaditya I.[31] The Western Ganga ruler Rachamalla I took advantage of the absence of the Rashtrakuta forces in Gangavadi, defeated the Banas and occupied Gangavadi 6000 in the course of his campaign.[32] The Banas had to face the hostility of another rising power, the Nolambas, who had matrimonial alliance with the Gangas of the main line.[33] When the Rashtrakuta power waned, it facilitated Pallava Dantivarman to grab parts of the Bana kingdom due to which Vijayaditya I became his subordinate.[34]

Malladeva (c. 845-46 A.D.) :

He succeeded his father Vijayaditya I. The Mudiyanur charter[35] issued by him is wrongly dated in Sake 261 and 23rd regnal year. This record has been assigned now to the 9th century A.D. on palaegraphical grounds as the characters of this record are akin to those of the Vakkaleri plates[36] of Chalukya Kirtivarman I dated Sake 679 (757 A.D.). This would be the earliest record to refer to his rule over the division of seven and a half lakh (*saptardhlaksha*) country containing twelve thousand villages, and also the earliest reference about this country.[37] He is also known as Vadhuvallabha Malladeve Nandivarman,[38] and he bore the title Jagadekamalla.[39]

Vikramaditya I (c. 846-83 A.D.) :

According to Pallava Nandivarman III's record[40] dated in his 17th regnal year (863 A.D.) Vikramaditya I succeeded his father Malladeva. He bore the title *Banavidyadhara,*[41] *Banakundarappa*[42] and *Jayameru*[43]. An inscription from Budidapalle,[44] in Kannada characters of 9th century A. D., records that, certain Mudhuderaguns-Menti of Minikki destroyed Kurunjeale and captured the cows from that place. In this scuffle a certain Periyanna fell, and another hero named Kelamudden (both from the Bana camp) was pierced and put to death. Another inscription,[45] almost in similar characters, which records the death of one Alamaren *alias* Kelemuldan in the course of an attack on the same place (i.e., Kurujjiyala or Kurunjeale) by a certain Mudunda of Miniki, belongs to the reign of a Mahavali-Vanarasa. He had two queens viz., Kundavvai ***alies***

Banamahadevi, daughter of the Western Ganga king Prithivipati I, [46] and Mahadeviadigal *alias* Maraka [ni] mmadigal.[47] The famous battle of Soremati[49] which took place during his reign between the Banas and the Vaidumbas on the one hand and the Gangas and the Nolambas on the other was an important event which considerably affected the political equilibrium of that period. Many herostones bear testimony to this.[50] However, the fort of Soremati was besieged by Vikramaditya I with his ally, Vaidumba Gandatrinetra. The victory thus achieved was shortlived and the Banas lost their hold over Soremati for Mahendra-Nolamba destroyed the power of the Banas and assumed the title *Mahabalivamsa -vidhvamsa*.[51] In the initial years he was mainly known through the inscriptions of his Pallava overlord and his subservient position is amply corroborated by the mention of the regnal year of his overlord viz., Pallava Nandivarman III.[52] But at a later date he seems to have declared his independence taking courage from the defeat of Pallava Nripatunga, the successor of Nandivarman, in the Sripurambiyam battle. A record from Balla[53] in Mulbagal taluk is dated in the second regnal year of this Bana ruler. Hence it may be discerned that he had control over the region around Mulbagal. The mention of his own regnal year shows the retrieval of his power and ascendancy. It can also be presumed that the Pallavas, at least temporarily, had lost their hold over the Banas.

Vijayaditya II (c. 888-909 A.D.) :

He was the son of Vikramaditya I and queen Mahadeviadigal *alias* Marakanimmadigal.[54] He is also known as Mahabali Vanarasa Virachulamani Prabhumeru.[55] He is referred to as Prabhumeru and Vijayaditya Prabhumeru in the Udayendiram[56] and Gudimallam[57] copper-plates respectively.

The Nolamba king Mahendra sent his two generals Kaduvatti-Muttarasa and Mriduva to invade Pulinadu of the Banas. Implicitly obeying the command of their master they burnt down Permavi town and destroyed Koyatur. Virachulamani i.e., Vijayaditya II Prabhumeru assisted by the Vaidumba chief Gandatrinetra repulsed the invaders.[58] Bana Virachulamani who fought in this battle was then probably a prince and represented his father. The second Kannada inscription[59] from Kalakottur, Pungenur Zamindari, Chittoor District, belonging to the reign of the Nolamba-Pallava chief Nolambadityarasa who was ruling over the Gangavadi - 6000 province, records the same event as referred to above in which a certain Tejamani was slain. The third Kannada record from Punganur[60] of the same District records the gift of a wet land of a *kanduga* in sowing capacity to the family of the deceased, Kalaianga Kandanarayana who slew nine thieves during the reign of Bana Vijayaditya II over the Vaduguvali 12000 province and east of Manne when Kaduvetti-Muttarasa had come to Koyatur on a raid. Both the father and the prince are referred to in the two records connected with local skirmishes.[61] An inscription in Kannada characters of the 9th century A.D., from Karshanapalle,[62] Punganur Taluk, refers itself to the reign of the Bana king Banarasa who was also incharge of the Gangavadi-6000 province when Ballaha i.e., the Rashtrakuta king whose identity is not known led a campaign against Kaduvetti, for not paying tribute. On this occasion, a servant of Banatattaran, who was under the servitude of Vijayitta i.e., Vijayaditya II, while returning on a horse near Kuntiala, lost his life after slaying Ganamurti. A Bana chief whose name is not mentioned, but who is referred to only by his title *Mahavali-Vanaraja* in an inscription from Tiruvallam [63] dated in Saka 810 is perhaps identical with Vijayaditya II Prabhumeru, for his inscriptions cite Saka dates from 820 onward. It may be surmised that he was the only Bana king known to have ruled independently as his records are dated in the Saka years without mentioning any overlord. Therefore, it may be presumed that the earliest date of Vijayaditya II is probably Saka 810 (888 A.D.).

Subsequently, Parantaka I, the Chola ruler, by force uprooted two Bana kings besides defeating a Vaidumba ruler and thereupon conferred the dignity of "The lord of the Banas" on the Ganga king Hastimalla, as evidenced by the Udayendiram plates of Prithvipati II.[64] The two uprooted Bana kings may be identified with Vijayaditya II Prabhumeru and his son Vikramaditya II, for during his period, Prithvipati II assumed the title *Sembiyan Mahavali Vanaraya* there by proclaiming his allegience to the Sembiyan (Cholas) as manifested in Pullamangai inscription.[65] An inscription from Manigatte-Gollahalli[66] dated Sake 831 (909 A.D.) mentions Bijayitta Banarasa and refers to the battle of Mulked in which a certain Posevayya fell fighting against the enemies. The Bijayitta Banarasa of this record can be identified w1ith Vijayaditya II. Another record from Chendattur,[67] dated Saka 832 (910 A.D.) mentions the death of a Mavali Vanaraya *alias* Kudiparitandikkamanar of Adaiyaru-nadu, residing in Igalmeraimangalam in a cattle raid. This Mavali Vanaraya has been identified with Vijayaditya II.[68] Therefore, it is evident that Vijayaditya II died in 910 A.D.

Vikramaditya II (c. 909-12 A.D.) :

He is the son and successor of Vijayaditya II. Both the Udayendram[69] and Gudimallam[70] copperplates mention his name. The latter grant confirms and ratifies the earlier gift of the village called Viprapitha to the Brahamanas by this ruler.[71] It states that it was re-issued with the consent of his father. He was probably assisted by his son Vijayaditya II *Pugalvippavaraganda.* After the battle of Vallala[72] these two probably had sought the help of the Rashtrakutas, as they had been deprived of their territory by Chola Parantaka I.

Vijayaditya III (c. second quarter of the 10th century) :

He succeeded his father and had the title *Pugalvippavaraganda.*[73] He meekly accepted the over lordship of the powerful chola king Parantaka I.[74] He seems to have led a peaceful life as there was no incident worthy of note during his reign.

Vikramaditya III (c. 940. A.D.) :

He took the reins of the kingdom after his father and bided for an opportunity to declare his independence from the Cholas. He allied himself with Rashtrakuta Krishna III during the latter's campaign against Chola Parantaka I. This cordial relationship is very well attested by the records as they style him as *Krishnarajapriyah.*[75] The grant of Vikramaditya Mavali-Vanaraja[76] dated 946 A.D. mentions no overlord. He may be identical with Vikramaditya III who probably asserted his independence after the death of Ganga Prithvipati II about 940 A.D. the date of this record. According to the Karhad grant[77] of Rashtrakuta Krishna III dated in 956 A.D., some of the territories were distributed to the Banas and the Vaidumbas who were his loyal feudatories. In other words, Vikramaditya III was restored to his ancestral dominions. After the decline of the Rashtrakuta power following the death of Krishna III, he once again re-established good relationship with the Cholas and further enhanced his position through matrimonial ties.[78]

Other Bana Chiefs :

A Bana chief Sambayya who was ruling from Bidrur under the overlordhip of Iriva-Nolamba, son of Mahendradhiraja is known from a record. He might have belonged to a collateral branch.[79]

We hear about some other Bana rulers viz., Chandiyanna[80] and Chilparasa[81] who did not probably belong to the main line. The latter was ruling in 1068 A.D. as *mahasamanta.* They ruled as the subordinates of the Chalukyas of Kalyana.

The Kaligi inscription[82] mentions two Bana rulers viz., Chandarasa and Bandarasa. The Tengali inscription[83] mentions Bibbarasa who was renowned for his bravery and religious devotion. He erected a temple of Siva at

Jivanikapura, which deity came to be known as Bibbarasa after him. A certain Bibbarasa with the title *mahamandalesvare* who is different from the above chief, figures in the record dated Chalukya Vikrama year 31 (1106 A.D.). [84] Viragonkarasa II, son of Udayaditya Virakalarasa and grandson of Viragonkarasa (I) is mentioned as the donor in an inscription[85] of the reign of the Kalachuri king Rayamurari Sovideva. All these Bana feudatories ruled Khandavamandala, comprising the unit of 100 villages situated in the region of Mannadadi 1000 as subordinates of the Western Chalukya kings. The Banas, after enjoying centuries of power appear to have steadily grown weak and finally drifted into oblivion. A synchronistic table with regard to the geneology of the Banas is given hereunder for easy reference and comparative study.

Table I[86]

Nandivarman or Jayanandivaraman

|

Vijayaditya I

|

Malladeva 'Jagadekamalla'

|

Vikramaditya I 'Jayameru', 'Banavidyadhara' m. Kundavvai daughter of the Ganga king Prithivipati I; and Marikanimmadi C. 872 - 90

|

Vijayaditya II 'Vira Chulamani', 'Prabhumeru' 898-910

|

Vikramaditya II heir apparent 898

|

Vijayaditya III 'Pugalvippavaraganda'

|

Vikramaditya III 'Vijaya Bahu', 'Krishnarajapriya' 937-66

Table II[87]

The legendary or mythological figures are dropped out

Nandivarman or Jayanandivarman c. 770-95

|

Vijayaditya I c. 795-835

|

Nalladeva alias Jagadekamalla c. 835-50

|

Vikramaditya I Jayameru Bana Vidyadhara c. 850-95

|

Vijayaditya II (Prabhumeru) Virachulamani c. 895-910

|

Vikramaditya II 'friend of Krishnaraja' c. 910-16

|

Vijayaditya III (Pugalvippavaraganda)

|

Vijayabahu Vikramaditya III c. 965 (?)

Table III[88]

Vikramaditya I Bana or Banavidyadhara 868-90

|

Vijayaditya

|

Vikramaditya II

|

Vikramaditya III

Table IV[89]

Mahabali

|

Banadhiraja - Nandivarman

|

Jayanandivarman

|

Vijayaditya Mahabali I 796-835

|

Malladeva-Jagadekamalla 835-50

|

Banavidyadharavikramaditya, Jayameru-Bana 850-95

|

Vijayaditya II - Prabhumerudeva 895-910

|

Prabhumeru (died early)

|

Vikramaditya II - Mahabali Bana 910-16

|

Vijayaditya III 916 ?

|

Pugalvippavaraganda Vijayabahu

|

Vikramaditya III 949 ?

|

Sambayya 916

Table V[90]

Virochana
|
Bali
|
Bana
|
Banadhiraja
|
Jayanandivarman 770-95
|
Vijayaditya I 795-820
|
Mallideva 820-50
|
Vikramaditya I - Jayameru 850 - 90
|
Vijayaditya II - Prabhumeru 890 - 910
|
Vikramaditya II 910-16
|
Vijayaditya III (Pugalvippavaraganda)
|
Vikramaditya III (Vijayabahu) 940-60

Table VI[91]

Bali

|

Nandivarman, Jayanandivarman c. 782-83 - 92

|

Vijayaditya (I) 793-845

|

Malladeva, Vadhuvallabha Malladeva - Nandivarman 845-46

|

Vikramaditya I Jayameru, Vikramaditya Vanavidyadhara, Vikramaditya Banakandarppan c. 846-83 *m.* 1. Kundavvai alias Banamahadevi 2. Mahadevi Adigal *alias* Marakanimmedigal

|

Vijayaditya II Prabhumeru 888-909

|

Vikramaditya II c. 909-12

|

Vijayaditya Pugalvipparaganda - Second quarter of the 10th century A.D.

|

Vikramaditya III c. 940

The genealogy of the Banas of Khandava mandala [92]

Brahma

Marichi

Kasyapa

Hiranyakasipu

Prahlada

Virochana

Bali

Bana

After many had ruled

Chamdarasa (I)

Bamdarasa

Bibba (I)

Chamdarasa (II)

Loka

Bibba (II) *m.* Rebbaladevi

Vira Goika (I) *alias* Banaradityadeva (*m.* Mailaladevei; known dates :1077 and 1102)

Kumara Malla *alias* Mallideva - Kumara (known date : 1102)

Gomka (II)

Katta

Gomka (III) (*m.* Mailalladevi; Known dates : 1122, 1123-24,1157, 1162 and 1172)

Udayaditya Vira Kalarasa *alias* Vira Kaladevarasa (known date : 1173 A.D.)

Gomka (IV) (known date : 1173)

REFERENCES

1. *E.I.*, XVII, p. 2, v. 9.

2. *ABSTE.*, 1890, No. 194; *Ibid.*, 1900, p. 31, para. 85; *Ibid.*, 1906-07, part II, p. 79, para. 46; *SII.*, II, p. 358; *NDI.*, part III, p. 1201.

3. *E.C.*, X (1904), Introduction, p. ii, iii, f.n. no. 5.

4.. *I.A.*, XIII, p. 7, v. 3: E.I., III, p. 74-76, v. 31.

5. M.D. Sampath : *CTA.*, pp. 34-35.

6. *E.I.*, VIII, p. 32, v. 15; *E.C.*, VII (1902), p. 200 f.

7. *E.I.*, XI, p. 230 ff. No. 5, *adade karan Brihad - Banapramukhad - bahun raja - mandalat.*

8. *MAB.*, 1936, p. 72. *Sandraka-Banabhaya-degada virapurusha-samakshame Kekaya-Pallavaram kaderidu.*

9. *E.I.*, III, p. 76, 11. 20-22. *Sa ratshaksha ti sma kshitim-ekavira Andhrat-pathah paschimato bali (l i) yan.* This has been wrongly read by V. Balambal, *FOSI*, p. 35.

10. *Vadugavali-merku, Vadugavaliyin-merku Vadugavali-pannirayairam, Vadugavali pannirchchasira* and *Vaduguyuliyinpuduva* ; *CTA.*, p. 77, f.n. No. 186.

11. *SII.*, II, p. 387, v. 13.

12. *E.I.*, XI, p. 233.

13. *I.A*, XIII, p. 7; *E.I.*, III, pp. 75-76.

14. *E.I.*, XVII, p. 1 ff.

15. *I.A.*, XV, pp. 172-77 and text; pp. 174 - 76; *E.C.*, X (1904), Mb. 157

16. *MAR.*, 1921, p. 18 ff.

17. (a) *KTA.*, (1968), p. 135.

(b) centra : In the genealogical list, V. Balambal has treated this Banadhiraja as an independent ruler and the predecessor of Jayanandivarman, op. cit., p. 196.

18. *I.A.*, XIII, p. 7; *E.I.*, III, pp. 75-76.

19. *E.I.*, XVII, p. 1 ff.

20. *Ibid.*, XI, p. 222 and 24-25; *SII.*, VIII, Nos. 524-25.

21. *SII.*, III, No. 42.

22. *FDSI.*, p. 40.

23. *E.I.*, XXXVIII, pp. 192 ff.

24. *Ibid.*, III, p. 78.

25. *Ibid.*, XVII, p. 3, v. 2.

26. *E.C.*, X (1904), Introduction, pp. iv-v.
27. *I.A.*, XI, p. 121.
28. *MAR.*, 1914, paras. 67-69.
29. *FOSI.*, p. 40.
30. *MAR.*, 1931-14, pp. 35-36; *E.C.*, XVII (1965), Cb. 66.
31. *FOSI.*, p. 40.
32. *E.C.*, X (1904), pp. 86.
33. *E.I.*, X, p.56. Rachamalla I married a Nolamba princess and gave his daughter in marriage to the Nolamba prince Nolambadhiraja Polelchora (828 A.D.).
34. *ARSIE.*, 1903, No. 226; E.I., XI, p. 234 B.
35. *I.A.*, XV, pp. 172 ff.; *E.C.*, X(1904), mb. 157.
36. *E.I.*, V, pp. 200 ff.
37. *SIHC.*, Prof. P.B. Desai Fel. Volume (Dharwar, 1971), *'Rattapadi Seven and a half lakh'* an article by K.G. Krishnan, pp. 270-71.
38. *I.A.*, XV, pp. 172 ff.; *E.C..*, X (1904), Mb. 157.
39 *E.I.*, III, p. 76, l. 28 and plate; *I.A.*, XV, p. 173.
40. *SII.*, III, pt. I, pp. 93-94. It is surmised that the Nolamba attacked the Banas soon after the death of Vijayaditya I and that his successor, Malladeva seems to have lost his life soon after his accession. Vikramaditya I was born in c. 846 A.D. soon after the death of his father, *CTA.*, p. 39.
41. *E.I.*, III, p. 78; *ARSIE.*, 1900, No. 571'.
42. *ARSIE.*, 1906, No. 569; *SII.*, IX, pt. I, No. 2.
43. *E.I.*, XVII, p. 6, v. 14.
44. *SII.*, IX, pt. I, No. 2.
45. *Ibid.*, No. 3. Nahavali Vanarasa of this inscription is identified with Mahavali Vanarayar Vikramaditya Banakandarppan of the Budidepalle record for the same event is recorded in both epigraphs - *CTA.*, p 40
46. *SII.*, III, pt. I, Nos. 47-48. This matrimonial alliance shows that the Gangas and the Banas were occasionally on friendly terms.
47. *E.I.*, XI, p. 227.
48. *MAR.*, 1914, Paras. 67-69; *Ibid.*, 1913-14, pp. 35-36; E.C., XVII (1965), Cb. 66.
49. The date of Soremati battle has been a bone of contention among scholars. M.D. Sampath places the date of the battle between 870 - 79. A.D. (*CTA.*, pp. 24 - 25) while V Balambal assigns it to about 875 A.D. (*POSI.*, pp. 44 - 49). M.S.Krishnamurthy puts the date of the battle in 878-83 A.D. (*The Nolambas,* pp. 73 - 84).

50. Sewell's List, p. 328.
51. *EC.*, XII (1904), Si. 24, 38; *E.I.*, X, p. 65.
52. *SII.*, III, pt. I, pp. 93-94.
53. *E.C.*, X (1904), Mb. 92.
54. *E.I.*, XI, p. 227 D; *ARSIE.*, 1903, No. 223.
55. *E.C.*, X (1904), Mb. 229.
56. *I.A.*, XIII, p. 7; *E.I.*, III, pp. 75-76.
57. *E.I.*, XVII, p. 1 ff.
58. *ARSIE.*, 1913, pp. 90-91; Sewell's List, pp. 38-39.
59. *SII.*, IX, pt. I, No. 20; *ARSIE.*, 1921, No. 306.
60. *SII.*, IX, pt. I, No. 5; *ARSIE.*, 1906, No. B 542.
61. *EC.*, X (1904), No. 243-44.
62. *SII.*, IX, pt. I, No. 6.
63. *Ibid.*, III, No. 44; *E.I.*, XI, p. 227.
64. *SII.*, II, pp. 383-84.
65. *E.I.* XXVI, p. 112.
66. *E.C.*, X (1904), Mb. 229.
67. *ARSIE.*, 1921, No. 168; pp. 94-95, para. 25.
68. *JOR.*, 1931, p. 308.
69. *I.A.*, XIII, p. 7; *E.I.*, III, pp. 75-76.
70. *E.I.*, XVII, p. 1 ff.
71. *Ibid.*, XI, p. 222 ff.
72. *Ibid.*, XXVI, p. 113; probably modern Tiruvallam.
73. *Ibid.*, III, p. 75 ff.
74. *JIH.*, XXIX, p. 221.
75. *E.I.*, III, p. 75.
76. *ARSIE.*, 1943-44, No. 160
77. *E.I.*, IV, p. 280.
78. *SII.*, XIII, No. 197.

79. *E.C.*, X (1904), Mb. 126; *FOSI.*, p. 57.
80. *E.I.*, XXXVIII, p. 119 ff.
81. *ARTE.*, 1947-48, No. B 5.
82. *E.I.*, XXXVIII, p. 231 ff.
83. *Ibid.*
84. *JOR.*, XXI, p. 100.
85. *ARTE.*, 1960-61, No. B 499; E.I., XXXVIII, p. 231 ff.
86. *HISI.*, p. 328.
87. *JIH.*, XXIX, p. 165.
88. *AIK.*, p. 535.
89. *KTA.*, p. 135.
90. *EOSI.*, p. 196.
91. *CTA.*, p. 47.
92. *E.I.*, XXXVIII, p. 231 ff.

III

THE SILAHARAS

Many scholars of earlier days and the recent past like Fleet, Desai, Mirashi and Gopal worked on the history of Silaharas[1] with the help of the evidences available to them during their time. This chapter is mainly based on the inscriptions published so far and published works of the scholar mentioned above.

The Silaharas are stated to be the descendants of the mythical Vidyadhara prince Jimutavahana, son of Jimutaketu. According to the *Brihatkathamanjari* of Kshemendra and the *Kathasaritsagara* of Somadeva, Garuda, the vehicle bird of Vishnu, forced the serpent king Vasuki to supply him one serpent a day for his food. Silahara means 'food on a slab', the victim serpent being made to sit on a stone slab awaiting Garuda. Once it was the turn of Sankhachuda to offer himself. When he was seen sitting on the stone Jimutavahana, the Vidyadhara prince, moved by compassion, resolved to take his place. As Sankhachuda had to be away for the *darsana* of lord Siva at Gokarna, Jimutavahana took his place and was carried away by Garuda. Garuda, after sometime, realised his mistake in eating Jimutavahana. On the prayers of the victim's wife the goddess Parvati revived Jimutavahana and there after Garuda gave up the eating of serpents.

According to a variant epigraphical anecdote, Silara was a great warrior who saved the Western Ocean when it was threatened by the arrow of Parasurama. His descendants consequently came to be known as Silaras.[2] This dynastic name is found written as *Silara*, *Sivalara* and Sailahara. Three branches of the Silaharas who ruled respectively from North Konkan, South Konkan and Kolhapur are dealt with in this chapter. The members of both the North Konkan and Kolhapur regions call themselves as *Tagarapuravaradhisvara* or *Tagarapuraparamesvara*. Mirashi is of the opinion that these members originally hailed from Tagara and were ruling there.[3] Tagara has been identified with Ter situated in the Osmanabad District of Maharashtra.[4] Ter, though now in Maharashtra, was, according to Gopal, then a part of the Karnataka Kingdom.[5] The Silaharas were of Karnataka origin as their titles *Malagalaganda, Gandaraganda, Gandavangara, Villavadanga, Induvaraditya, Avvanasinga*, etc. are all in Kannada.[6]

Silaharas of North Konkan :

The region around the Kolaba and Thana Districts of Maharashtra, which was originally described as a province of 1400 villages with Puri, the identification of which is in controversy, as its early capital, was known as North Konkan. At a later stage the Silaharas made Sthanaka (i.e., modern Thana) their capital. Surparaka (i.e., Sopara in Thana District) is also said to be another and earlier capital of the Silaharas.[7]

The political condition of North Konkan during this period is noteworthy. Chalukya Pulakesi II, after conquering the region around Puri, annexed it to his empire and it continued to be under Chalukya sway till the middle of the 8th century A.D. Afterwards this region was conquered by Rashtrakuta Dantidurga (752-56 A.D.). The Rashtrakutas retained their hold over this region upto the reign of Govinda III (793-814 A.D.).[8]

Kapardin I (c. 800-25 A.D.) :

It is surmised that he assisted his Rashtrakuta suzerain in extending his rule in the region due to which act this region came to be designated as Kapardika-dvipa or Kavadi-dvipa-a name given in his honour.[9] We do not know much about him as he does not seem to have left behind any records.

Pullasakti (825-50 A.D.) :

His only known inscription is also the earliest among the available epigraphs pertaining to this dynasty. He was the son and successor of Kapardin I. He is supposed to have ruled from 825-50 A.D. as his record is dated in 843-44 A.D.[10] He had the titles *mahasamanta* and *Konkanavallabha* by the grace of Amoghavarsha I (814-80 A.D.), the Rashtrakuta ruler. He is described as meditating on the feet of Kapardin (*Kapardi-padanudhyata*) and as ruling over the whole of Konkana including Puri (*Puri-prabhriti-Konkana-vishaya*). He had a minister (*amatya*) named sarvadhyaksha Vishnugupta, son of Purnahari.

Kapardin II (850-80 A.D.):

He succeeded his father Pullasakti in c. 850 A.D. In the later records he is described as *Laghu Kapardi*. His two records dated in 851 and 877-78 A.D.[11] respectively refer to the rule of Amoghavarsha I (814-80 A.D.). The earlier of the two records gives information that Pullasakti had obtained the entire Konkana country by the grace of Amoghavarsha I and then it refers to Kapardin. Both these members are associated with the title *mahasamantasekhara*. It is surmised that Kapardin II must have come to the throne when quite young because of the evidence of the Thana plates of Arikesari referring to his receiving homage from his enemies though he was only an infant. [12] This surmise is further strengthened by the gap of more than 25 years between the dates of his two records referred to above.

Vappuvanna (c. 880-910 A.D.):

We do not get much information about Vappuvanna who succeeded his father. But this much is certain that during his reign, Madhumati, an Arab subordinate of Rashtrakuta Krishna II (880-915 A.D.), rose to great prominance by receiving charge of Samyana-mandala, the region around modern Sanjan of Surat District, Gujarat. Madhumati (Mohammed), Sahiyasahara (Shahariyar) and Sugatipa (Subakta) ruled successively over that *mandala* till the decline of the Rashtrakutas. They often fell out with and fought against the Silaharas. Aparajita finally subdued them and annexed their territories.[13] Vappuvanna had two sons, Jhanjha and Goggi.

Jhanjha (c. 910-30 A.D.) :

He was governing Samur (Chaul in Kolaba District) in c.916 A.D.[14] He is credited with building twelve temples for the god Siva, apparently indicating his devotion for that god. We know a little about his younger brother Goggi (c. 930-45 A.D.) and his son Vajjada I (c. 945-65 A.D.) who succeeded him. The undated record belonging to him but actually issued by his successor Chhadvaideva refers to a religious gift known to have been made by Vajjadadeva I.[15]

Chhadvaideva (c. 965-75 A.D.) :

He was the brother of Vajjada I and was the executor of the Prince of Wales Museum plates.[16] He is described as a *mahasamanta* of Rashtrakuta Krishna III. Mirashi surmises that the grant promised by Vajjada I had not been reduced to writing during his life-time. On coming to know of it Chhadvaideva granted the charter recording the details of the religious gift made by Vajjada I. The significance of his copper plate grant has already been referred to while dealing with the origin of the Silahara family. He has been considered as an usurper since no other record of this family refers to him except his own record[18] which states that he succeeded his brother Vajjada I evidently depriving the latter's son Aparajita of his rightful chance.

Aparajita (c. 975-1010 A.D.) :

He succeeded his uncle in c. 975 A.D. The records belonging to his reign furnish the genealogy of the imperial Rashtrakuta family and regretfully state that Kakkala, the last king, was through misfortune, destroyed by the mighty Tailapa "even as a bright lamp is put out by a strong storm and the kingdom of the Rattas was reduced to a tale."[19] This obviously refers to the fact of the Chalukyas of Kalyana supplanting the Rashtrakutas. Aparajita I seems to have taken advantage of the political chaos which prevailed at the time of the commencement of his rule to improve his own position and status. This is proved by his assuming high-sounding titles such as *mahamandalesvara* and *mahasamantadhipati, abhimanamahodadhi, paschimasamudradhipati, suvarnagarudadhvaja, mandaliketrinetra, gandarasganda,* etc. Other titles like *pusiganjuvata* and *nannisamudra* indicate his Kannada bias.[20] He claims to have conquered the Samyana country (the region around Sanjan which was under Arab rule as shown above) and made the large Punaka country (modern Poona District) submissive to him. He is also stated to have been administering the Sasya territory which has lovely surroundings, Sangamesvara (Ratnagiri District) won by his solidiers and the Chipulana (Chiplun, also in Ratnagiri District) territory which submitted to him the moment his name was mentioned.[21] Aparajita had raided Chandrapura, modern Chandor, and defeated the ruler there of, who was probably Guhas adeva I (Guvaladeva I).[22] His kingdom, on the basis of available records, extended from Latadesa (southern Gujarat) in the north, to Chandrapura (Chandor in Goa) in the south, and from the Western Sea to Bhillamiyadesa (Khandesh) in the east.

He is said to have offered shelter to Gomma, established Aiyapa on the throne and gave security from fear to Bhillama, Ammana and Mumbuva.[23] Among the members referred to above, Bhillama is to be identified with Yadava Bhillama II. We know well that the Silaharas were the loyal feudatories of the Rashtrakutas. Hence Aparajita, not forgetting the days of friendship with the Rashtrakutas was hesitant to transfer his subordination to the Chalukyas and preferred to remain in isolation. This is attested by his Janjira plates (2 sets) and the Bhadana plates issued in 997 A.D. which do not refer to any suzerain.[24] But, ultimately, he was defeated by Chalukya Satyasraya who came to the throne in 997 A.D.[25] Aparajita I had two sons viz., Vajjada II and Arikesari (Kesideva I).

Vajjada II (c. 1010-15 A.D.) :

He has been identified with Vachchaya of Thana whose daughter became the queen of the Kadamba chief Chattayya (i.e., Shashtha II mentioned in a record from Hangal).[26] He ruled for a period of 5 year only.

Arikesari (Kasideva I - c. 1015-22 A.D.) :

He succeeded his brother Vajjada II and ruled for a period of 7 years. According to the Thana plates, when he was a young prince, he marched with his army on the advice of his father to see the god Somesvara (Somanatha in Saurashtra) and offered to that god all his conquests.[27] His reign witnessed some important political developments. On the one hand he was forced by Jayasimha II (1015-43 A.D.) to accept the suzerainty of the Chalukyas. On the other, Paramara Bhoja seems to have formed a coalition with Kalachuri Gangeyadeva and Chola Rajendra against Chalukya Jayasimha, and conquered Konkana some time between 1018 A.D., the date of his Mahudi plates and 1019 A.D. the date of the Betma plates.[28] However, Bhoja lost his hold over Konkana in 1024 A.D. as, in that year, Jayasimha, according to the Miraj plates, was camping at Kolhapur in the course of his campaign against North Konkan.[29] Jayasimha's return meant Arikesari's return to the Chalukya fold. Arikesari had three sons viz., Chhittaraja, Nagarjuna and Mummuni.

Chhittaraja (c. 1022-35 A.D.) :

As soon as he occupied the throne, Kadamba Shashthadeva of Goa successfully attacked Kavadidvipa to take revenge against Aparajita at whose hands his father Guhalladeva I had suffered defeat. Chhittaraja, after his defeat in this encounter, had no choice but to accept the suzerainty of the Kadambas of Goa. in recompense, Kavadi-dvipa was restored to him.

Nagarjuna (c. 1035-45 A.D.) :

He succeeded his elder brother Chittaraja in c. 1035 A.D. Nothing is known about him.

Mummuni (c. 1045-70 A.D.) :

Nagarjuna was succeeded by his younger brother Mummuni in c. 1046 A.D. Chalukya Somesvara I who was the most powerful ruler of his days in Karnataka attacked the Silahara territories with the help of his subordinates and generals even as early as 1046 A.D. as a result of which the three families of the Silaharas viz., those of North and South Konkana as also of Kolhapur were forced to accept the suzerainty of the Chalukyas.[30] In this connection it is indicated that it was not Kadamba Shashtha (Chattayya) alone that attacked the Silaharas, but even some of the subordinates and generals of Chalukya Somesvara I like *mahamandalesvara* Revarasa of the Haihaya family who described himself as a submarine fire to the ocean which was Mummuni of Konkana (*Mummuni-Konkaniga-Jaladhibadavanala*) and another chief named Pulakesi who also claims to have subdued Mummuni.[31]

Anantadeva I, Anantapala (c. 1070-1125 A.D.) :

He was the son of Nagarjuna and nephew of Mummuni. He is described as *paschima-samudradhipati* in his copper-plate grant[32] dated 1094 A.D. apparently indicating that he extended his sway over the entire Konkana country. His Kharepatan plates[33] state that he drove out the enemies who had occupied the enemy country and plundered it, 'at a time of misfortune from relatives that had become hostile". The expression *dayada-vairi-vyasana* may refer to the internal quarrels among the three brothers viz., Chittaraja, Nagarjuna and Mummuni or among their sons.[34] He was killed by Jayakesi II, the Kadamba chief of Goa and a subordinate of Vikramaditya VI in an encounter against the latter. The cause for this encounter is not known; but it is presumed that his recalcitrance led to the battle which cost him his life.

Aparaditya I (c. 1127-48 A.D.) :

He was the son of Anatadeva I. He recovered the kingdom probably with the help of Vijayaditya, son of Gandaraditya, the Silahara chief of Kolhapur. He was a learned man and wrote a commentary on the *Yajnavalkya-smriti* entitled '*Apararka-tika*'. He had two sons, viz., Vikramaditya and Haripaladeva. Vikramaditya figures as the executor of a grant made by his father in 1139 A.D. [35]

Haripaladeva (c. 1145-55 A.D.) :

He succeeded his father Aparaditya I in c.1148 A.D. After him Mallikarjuna (c. 1155-70 A.D.) and Aparaditya II (c. 1170-97 A.D.) successively had their sway over Konkan. The relationship between these members is very difficult to ascertain. The Silahara rule over Konkana had by then begun to decline. The Chaulukya ruler Kumarapala of Gujarat defeated and killed Mallikarjuna in a battle. According to the evidence of an epigraph[36] from Chaudharpada, Kesideva II (c. 1200-45 A.D.) was a son of Apararka, identical with Aparadity II. Anantadeva II (c. 1198-1200 A.D.) is regarded as the elder son of Aparaditya.[37] In what way Anantadeva III (c. 1245-53 A.D.) and Kesavadeva II are related is not known. Somesvara (c. 1255-65 A.D.) was the last ruler of this family and he was defeated at the hands of the Yadava king Mahadeva in c. 1265 A.D. who ultimately annexed North Konkana to his kingdom.

The genealogy of the Silaharas of North Konkan[38]

- Kapardin I (c. 800-25 A.D.)
  - Pullasakti (c. 825-50)
    - Kapardin II (c. 850-80)
      - Vappuvanna (c. 880-90)
        - Jhanjha (c. 910-30)
        - Goggi (930-45)
          - Vajjada I (c. 945-65)
            - Aparajita (c. 975-1010)
              - Vajjada II (c. 1010-15)
                - Chhittaraja (c. 1022-35)
                - Nagarjuna (c. 1035-45)
                  - Anantadeva I (c. 1070-1125)
                    - Aparaditya I (c. 1127-48)
                      - Vikramaditya
                        - son (?) Anantadeva II (c. 1198-1200)
                          - Anantadeva III (c. 1245 58)
                            - Somesvara (c. 1255-65)
                      - Haripaladeva (c. 1145-55)
                        - Mallikarjuna (c. 1155-70)
                          - Aparaditya II (c. 1170-97)
                            - Kesideva II(c.1200-45)
                - Mummuni (c. 1045-70)
              - Arikesari (Kasideva I) (c.1015-22)
          - Chhadvaideva(c. 965-75)

Thus the Silaharas of North Konkan had a long and chequered history for over 465 years; having originally commenced their rule as the subordinates of the Rashtrakutas, they shifted their allegiance to the Chalukyas due to changed political circumstances and ultimately were defeated by the Yadavas in about 1265 A.D. Some of the members of this family successfully asserted their independence from time to time; however, their independence as rulers was always of the nature of temporary interludes.

The Silaharas of South Konkan

The region consisting of the parts of present day Goa and the Ratnagiri District of Maharashtra is known as 'South Konkana'. It was known in the medieval period as Konkana-900 and was ruled over by the Kadambas of Goa as subordinates of the later Chalukyas. this region was under the leadership of a branch of the Silahara family. The Kadambas had their sway over this land much earlier when the Rashtrakutas were ruling Karnataka.[39]

The history of this family is known to us from three copper-plate records belonging to the members of this branch. Of the three, two records viz., the Pattanakudi plates [40] dated 988 A.D. and the Kharepatan plates [41] of Rattaraju dated 1008 A.D. furnish the genealogy of this family differently as follows.:

Pattanakudi Plates	**Kharepatan Plates**
Dhammiyara	Sanaphulla
Ammalla	Dhammiyara
Aiyapa	Aiyapa
Adityavarma	Avasara I
Avasara I	Adityavarma
Indraraja	Avasara II
Bhima	Indraraja
AvasaraII	Bhima
	Avasara III
	Ratta

Both the plates give the genealogy of their overlords - the Rashtrakutas and describe the Silaharas as the descendants of Jimutavahana, who is stated to have offered himself, according to the Pattanakudi plates, to Garuda for the protection of the Nagas "Thinking his life as no better than a blade of grass".

Gopal has carefully studied both the Pattanakudi and Kharepatan plates and has solved the discrepancies that are found in the latter record. He gives the real position of the members of this family after analysing Mirashi's wrong surmises made on the basis of the Kharepaten plates. He has also drawn the conclusion that the earlier Pattanakudi plates of 988 A.D. are more reliable as, according to him, the royal draft of the Kharepatan plates came to be considerably revised during the period of Rattaraja.[42]

Sanaphulla (c. 965-90 A.D.)

He is referred to in the Kharepatan plates and not in the Pattanakudi plates. The former charter states that he enjoyed the favour of Krishnaraja (Krishna I-756-75 A.D.) and occupied the country stretching from the ocean shore to the Salya mountain. It also states that the Silahara family was the best among the royal families of Simhala, identified either with Lanka referred to in the Degamve inscription, or with the Goa island.[43] The opinion of Mirashi that Goa was the original home of this family[44] has been refuted elsewhere on the ground that neither the Pattanakudi plates nor any other records belonging to the Silahara branches make mention about it.[45]

Dhammiyara (c. 790 A.D.) :

Both the aforesaid records assert that he founded Balipattana i.e., Kharepatan. It may therefore be concluded that he was the first effective member of this family. He was succeeded by Ammala and other chiefs successively.

Avasara II (988 A.D.)

His Pattanakudi grant[46] dated 988 A.D. which is the earliest known record of the Silaharas of South Konkan, contains the genealogy of the erstwhile overlords, viz., the Rashtrakutas. In this record, Avasara II is stated to have obtained 40 *dinars* as a present (*pada-puja*) from three merchants named Nagai-sreshthin, Lokkai-sreshthin and Adityavaraman for the confirmation of certain hereditary rights over Kinjala and Pulisa.

It has already been stated that the records of this family invariably furnish the genealogy of the Rashtrakutas even after they were supplanted by Chalukya of Kalyana. The reason for this attitude is probably to be traced to their loyalty to this erstwhile imperial dynasty.

Rattaraja (1010 A.D.):

His record[47] is dated in 1008 A.D. It is assumed that he ruled upto 1010 A.D. He is stated to have been the subordinate of the Chalukyas as he describes himself as a *mandalika* meditating on the feet of *paramabhattaraka-maharajadhiraja* Satyasraya.

After the rule of Rattaraja, the Kadambas of Goa gained power over South Konkana. This shows that the Silaharas of South Konkana fell out with the Chalukyas, and gradually fell into oblivion.

The Silaharas of Kolhapur

The members of this family are also referred to as the Silaharas of Karad, the Karahata country which included the districts of Satara, Sangli and Kolhapur in Maharashtra and the Belgaum District of Karnataka. They had, besides Karad, two other capitals viz., Panhala near Kolhapur and Kshullakapura i.e., Kolhapur. They are described as the lords of Tagarapura (*Tagarapuravaradhisvara*) bearing the royal emblem of the golden bull (*suvarna vrishabha*) and as the worshippers of goddess Mahalakshmi of Kolhapur. The first three princes of this family viz., Jatiga I, Nayivarma and Chandraraja are known only from two later records of Gandaraditya.[48] Jatiga I is stated to be the lord of Gomanta identical with the hill of that name on which the capital Chandragupti or Chandragutti (in Shimoga District) was situated.[49]

Jatiga II (c. 100-1020 A.D.) :

He is the first member of this family to occupy the fort of Pannala[50] and is described as the lion of the hill fort of Panhala (modern Panhala, about 12 miles north-west of Kolhapur; *Pannaladurgadrisimhah*) and the lord of the city of Tagara (*Tagaranagara-bhupalaka*).

Gonka I (c. 1020-50 A.D.):

His first son Gonka I was ruling over Karahata (Karhad), the Kundi region (the region around modern Belgaum), Mirinja-desa (comprising the territory around modern Miraj) and the whole of Konkana. The assumption of Mirashi[51] that he assisted Chalukya Jayasimha II in his conquest of Konkana in c. 1024 A.D. has rightly been rejected in the light of the statement made in the grant of Marasimha that his brother i.e., Guhala I was a favurite of Chalukya Satyasraya[52] (997-1008 A.D.). We do not know much about Kirtiraja and Chandraditya, the other two sons of Jatiga II, except that they are simply referred to as kings in later records probably because they after all belonged to the royal family.

Marasimha (c. 1050-75 A.D.)

He was the son and successor of Gonka I. He was a *mahamandalesvara.* He had many titles.[53] Surmises with regard to Marasimha made by Mirashi have also been discussed and discarded by Gopal giving proper reasons for the same.[54].

According to Bilhana Marasimha's daughter was Chandaladevi or Chandralekha who married Chalukya Vikramaditya VI in a *Svayamvara.* Gopal is of the opinion that Marasimha might have been defeated by Somesvara I (1043-63 A.D.) in the course of his movements northward.[55] But it is very difficult to say whether he was really defeated as there is no sufficient ground to prove it. On the basis of his Miraj plates[56] dated 1058 A.D. which do not refer to any overlord, Gopal is of the opinion that Marasimha probably asserted himself and adopted a defiant attitude.[57]

Guhala II, Ballala, Gonka II, Bhoja I and Gandaraditya, the sons of Marasimha succeeded one another in that order. It is surmised that Guhala II was subdued by the Chalukya prince Jayasimha III as the latter is stated to have been camping at Pannaleya-kote, the fort of Pannala, (same as Panhala, near Kolhapur) in 1079 A.D.[58]

Bhoja I :

Bhoja I is described in the Kolhapur plates of Gandaraditya dated 1115 A.D.[59] as having defeated the Santara and Kongaja chiefs and Bijjana, Kokkala and Govinda. Santara whose head Bhoja I is stated to have offered to his overlord Vikramaditya VI is described as belonging to the Kadamba family. Mirashi identified this Santara chief as Santivarman II of Kadambas of Banavasi.[60] This view has been clearly brushed aside by Gopal stating that Santivarman was in no way inimical to the Chalukya ruler.[61]

On the other hand, the scholar establishes that Bhoja I was defeated by Vikramaditya as he had exhibited an independent spirit.[62] His view is strengthened by the following records. The Raibag inscription assignable to c. 1089 A.D. refers to *mahamandalesvara* Komagajarasa fighting against *mandalika* Bhoja, the Silahara.[63] Another inscription from Malghan dated 1100 A.D. states that Vikramaditya was camping on the Bhimarathi while he was proceeding to the west against Bhoja, identical with this Silahara chief.[64] From the above fact it is certain that this Bhoja had been independent during this period and was defeated only after 1100 A.D., probably by Achugi, the Sinda chief.[65] Gopal has identified Kongaja referred to in the Kolhapur plates of Gandraditya with Komagajarasa of the Raibag inscription.

Gandaraditya succeeded his elder brother Bhoja I. By this time he had accepted the suzerainty of the Chalukya Vikramaditya VI. *Samanta* Nimbarasa, subordinate, is said to have constructed the Rupanarayana *basadi* at Kolhapur.

Vijayaditya I, son of Gandaraditya, seems to have assisted Kalachuri Bijjala in ousting Chalukya Tailapa III, probably in order to declare his independence. The callousness on the part of Vijayaditya I was not tolerated by Bijjala for there was a battle wherein, however, the Silahara general Boppana fought courageously and defeated Bijjala. In a battle that took place between Vijayaditya (Vishnuchitta) son of Jayakesi II of the Kadambas of Goa and Kalachuri Ahavamalla, this Silahara Vijayaditya I is said to have saved the former.[66]

Bhoja II :

Bhoja II, successor of Vijayaditya I, was made to rule independently due to which he had to face the attack of Yadava Singhana II. This has been attested to by epigraphs dated c. 1216 A.D. which refer to the defeat of Bhoja II, the destruction of the fort of Pannala and the occupation of Khidrapura by Singhana II.[67] This event is placed sometime before 1212 A.D. by Mirashi.[68] This defeat considerably weakened the Silahara power.

Vijayaditya II, son and Successor of Bhoja II, was the last member of this family. He was in no way a match to the Yadavas, and the Silaharas of Kolhapur finally lost their kingdom to the Sevunas.

The Silaharas of Taravadi

This branch is known from the Hire Bevinur inscription dated 1124 A.D.[69] This family is an offshoot of the Kheda family of Silaharas. The members belonging to this family are stated to be the worshippers of the goddess Chamundika. They are also said to be the lords of the city of Karabbetta Kalanjara (*Karabetta – Kalanjarapuraparamesvara*). *Mahamandalesvara* Dakarasa, whose genealogy is given in this record, was a subordinate of Chalukya Vikramaditya VI. Their genealogy is as follows :

Piriya Govanarasa of Tarddavadi
|
Dakarasa I
|
Kiriya Govanarasa
|
Indarasa
|
Ahumallarasa
|
Dakarasa II

Gopal has identified Piriya Govanarasa with his namesake of the kheda and Akkalkot branches and Dakarasa as another of his sons, besides Dhanasangraha II. He also points out the nature of relationship between the rulers from Piriya Govanarasa to Indarasa on the basis of last three members' relationship.[70]

The record cited above, registers a gift of land, money, etc., to Devasakti-Pandita on the occasion of the consecration of the image of Bhogesvaradeva at Hiriya-Bevinur by *Mahamandalesvara* Dakarasa II.[71]

REFERENCES

1. Fleet : *Bombay Gazetteer*, I, Pt. II, pp. 535-49; *Ep. Ind.*, XXXVII, pp. 65 ff; *CII.*, VI and B.R. Gopal : *MDSIK.*, I, pp. 135 ff.
2. CII., VI, p. 11.
3. *Ibid.*, Introduction, pp. IV-VI
4. *Ibid.*
5. B.R. Gopal : *op. cit.*, p. 136
6. *Ibid.*, p. 137.
7. *CII.*, VI, Introduction, p. I.
8. B.R. Gopal : *op. cit.*, p. 137
9. *Ibid.*
10. *Ibid.*, p. 138
11. *CII.*, VI, pp. 3 and 6 ff.
12. *Ibid.*, Introduction, p..x. pp. 44 ff.
13. B.R. Gopal : *op. cit.*, p. 139.
14. *CII.*, VI, Introduction, p. xi.
15. *Ibid.*, p. 8 ff.
16. *Ibid.*,
17. *Ibid.*, p. 9.
18. *Ibid.*, p. 11.
19. *Ibid.*, p. 25.
20. B.R. Gopal : *op. cit.*, p. 140
21. *CII.*, VI, p. 26
22. *Ibid.*, Introduction, p. XIII.

23. *Ibid.*, Introduction, p. XII and p. 82ff
24. *Ibid.*, pp. 22 and 36 ff.
25. B.R. Gopal : *Chalukyas of Kalyana and the Kalachuris*, pp. 96-97.
26. *Indian Culture*, II, p. 408.
27. *CII.*, VI, pp. 44 ff.
28. B.R. Gopal : *MDSIK.*, I, p. 141.
29. B.R. Gopal : *Chalukyas of Kalyana and the Kalachuris*, pp. 129-32.
30. *Ibid.*, pp. 174-76.
31. *Ibid.*
32. *CII.*, VI, pp. 115 ff.
33. *Ibid.*
34. B.R. Gopal : *MDSIK.*, I, pp. 141-42.
35. *CII.*, VI, pp. 133 ff.
36. *Ibid.*, pp. 169 ff.
37. B.R. Gopal : *MDSIK.*, I, p. 144.
38. Genealogy as given in *CII.*, VI, Introduction, pp. ix-x.
39. B.R. Gopal : *MDSIK.*, p. 144.
40. *Ep. Ind.*, XXXVII, pp. 56 ff.; CII., VI, p. 178 ff.
41. *CII.*, VI, pp. 183 ff.
42. B.R. Gopal : *MDSIK.*, p. 146.
43. *CII.*, VI, pp. 186-87.
44. *Ibid.*
45. *Ep. Ind.*, XXXVII, pp. 57-58; B.R. Gopal : *MDSIK.*, p. 145.
46. *CII.*, VI, pp. 178 ff.
47. *Ibid.*, pp. 183 ff.
48. *Ibid.*, pp. 214 and 224 ff.
49. *Ibid.*, Introduction, p. XXVIII.
50. *Ibid.*
51. *Ibid.*, Introduction, p. XXIX
52. B.R. Gopal : *MDSIK.*, p. 148.
53. *CII.*, VI, p. 202.
54. B.R. Gopal : *MDSIK.*, p. 148; and *Chalukyas of Kalyana and the Kalachuris*, p. 167 ff.
55. B.R. Gopal : *MDSIK.*, I, p. 148.
56. *CII.*, VI, p. 200 ff.

57. B.R. Gopal, *MDSIK.*, I, p. 149.
58. E.C., VII (1902), Sk. 297; B.R. Gopal : *MDSIK.*, I, p. 149.
59. *CII.*, VI, pp. 214 ff.
60. Ibid., p. 215.
61. B.R. Gopal : *MDSIK.*, I, p. 149
62. *Ibid.*
63. *Ep. Ind.*, XXXVIII, pp. 106 ff.
64. *SII.*, XX, No. 64.
65. For further details see B.R. Gopal : *Chalukyas of Kalyana and the Kalachuris*, pp. 254-57 and 271.
66. B.R. Gopal : *MDSIK.*, I, p. 150.
67. S.H. Ritti : *The Sevunas*, pp. 117-18.
68. *CII.*, VI, Introduction, p. XXXIV.
69. *SII*, XX, No. 85
70. B.R. Gopal : *MDSIK.*, I, p. 156, for further branches of the Silaharas see *Ibid.*, pp. 151-55, 156-64.
71. *SII.*, XX, No. 85.

IV

THE SANTARAS OF SANTALIGE

The history of the Santaras[1] is dealt with in three periods, the early Santaras, the medieval Santaras and the later Santaras who held sway over Santalige-1000 province. This system is adopted on the basis of the availability of the epigraphs in different regions like Shimoga and Chikamagalur Districts[2] and also on the basis of the genealogical account provided in those records. Some of the records found at Nagar, Tirthahalli, Sagar and Shikaripur, all situated in Shimoga District, are very important for they provide the genealogical account of this family in unambiguous manner. The origin and history of the Santaras have been reconstructed in this chapter with the help of these epigraphs.

The chiefs of this family started their rule over the province of Santalige-1000,[4] which corresponds to the western parts of Shimoga and Chikkamagalur Districts, from about the middle of the 9th century A.D.[5] from their capital Pombuchchapura i.e., modern Humcha in the Nagar Taluk of Shimoga District. This capital is also known by several other names such as Pombuchcha, Pombulcha, Patti-Pombuchcha and Kanakapura. The rule of the Santaras over this province lasted for more than four hundred years as we shall see in this chapter. The Alupas seem to have lost Santalige province to the Santaras after their defeat at the hands of the Rashtrakuta king Krishna II.[6] The Santaras who were *mahamandalesvaras* under the Rashtrakutas were entitled to the honour of *Panchamahasabdas.* They had the epithet 'the lord of northern Madhura' *(Uttara Madhuradhisvara).* It is interesting to note that though they are known as Santaras they seem to take pride in calling themselves as having originated from *Ugravamsa (Ugravamsodbhavar)* throughout their history inspite of the fact that *Ugr-anvaya* came to be called *Santaranvaya* ever since Jinadatta assumed the secondary name of Santara.[7] Other epithets borne by the chiefs of this family are as follows :

The lord of the city of Patti Pombuchcha[8] *(Patti - Pombuchcha puravaradhisvara)*, obtainers of the boon from the goddess Padmavati *(Padmavati - labdha - varaprasada)* and thunderbolt to the race of Tondamandalikas[9] *(Tondamandalika - kulachala - vairadanda)*. They had the banner of monkey *(vanara-dhvaja)* and a lion as their crest *(mrigaraja - lanchchana)*.[10]

The Early Santaras

Raha is stated to be the progenitor of this family. He is said to have played a victorious role in the Mahabharata war fought at Kurukshetra and that, in appreciation of his valour, Lord Narayana bestowed upon him the insignias of *ekasakha* and *vanara - dhvaja*.[11] This description appears to be unhistorical as he and his successors professed the Jaina faith throughout their known history. He, in fact, belonged to the Parsvanathasantana.[12] Sahakara came after many generations. He was a cannibal by vow[13] *(atamaramamna-vratan-age)*.

Jinadatta was his successor.[14] He was like a lion on the great mountain of the celebrated *Ugr-anvaya* and before him all the kings in the world were like deer. He is also said to have participated in the Mahabharata war and obtained *ekasankha* and *vanara-dhvaja* from Vishnu.[15] This description once again is nothing but a repetition of mythology as it has already been referred to above in connection with Raha.[16] Jakkiyabbe (obviously derived from Sanskrit *Yakshini*) bestowed upon Jinadatta, the *Simha-lanchchhana* in appreciation of his victory on his way to the south over the demon Simharatha. Further Jinadatta is said to have fought with and killed the demon Andhasura; freed the fort of Kunda from the clutches of the demons Khara and Dushana.[17] The epithet *Padmavati-labdhavara-prasada* denotes that the Santaras were devout worshippers of the goddess Padmavati. This is further corroborated by the statement that, pleased with the achievement of Jinadatta, she came to stay on the *lokki* tree in the city of Kanakapura (i.e., Humcha)[18] due to which she came to be known later on as Lokkiyabbe. Humcha was declared by her to be the headquarters (rajya-sthana) of Jinadatta's kingdom.[19] This family hitherto known as *Ugranvaya* came to be called *Santar-anavya* ever since Jinadatta assumed the second name, Santara.[20]

Srikesi and Jayakesi, two brothers, succeeded to the Santara throne after the rule of Jinadatta and a number of others whose names are not given.[21] These two brothers were the earliest historical figures of this family while Raha, Sahakara and Jinadatta were only mythical ancestors.[22]

Jayakesi (825-50 A.D.) :

Srikesi was succeeded by Jayakesi. An undated epigraph,[23] in characters of the middle of the 9th century A.D. and of the reign of Rashtrakuta Nripatunga Amoghavarsha (Amoghavarsha I, 814-80 A.D.), states that Jagesi of Chantarajakula (i.e., Santar-anvaya) was adminstering the entire Santalige region. Jagesi of this record has been identified elsewhere with Jayakesi.[24] Ranakesi, son of Srikesi and Mahadevi, succeeded Jayakesi, his uncle. He was followed by a number of rulers.[25] Then came Vikramasantara.

Vikramasantara (890-920 A.D.) :

Vikramasantara was one of the most powerful rulers of this family. He consolidated his hold over Santalige-1000 by driving out all rival chieftains. He thus became the unquestioned king of his country which was bounded on the south by the river Sula, on the west, by Tavanasi and on the north by Bandaga. He is said to have performed *hiranyagarbha* in which he offered several gifts.[26] He is credited with the founding of the Santalige kingdom.[27] He is called Tolapurasha-Vikramaditya-Santara in his earliest dated record[28] of 898 A.D. This leads us to surmise that he should have also performed the *Tulapurusha-dana.* He figures as a subordinate of Rashtrakuta Krishna II in 903 A.D.[29]

An inscription [30] assigned to 890 A.D. by Rice refers to the rule of a Santara chief who was a subordinate of Rashtrakuta Krishna II (*Prithvivallabha* Kannarasa). This record has been assigned doubtfully to the rule of Vikramasantara and to that of his immediate predecessor whose name is not known.[31] On the basis of the two records[32] referred to above we are inclined to attribute it only to the rule of Vikramasantara, for he was already known to have been a feudatory of Krishna II (880-915 A.D.).

Chagisantara (920-45 A.D.) :

Vikramasantara was succeeded by his son Chagisantara who got excavated a tank named after himself as Chagisamudra probably at Humcha.[33] Three epigraphs[34] dated 933-34 A.D. and belonging to the rule of Suvarnavarsha (Rashtrakuta Govinda IV - 930-34/35 A.D.), make mention of a Santara chief Chaladamka-Ramasantara who was wielding his power over Banavasinadu. These three records can be assigned to the reign of Chagisantara on the basis of the duration of the rule suggested for him.[35]

Jinadatta, who is described as *kanaka-kulodbhava* and *kalasa-rajyanvaya* in an inscription[36] assigned to 950 A.D., has been identified with Chagisantara.[37] But he cannot be associated with this family for (1) the beginning portion of the record does not contain the usual epithets and desriptions of the Santara chiefs; (2) Jinadatta belonging to this family was of a more mythical nature[38] and (3) the Kalasa region referred to in this record figures as a *rajya* in the 12th century A.D.[39]

Virasantara (945-70 A.D.) :

Virasantara succeeded his father Chagisantara. Kannarasantara and Kavadeva were his two sons. The former appears to have predeceased the latter. Then Kavadeva was succeeded by his son Tyagisantara.

Nannisantara I (1020-30 A.D.) :

Nannisantara I was the son and successor of Tyagisantara.[40] An inscription[41] dated 1027 A.D. refers itself to the rule of Annaladeva who had several epithets including Nannisantara[42] *(Nannisantara-namadi samasta-prasasti-sahitam).* Another record[43] of the same date refers to the reign of Vikramasantra. Vikramasantara mentioned herein may be identical with Nannisantara I *alias* Annaladeva[44] referred to above.[45]

The reign periods fixed elsewhere for the Santara chiefs from Jayakesi to Tyagisantara by K.V. Ramesh and Madhav N. Katti[46] have been largely adopted here. But we differ from them in regard to the reign period fixed for Nannisantara as it seems to be too long for him. The first available record[47] of Virasantara III *alias* Viradeva is dated 1016 A.D. We have to accommodate four chiefs who preceded him before 1060 A.D. Therefore, the duration of the rule of Nannisantara I and his successors can be fixed as follows :

Nannisantara I c. 1020-30 A.D.

Rayasantara c. 1030-35 A.D.

Chikkavirasantara (Virasantara II) c. 1035-40 A.D.

Ammana c. 1040-50 A.D.

Tailapadeva I c. 1050-60 A.D.

Virasantara III (Viradeva or Biruga) c. 1060-70 A.D.

Rayasantara (1030-35 A.D.) :

Rayasantara succeeded his father Nannisantara I.[48] A much demaged inscription[49] dated 1058 A.D. mentions *mahamandalesvara* Rayasantara-deva. This Rayasantaradeva has been identified elsewhere with Virasantara III who married the daughter of Pattiyadeya *alias* Alvara.[50]

Virasantara II (1035-40 A.D.)

Rayasantara was succeded by his son Chikka-virasantara (i.e., Virasantara II) and in turn he was succeeded by Ammana.[51] We do not know much about them due to the paucity of their records. However, Odd-Ammana figuring in a record[52] of 1007 A.D. was identified with Ammana[53] who was referred to in the genealogical account of the Santaras.[54] Further his reign was fixed from 1000 to 1030 A.D. on consideration of the matrimonial alliances between the Santaras and the Alupas.[55] Both the identification as well as the rule fixed for him cannot be accepted because it has already been shown that during this period Tyagisantara (905-1020 A.D.) and Nannisantara I (1020-30 A.D.) were respectively wielding power over Santalige-1000 province. Therefore, the proper course will be to presume that Odd-Ammana was another name for Tyagisantara.[56]

Ammana (1040-50 A.D.) :

Ammana gave his daughter Biraladevi to Bankeya i.e., Bankideva I (1020-50 A.D.) in marriage and brought the younger sister of the latter viz., Mankabbarasi as the wife of his son Tailapadeva I who succeeded him.[57]

Tailapadeva I (1050-60 A.D.) :

The period of Tailapadeva I, on the basis of the marital alliance as shown above, has been fixed from 1030 to 1060 A.D.[58] This sort of fixation of the period for him poses some problems in the light of the record of Virasantara III who succeeded Tailapadeva I in 1060 A.D.[59] In view of this, reign period for Tailapadeva I can be fixed from 1050 to 1060 A.D.

Virasantara III (1060-70 A.D.)

Virasantara III succeeded his father Tailapadeva I to the Santara throne in 1060 A.D. He is also known as Biruga and Viradeva. In that year he was adminstering Santalige-1000. He offered gifts to the goddess Nokkiyabbe[60] i.e., Lokkiyabbe. The hostility that existed between this Santara chief and the Hoysalas can be gleaned from an inscription[61] wherein an encounter is referred to with the Hoysala forces in which Kumbara Siriyama lost his life in c. 1062 A.D. This is further attested to by the statement that Virasantara freed the kingdom from those who had no claim to it [62] *(nirdayadamum nishkamtakamum nirakulamum madi)*. His epithet *trailokyamalla-Santaradeva*[63] denotes that he was a subordinate of Chalukya Somesvara I (1043-68 A.D.).

An inscription[64] dated Ṣaka 1011, Kilaka refers to a battle against a Nayaka of the Hoysala ruler. In this battle Ketamalla Sahani lost his life while fighting for Virasantara. the Saka date given in this record seems to be wrong as the cyclic year Kilaka actually falls in 1068 A.D. Therefore, undoubtedly Virasantara of this record was none other than Virasantara III. Bijjaladevi, according to the genealogical account provided in an inscription[65] dated 1077-78 A.D., was his wife. But another record[66] dated 1062 A.D. refers to Chagaladevi as his wife. She is stated to have set up a *makara-torana* in front of a *basadi* of Nokkiyabbe i.e., Lokkiyabbe the family goddess and also to have got constructed a temple for Chagesvara at Balligame.

Virasantara III had two brothers viz., Singideva and Barumadeva[67] whose inscriptions have not so far been discovered. He also had four sons from Viramahadevi, *alias* Kamchaladevi *alias* Biraladevi.[68] They are : Tails II *alias* Bhujabalasantara, Nannisantara II; Odduga and Barmma II.[69] Virasantara III died in c. 1070 A.D.[70]

Taila II (10780-96 A.D.) :

An epigraph[71] assigned to c. 1077 A.D. by Rice mentions Virasantaradeva as a subordinate of Tribhuvanamalladeva (i.e., Vikramaditya VI). Another inscription [72] of the same date refers to Bhujabala-santara. Virasantara and Bhujabalasantara of these records may be identified with Tailapa II as he had the title *Bhujabalasantara.*[73]

Nannisantara II (1076-1105 A.D.) :

Santaradeva[74] who is stated to have laid seige to some place in 1076 A.D. can be identified with Nannisantara II, the younger brother of Bhujabala-santara.

Nannisantara II seems to have succeeded his father Virasantara III since the rule of his elder brother is not mentioned in any inscriptions. He is described as a greater personality than Ganga Butuga Permadi as the emperor (*chakravarti,* probably meaning Vikramaditya VI) himself came to meet him half way and offered half of his seat on the metal throne *(loha-vistara)* to him. Though there may be some exaggeration in this description it is neverthe - less indicative of his greatness. His record[75] dated 1077 - 78 A.D. is very important as it vividly contains the information as well as the genealogy of the members of this family without any interruptions. Further the significance of this record lies in the fact that it also throws much light on the history of some contemporary chiefs like tha Alupas, the Gangas, the Bayalnad chiefs, the Kadambas and the Nolambas who had matrimonial relationships with the Santaras. It also furnishes the genealogy of Rakkasaganga,[76] who was a grandfather of Nannisantara II in whose lineage Viramahadevi *alias* Kamchaladevi, the mother of Nannisantara II, was born.

Nannisantara II is stated to have defeated the enemies who were a menace to his kingdom *(rajya - kantakaram - nishkamtam madi)* and secured for himself the land (i.e., kingdom) which was earlier in the hands of enemies *(Palakaladim paravattam ada - bhumiyam svayattam madi)*. He got the name Nannisantara because he was the very embodiment of truth.[77] It is very interesting to note from this inscription that Chattaladevi, an elder sister of Viramahadevi, claims to be the mother of Nannisantara II which indicates the demise of Viramahadevi by the time of this record, as it records the gift of some villages to the *Pamchakuta - basadi* known as *Uruvitilaka* by Chattaladevi along with the three sons[78] of his younger sister for the merit of the parents of Chattaladevi viz., Arumulideva (i.e., Pakkssaganga) and Gavabbarasi as well as the parents of Nannisantara II, Viraladevi and Rajaditya[79] apparently another name of Virasantara III respectively.

As we often find the names of Tailapa II and Odduga *alias* Vikramasantara in association with Nannisantara II, it is presumed that they were assisting their brother Nannisantara II in his administration. That some times one of these chiefs individually granted some gifts during this period is evidenced by an inscripiton[80] of Odduga *alias* Vikramasantara. He offered the gift of some villages with remission of all the taxes to the *Panchakuta - basadi* for its maintenance etc., in 1087 A.D. An inscription dated 1096 A.D. of the reign of Vikramaditya VI refers to a was and mentions Tailapa II as his subordinate.[81]

An epigraph[82] of Nannisantara II dated 1103 A.D. furnishes the genealogy down to four sons of Virasantara III. Nannisantara is also called as Tribhuvanamalla Santara which denotes his subordination to Vikramaditya VI. The above record mentions the construction of a *basadi* by Chattaladevi in association with the four sons of her younger sister, opposite to *Panchakuta - basadi* which was already in existance at Pombuchcha.

Odduga (1100-30 A.D.) :

Odduga appears to have succeeded his elder brother Nannisantara II. He is known by several names such as Odduga, Kumara Roddamarasa,[83] Nodduga and Vikramasantara.[84]

That Tailapa II, a chief belonging to the family of the Kadambas of Banavasi was engaged in hostilities with the Santaras is indicated by a reference to an encounter that took place in 1127 A.D. against the Santaras.[85] Nothing is known about Barman II, an younger brother of Odduga.

Taila III (1130 - 45 A.D.) :

Odduga was succeeded by his son Taila III who is also known as Tribhuvanamalla Santara.[86] It is not possible for us to know further details about these chiefs as they do not seem to have left behind any records of their own.

Srivallabha (1145 - 57 A.D.) :

Taila III had a daughter by name Pampadevi and a son, Srivallabha *alias* Vikramasantara II. The rule of both the sister and her brother is recorded in 1147 A.D.[87] In the same year both are stated to have consecrated the northern *Pattasale* of the *Pancha - basadi* and granted some gifts to it, Pampa - devi is credited with the title of *Nutana Attimabbe* as she was very much immersed in activities connected with Jainism. She had a daughter named Bachaladevi.

Virasantara IV (1157 - 1200 A.D.) :

Bhujabala Virasantara IV was the son and successor of Srivallabha. The relationship of father and son is shown in a very peculier manner. In other words, Bachaladevi wife of Bhujabala Virasantara is mentioned as a daughter - in - law *(sose)* of Srivallabha in an inscription[88] dated 1157 A.D. In fact, it is very interesting to know that she was the daughter of his elder sister Pampadevi. Some of the records[89] of Bhujabala Virasantara IV dated 1173, 1189 and 1191 A.D. respectively do not mention his overlord. But his record[90] dated 1197 A.D. mentions Trailokyamalla Somesvara IV (1184 - 1200 A.D.) as his overlord. From this account we may surmise that he enjoyed an independent status for some time. Further *Mahaprdhana Kumara* Sroyama, Pattasahani Bamayya etc., are mentioned as his subordinates.[91] In an incomplete record[92] he is referred to as Tibhuvanamalla - Bhujabalapratapa - Santiyadevarasa. Another epigraph[93] of 1191 A.D. refers to a battle in which Ekkalarasa of Uddhara marched against the Santaras but fled from the battle field. This Ekkalarasa has been indentified with a local chief who was then ruling over Banavasi.[94].

Kundana (1220 - 30 A.D.) :

After a gap of nearly 20 years we find an inscription[95] belonging to the rule of Tribhuvanamalla Santara and his brother Kundana. The importance of this record lies in the fact that it furnishes the genealogy of the Alupa rulers on the one hand and, on the other, reveals the names of two chiefs of the Santara family who are otherwise unknown. Tibhuvanamalla Santara of this record has been identified with Virasantara IV.[96] He had the title *Pamdita - pandya* and *Pandya - Dhananjaya* as also the epithet *Hurmadi Chakravarti*. His two brothers were Virabhupala and Kundana. Of the two, Kundana suceeded the Alupa ruler Kulasekhara (c. 1160 - 1220 A.D.). The circumstance that led him to adorn the Alupa throne has been elsewhere correctly assessed and on that basis the duration of his regin has been fixed from 1220 to 1230 A.D.[97] According to the available epigraphs of the early Santaras, Kundana was the only Santara chief who had the opportunity of ruling over Aluvakheda.

The dates for the above Santara chiefs, arrived at on the basis of their records, are given below :

Taila II, Bhujabalasantara 1070 - 96 A.D.

Nannisantara II 1076 - 1105 A.D.

Odduga, Vikramasantara 1100 - 30 A.D.

Taila III, Tribhuvanamalla Santara 1130 - 45 A.D.

Pampadevi (daughter of Taila III) 1147 A.D.

Srivallabha, Vikramasantara 1145 - 57 A.D.

Bhujabalavirasantara IV, Tribhuvanamalla 1157 - 1200 A.D.

Kundana 1220 - 30 A.D.

The Medieval Santaras

The Santara chiefs of this period are stated to be the descendants of Brahma, who was born on the lotus sprouting from the naval of Vishnu. They were called Santaras because of their equanimity as well as the fact that they were successful in conquering the external enemies viz., the enemy kings, and internal enemies viz., the qualities of fear and greed. The record[98] containing the above narration is dated in 1149 A.D. and belongs to Jagaddevarasa. An important point to be borne in mind, especially while dealing with these Santara chiefs, is that no single record refers to them as having belonged to the ugranvaya which is quite common in the case of the early Santaras.

The earliest chief of this branch was Jagaddevarasa who traces his descent from Ammana who, in all likelihood, was an early Santara chief. According to the genealogy provided in his record, Singi was a brother of Ammana. The son of the latter was Taila (apparently Taila II) whose son was Kama. Jagaddeva and Singideva were his two sons. Further, Vijayadityadeva and Chattaladevi, a sister of Bijjaladevi, the wife of Kama, had a son viz., Jayakesideva, who has been reckoned as an elder brother of Jagaddeva.

Jagaddevarasa (1146 - 80 A.D.) :

Jagaddevarasa, a mahamandalesvara, has been described as the lord of Patti - Pombuchchapura (Patti - Pombuchcha - puravaradhisvara), and as the obtainer of a boon from the goddess Padmavati (Padmavati - labdha - varaprasada). He had the title Tribhuvanamalla, pointing to his subordination to the Chalukya emperor Jagadekamalla II.

Jagaddevarasa was ruling from his residence at Setu (i.e., Setunad) situated in the south - west of Sagar Taluk in Shimoga District.

A record[99] dated 1159 A.D., of the reign of Chalukya Tribhuvanamalla apparantly Taila III (1149/50 - 63 A.D.), refers to Raya Tailahadeva obviously Jagaddevarasa. The genealogy given in this record differs from that of the fore - said inscription, though the chief of both the records is the same. In contradiction to the former record, the descent of Jagaddevarasa in this record is traced from Raya Tailahadeva who in all probability is identifiable with Rayasantara of the early family as he is stated to have had a wife by name Akkhadevi (corrupt form of Akkadevi). This identification is further proved by the mention that she was the younger sister of Nannisantara apparently Nannisantara I. The genealogical portion of this record furnishes the names of the following chiefs, viz. Kama, Simha (Singi), Ammana who were the three sons of Raya Tailahadeva. Bijjaladevi, of the lineage of the Pandyakula, was the wife of Kama. They had two sons and one daughter viz., Jagaddeva; Simgideva and Aliyadevi. The latter had been given in marriage to Honneyarasa, born in the Ganga- vamsa and from her was born their son Jayakesideva.

It has already been stated that the genenlogical account given in this record differs from that of the former[100] which is dated in 1149 A.D. It is very surprising to note this change within a short span of ten years. The discrepancy about the parents of Jayakesi has also crept in by then. Though the name of Jayakesi occurs in both the records,[101] the names of his parents are different. From a careful study of the present record it appears that the chiefs of this medieval family tried to associate themselves as for as possible with the early chiefs of the Santaras in order to enhance their power and prestige. Akkadevi wife of Tailapa is connected with the younger sister of Nannisantara I (?) about which the records of early Santaras are silent.

The tendency of incorporating unhistorical matter into the text of later records is quite evident from observations made elsewhere.[102] The record in question is not an exception to this as far as its corrupt genealogy is concerned.

An inscription[103] of the reign of Chalukya Tribhuvanamalla Jagadekamalla III (1163 - 83 A.D.), dated 1164 A.D., refers to *mahamandalesvaras* Rayasantara and Tailapadeva. We have already known from a record[104] dated 1159 A.D. that Raya Tailapadeva had a son named Kamadeva. On the basis of this record we may conclude that *mahamandalesvara* Rayasantara and Tailapadeva, who seem to have been mentioned separately in this epigraph, are one and the same and also identical with Jagaddeva.

Jagaddevarasa was forced by Kakatiya Prola II to withdraw his army while he marched with his master Chalukya Taila III in 1153 A.D. against Warangal to punish the rebels.[105]

The battles fought at Avaraguppe in 1160 A.D., indicate some political distrubances that prevailed during the reign of Jagaddevarasa.[106]

Transfer of Jagaddeva's allegiance from the Chalukyas to the Kalachuris is gathered from a record[107] of the reign of Rayamurari Sovideva (1167 - 76 A.D.). The reason for the acceptence of the supremacy of the Kalachuris may be his defeat at the hands of Bijjala in about 1162 A.D.[108]

An inscription[109] dated 1164 A.D. refers itself to the 19th regnal year of Virasantaradeva, a subordinate of Kalachuri Bijjala. Jagaddeva and Singideva are also referred to in this record. We know well that epigraphs belonging to Jagaddeva are dated before and after the date of this record. Virasantara of this record is therefore none other than Jagaddeva himself. His earliest availabel record[110] is dated in 1149 A.D. The 19th regnal year given in this record of 1164 A.D. shows that he commenced his rule in 1146 A.D. It is only rarely that inscriptions refer themselves to the regnal years of a mere chieftain. Does it indicate here that Jagaddeva was enjoying the full powers of his master ? May be so, because the records issued in 1164 - 67 A.D. hint at the enmity which arose between the Santaras and the Kalachuris on Bijjala attacking Jagaddeva with his followers. However, reverting to the record in question, it refers to a battle in which the forces of *hiriyadandanayaka* Aralaya, the governor of Banavasi - 12000, Birarase the chief of Hosagunda, Singideva of Hombuchcha, the Alupa king from below the ghats and Jagaddevarasa were involved.

Due to the wrong interpretation of the text of this epigraph, Jagaddevarasa of the present record had been considered as the successor of Kavi Alupendra by Saletore.[111] Singideva of Hombuchcha and Jagaddevarasa referred to above have been treated as the grandsons of Virasantara by Ramesh.[112] This relastionship is not acceptable for the genealogical account of the early Santaras which runs down to Bhujabalavirasantara does not refer to these names at all. Further these two chiefs who claim their descent from Ammana, according to the genealogy of the medieval Santaras, were the grandsons of Taila.[113] Birarasa of Hosagunda deemed to be a feudatory of Bhujabalavirasantara IV, has been indentified with his namesake Birarasa of an epigraph[114] of 1179 A.D.

Singideva seems to have been associated with the administration of his elder brother Jagaddeva. Two of his records are assigned to c. 1165 A.D. by Rice. One of them refers to a cattle raid[115] and another refers to him as Virasantara Siggi and abruptly ends after giving his epithets.[116]

Some of the epigraphs of this period belonging to the Santara chief Singideva as well as Kalachuri Bijjala refer to the constant war between them during 1164 and 1167 A.D. Kalachuri Bijjala marched against Jagaddeva on more than one occasion. Bijjala was assisted in these battles by the following chiefs, Kirtideva, Bamma, Uddhareya Ekkala, Satyavadili Vikramadityadeva, Bandalikeya Soyideva and Guttimandalika Birarasa.[117] In the last attack that took place in 1167 A.D. Kalimaraya is stated to have bravely fought and repulsed the enemies on behalf of the Santaras.

From the above account, we learn that Jagaddevarasa and his brother Singideva were so powerful as to face the attack of a band of chiefs under the orders of Kalachuri Bijjala. Further we may conclude that these Santara chiefs tried their best to throw off the yoke of the Kalachuris and that Bijjala, by his constant attacks, struggled hard to curtail them.

As far as the identification of the chiefs who participated in the above wars is concerned, Kirtideva has been identified with the Kadamba chief of the same name viz., Kirtideva III and Bamma with his nephew.[118] Ekkalarasa of Uddhare may be identified with a local ruler who was then ruling over Banavasi[119] and Uddhare is identical with modern Udri in Sorab Taluk, Shimoga District.[120] Soyideva of Bandalike may be identified with his namesake, a Kadamba chief of Hangal, who was a subordinate of Kalachuri Bijjala.[121] Bandalike, the place - name associated with Soyideva, is identical with the village of the same name situated in Shikaripur Taluk.[122] It is not possible to identify the other chiefs mentioned in this record.

Jagaddeva, who showed his prowess in 1167 A.D. during the attacks of the Kalachuri ruler, was however forced to accept the suzarainty of the Kalachuris in 1175 A.D.[123] as may be gathered from an inscription of 1175 A.D. Within a short span of nearly 5 years he once again transferred hiss allegience to the Chalukyas.[124]

Simgideva (1175 - 1190 A.D.) :

As we do not find the records belonging to Jagaddevarasa after 1175 A.D. it may be presumed that he was succeeded by his brother Simgideva. Isvaradeva II (c. 1155-85 A.D.), the Sinda chief of Belagutti, had acquired the northern districts of Santalige-1000[125] during this period. This event provoked Simgideva to march against the above mentioned Sinda chief in order to release the Santalige province from his clutches. The herostones[126] of the time of Isvaradeva II refer to the raids carried on against him by Simgideva. Isvaradeva II ably resisted the aggression of the Santara chief and continued his sway over Santalige.[127]

From the above narration, it is proved that there existed hostility between the Sindas and the Santaras. Meanwhile, the cordiality of Santaras with the Guttas was further strengthened through marital alliance when Simgideva married Vijayamahadevi, the sister of Gutta Vikramaditya II[128] (1180-1235 A.D.). Simgideva's record dated 1189 A.D. does not mention any everlord. Hence it can be surmised that he was then ruling independently.[129]

Ballal is surmised to be the son of Simgideva. He has been identified with Ballalabhupa of the Kuruvatti record.[130] He married Tuluvaladei, daughter of Vikramaditya II. Their son was Bamma.[131]

In the absence of the records of Bammarasa, the son of Jagaddevarasa as well as Bamma, the son of Ballala it is very difficult to be certain about their succession to the Santara throne after the rule of Simgideva. Santara family comes to a close after Simgideva.

Among the members figuring in the genealcgical account of this family, Jagaddeva ruled in association with his younger brother Simgideva who succeeded him. On the basis of the available epigraphs the reign period for both of them may be fixed as shown below. :

Jagaddeva 1146 - 75 A.D.

Simgideva 1175 - 90 A.D.

The Later Santaras

The sway of the later Santara chiefs over the Kalasa kingdom roughly started about 1216 A.D. They had epithets like *Adataraditya, Adiyarakulatilaka* and are described as worshippers of the feet of the god Adibillesvara of Hombuchcha [132] *(Hombuchchada - Adibillesvara - deva - sripulu - padmaradhaka), Pombuchchapura - varesvara,* etc.

It is stated by Desai that the Santaras had shifted their capital from Pombuchcha to Kalasa in the Mudigare Taluk of Chikmagalur District in 1215 A.D. in the wake of the expeditions of the Hoysalas.[133] In this lineage *mahamandalesvara* Jagadevapandya appears in 1217 A.D. His record[134] refers to a battle in which Kavadeyabimma lost his life. Pandyadevarasa's son was Biradevarasa and his son Bammarasa.

An inscription of the time of Isvaradeva III, the chief of Belagutti Sindas, states that he descended on Abbaluru (in Dharwar District) together with the Nayakas of Santalige District.[135] In this connection Desai states that Isvaradeva with the support of the Yadava general Mayideva encroached upon the Santara territory and thus extended the southern borders of his kingdom.[136] Desai's opinion is purely based on imagination as it is not evidenced by any record. The epigraphs belonging to the Santaras of this period do not make any reference to this effect. Further he states that the Nayakas referred to in the record of Isvaradeva III were the local chiefs who were appointed by him to rule over the newly acquired Santalige District.[137] This statement also seems to be incorrect as the rule of the Nayakas of Santalige (not the local chiefs as such) had started only in 1288 A.D. as will be shown below.

Mahamandalesvara Kumara Biradevarasa succeeded his father Pandyadeva. His record,[138] assignable to 1241 A.D. on the basis of the cyclic year Saravari mentined therein, referes to a battle between Soyideva who may probably be identical with the chief of the same name who participated in a battle during 1167 A.D.[139] and Bokora Madaga-nayaka etc., at Bayalahalli. Ramenayaka attacked the enemies, slew many and lost his life probably on behalf of the Santara chief.

Another epigraph[140] of 1248 A.D. refers to a battle of Biradeva against the chief Bommarasa of Hombuchcha. When Biradeva was returning after plundering Humcha, Jakkeya-nayaka fought against the Kalasa army, killed some of the soldiers and horses and ultimately sacrificed his life for the cause of his master. His other two records[141] dated 1248 and 1255 A.D. also mention some of his encounters.

Biradeva was succeeded by *mahamandalasvara* Bommarasa in 1266 A.D.[142] The hostility between the Santaras and the Hoyasalas led to a battle in 1266 A.D. Narasimha III seems to have subjugated Bommarasa in this encounter as we see that the latter fought for the Hoysalas against Goveya Chattayadeva in 1267 A.D. i.e., Shashtha III of the Kadambas of Goa, a subordinate of the Yadavas.[143] The struggle for supremacy between two major powers viz., the Hoysalas and the Yadavas was not without effect on the Santaras. In a way, it compelled the Santara chief, as a subordinate of the Hoysalas, to participate in another war against the Yadavas in 1270 A.D.[144] After this incident Bommarasa appears to have declared his independence probably taking advantage of the misunderstanding between the two Hoysala brothers, viz., Narasimha III and Ramanatha.

Mahamandalesvara Tammarasa succeeded his father Bommarasa. The two records[145] of the former dated 1282 A.D. refer to a raid on Hosagunda by *mahamandaleavara* Birarasa. An inscription[146] of 1287 A.D. gives an elaborate description of Tammarasa. Some of the titles which he bore are as follows : Breaker of the pride of the Lola king *(Lola - raya - mana - mardana)*, destroyar of the Kadamba king *(Kadambaravya - vibhada)*, Hunter of the Konkani king *(Konkaniga - raya - bemtekara)*, establisher of the Tulu king *(Tulu - raya - pratishtha - charya)*, master of the Western Ocean *(Paschimasamudradhipati)*, Lord of Patti - Pombuchchapura (Patti - Pombucha (chcha) puravaradhisvara) and worshipper of the devine lotus feet of the god Billesvera.

(Billesvaradeva - divya - sripadapadmaradhaka). He is said to have been ruling from Hosagunde. His genealogy given in this record is as under :

Sahakara and others

Jinadatta

Virasantara and others

Cholama

Bira

Brahma or Bammarasa

Tammarasa

The first three chiefs of the above genealogy were early Santaras. Nothing is known about Cholama. But on the consideration of the record of Jagadevapandya who was the first chief of this family, and whose name does not figure in the above list, he may be identified with Cholama. His two successors have been already dealt with. The last chief of this family is Tammarasa of the present record. It has been suggested elsewhere that he ruled Santalige as a subordinate of Yadava Ramachandra (1271 - 1311 A.D.).[147] It may not be so because his records do not mention any overlord and hence we can presume that he ruled as an independent chief.

From the study of the available records pertaining to the later Santaras the duration of the reigns of the chiefs can be fixed as follows. :

Jagadevapandya	1217 - 35 A.D.
Biradeva	1235 - 60 A.D.
Bommarasa	1260 - 78 A.D.
Tammarasa	1278 - 87 A.D.

From 1288 A.D. we notice the rule of the Nayakas belonging to the Santara clan. Soveyanayaka, also known as Someyanayaka, and Kotinayake, are stated to have been ruling over eighteen Kampanas.[148] Their records dated 1288 and 1290 A.D. refer to some religious grants and military encounters. Hoysala Ballala III is said to have taken Hosagunda, captured Kotinayaka and carried off his elephants in 1300 A.D.[149]

Yadava Ramachandra renewed his hostilities with the Hoysalas due to which his general Yobaranayaka attacked the Santara chief, a subordinate of Ballala III, at Nulagiri.[150]

An inscription[151] from Hosala dated 1334 A.D. in the reign of the Hoysala Ballala III refers to Lokanathadeva of the line of *(bali)* Dattaluva,[152] among those attending upon his queen Chikkayi Tayi. The former has been identified with Lokanathadeva of the record of the same year.[153] He bore imperial titles such as *Samasta - bhuvanasraya, Prithvivallabha, Maharajadhiraja, Paramasvara* and *Paramabhattaraka* along with the feudetory title *Mahamandalesvara.* He also had the typical Santara epithets like *Patti Pombuchcha - puravaradhisvara* and *Mahogra-vamsa - lalama* etc. That he was a subordinate of the Hoysala monarch Ballala III is indicated by his description as 'an object of admiration for the Hoysala emperor' *(Ballala - raja - Chittachamatkara).*[154] By this time South Kanara was under the control of the Hoysalas, as whose subordinate Lokanatha was permitted to add the Karkala region to his own principality of Santalige - 1000.[155] Bommideva and Siddaladevi were his parents. Bommaladevi and Somaladevi were his two sisters.[156] Lokanathadevarasa, a powerful feudatory of the Hoysalas, was probably the last chief of this family.

However, we hear of one more family having the appellation 'Santaras' which came in to existence in the beginning of the fifth century. The members of this family trace their descent from Nannisantara a chief of the early Santaras. The earliest chief of this family was Bhairava I who is credited to be the first ruler of Kalasa to establish his family's seat of power at Karkala. We are not entering into further details of this family as its history has already been elucidated by Ramesh.[157]

The Genealogy of the Santaras[158]

1. Vikramá c. 800 A.D.

2. Chagi c. 835

3. Vira I c. 850

Kannare — 4. Kavadeva c. 875

5. Tyagi c. 900

6. Nanni. c. 925

7. Raya c. 950

8. Chikka Vira c. 975

9. Ammana c. 1000

Birabbrasi, Biraladevi Daughter — 10. Taila or Taila I c. 1025

11. Vira II — Singideva — Barmmadeva I or Bamma

12.Taila or Tailapa II 1077 — Goggiga or 'Nannisantara' or 'Govindara' — Odduga or Vikramasantara — Barmmadeva II or Bomma II

Pampadevi Daughter — 13. Srivallabha 'Virama- Santara' 1096 — 14. Taila III 'Tailuga' (1089- 1096) — Goainda 'Raya - Santara'1096 — Boppuga

15. Taila IV or Tailapa 1115-16, 1162

16. Kamadeva — Simha — Ammana

17. Jagadeva 1160 — Singideva — Aliyadevi daughter

Jayakesi — Santeyadeva

The Genealogy of the early Santaras reconstructed

Brahma

Raha

After many rulers

Sahakara

Jinadatta

After many rulers

Srikesi — Jayakesi 825 - 50 A.D.

Ranakesi and some unnamed rulers (850-90)

Vikramasantara 890 - 920

Chagisantara 920 - 45

Virasantara I 945 - 70

Kannarasantara — Kavadeva 970-95

Tyagisantara 995 - 1020

Nannisantara I 1020-30

Rayasantara 1030-35

Chikkavira-santara II (Virasantara II) 1035 - 40

Ammana 1040 - 50

Birabbarasi; Biraladeve — Tailepadeva I 1050-60

Virasantara III Viradeva or Biruga 1060-70 — Singideva — Barmmadeva I

contd.

Virasantara III

- Taila II, Bhujabalasantara 1070-96
- Nannisantara II, Goggi Govindaradeva, Piriya Nannisantara-deva, 1076 - 1105
- Odduga, Odduga, Nadduga, Vikrama Santara, Kumara Roddamarasa 1100-30
  - Taila III, Tribhuvanamallasantara 1130-45
    - Pampadevi 1147
    - Srivallabha, Vikramasantara 1145-57
      - Bhujabalavira Santaradeva IV 1157-1200
        - Kundana 1220-30
- Barmma II

The genealogy of the Medieval Santaras as furnished in two records

I. E.C., VII, Sk. 103 - 1149 A.D.

Ammana

Taila

Kama *m.* Bijjaladevi

- Jayakesi, son of Vijayaditya and Chattaladevi, sister of Bijjaladevi
- Jagaddeva
  - Bammarasa
- Singideva

II. *E.C.*, VIII, Sa. 159 - 1159 A.D.

Taila *m.* Akkadevi younger sister of Nannisantara (I ?)

Kama | Singi | Ammana

Jagaddeva 1146-75 A.D. | Singideva, Tribhuvanamalle Bhujabalapratapa santaradeva 1175-90 A.D. | Aliyadevi *m.* Honneponna or Honneyarasa of Ganga vamsa

Jayakesideva

The genealogy of the later Santaras

Sahakara and others

Jinadatta

Virasantara and others

Cholame (Jagadevapandya) 1217-35 A.D.

Biradeva 1235-60

Bammarasa (Brahmma) 1260-78

Tammarasa 1278-87

THE MATRIMONIAL ALLIANCES OF THE SANTARASAS

The study of the epigraphs[159] of the Santaras throws much light on the matrimonial alliances they forged with the contemporary chiefs which were intended mainly to strengthen and consolidate their position.

To begin with, Vikramasantara (890-920 A.D.) married Lakshmidevi daughter of Kamadeva, the ruler of Banavasi, whose identification is uncertain. However, it is opined that he may have been a scion of the Kadamba family.[160] Vikramasantara's grandson Virasantara I (945-70 A.D.) is stated to have married Jakaladevi, daughter of a certain Santivarma whose name and the family to which he belonged are not known.[161] Kavadeva successor of Virasantara I had the connection of Vira-Bayalnatha by offering his daughter Chamdalacevi in marriage.[162]

Though the entry of the Santaras into the Aluva-kheda can be dated back to the reign of Chitravahana II[163] (765-800 A.D.) on the basis of an inscription available at Udiyavara,[164] their relation with the Alupas actually started during the chieftaincy of Chagisantara (990-45 A.D.) by getting Enjaladevi daughter of Rananjaya[165] (900-30 A.D.) in marriage. This sort of relationship has been once again renewed after 90 years by striking matrimonial alliances between them. At this juncture, the Santara chief Ammana (1040-50 A.D.) gave his daughter Biraladevi to Bankeya[166] i.e., Bankideva I (1020-50 A.D.) and brought Mankabbarasi, the younger sister of the latter, to his son Tailapadeva I. The same trend was kept up till the time of Virasantara III though Tailapadeva I had married Keleyabbarasi the daughter of Ganga-Palayadeva. Pattiyodeya[167] (1050-80 A.D.) an Alupa ruler offered his daughter Achaladevi to the former chief. Apart from marrying Achaladevi Virasantara III, extended his influence over some of the dynasties such as the Gangas, the chiefs of Kanchi and the Nolambas.

Chattaladevi and Kamchsaladevi were two daughters of Rakkasaganga who had the title Arumuli and Gavabbarasi. Chattaladevi married Kaduvatti, a chief of Kanchi. Kamchaladevi also came to be known as Viramahadevi after her marriage with Vikramasantara III, who had four sons, viz., Taila II, Nannisantara II, Odduga and Barmma II. Treating the afore - said four members as sons of Chattaladevi who was eulogised at length indicates that she did not have any issues of her own in Kaduvetti whose death might have taken place before 1077-78 A.D. as we do not find any reference to him thereafter. Virasantara III further extended his hands to Bijjaladevi, a daughter of Nolamba Narasimha, who has been identifird with a subordinate of the same name under Chalukya Somesvara I (1043-63 A.D.).[168]

Harivarma of Kadamba lineage was stated to have given his daughter Nagaladevi to Tyagisantara (995-1020 A.D.). It is surprising to note in this connection that no ruler of the name of Harivarma belonging to the family of the Kadambas was in existence during that period.[169]

Nannisantara I (1020-30 A.D.), son and successor of Tyagisantara had followed a different policy and struck an alliance with the Silaharas of North Konkan.[170] He married Siriyadevi a daughter of Arikesari who was ruling over Palasige-nadu.

Odduga also known as Vikramasantara (1100-30 A.D.) had a raltionship with the Pandyas as he was said to have married Chamdaladevi, a Pandya princess, the name of whose father, however, is not known.[171]

We know the system of getting a daughter of a sister in marriage *(Sodarike).* But here we find another type of marriage werein Pampadevi offers her daughter Bachaladevi to Virasantara IV (1157-97 A.D.) son of his younger brother Srivallabha. Further, it is very intersting to note in this connection that the relationship of a son and father is shown through Bachaladevi who was called as daughter - in - law *(sose)* of Srivallabha.[172]

Besides the marital alliances of the Santaras with the contemporary chiefs, we do come across a reference made to the Guttas of Guttavolal also. Simgideva (1175-90 A.D.) brother of Jagadeverasa, chief of the medieval period, married Vijayamahadevi who was stated to be a sister of Vikramaditya II (1180 - 1235 A.D.).[173] Thus, the secret of the sway of the Santaras over Santalige - 1000 province etc., for more than four hundred years according to our notion, was firmly based upon matrimonial alliances which they forged with various contemporary chiefs.

REFERENCES

1. The significance of the name 'Santara' has been made known in an article entitled 'The Origin and History of the 'Santalige - 1000' by K.V.Ramesh and Madhav N. Katti. See *QJMS.*, LVII, pp. 25 ff. Before this, the members of this family and the province Santalige on which they ruled are spelt as 'Santaras and the Santalige'. See *The Struggle for Empire,* p. 926, *HISI.*, p. 441.

2. *E.C.*, VI (1901), VII (1902) and VIII (1904).

3. *Ibid.*, VIII (1904), Nr. 35, Ti. 192, Ss. 95, 159 and VII (1902), Sk. 103 and 312.

4. Cf. *SII.*, XVIII, Introduction, p. xxvii; *The Struggle for Empire,* p. 188.

5. The three records (*E.C.*, VI (1901), Kp. 40 and Cm. 92 - 93) which are said to be the earliest and attributed to the Santaras. The dates of which have been assigned by Rice from 700 and 750 A. D. have not been taken into consider ation in this chapter for the reason that their history as the chiefs of Santalige-1000 has been known only from about the middle of the 9th century A. D. However,there is an earliest reference to a Santara chief (*SII*, VII, No. 294) in an inscription assigned to the rule of Chitravahana II (765- 800A.D.) on Alupa ruler. See K.V.Ramesh : *A History of South Kanara*, p. 79.

6. K. V. Ramesh : *op.cit.*, p. 79.

7. *E.C.*, VIII (1904), T1. 192.

8. *Ibid.*, Nr. 35.

9. The province ruled over by the Choles is known as Tondamandala. Therefore Tondamandalikas referred to in these records of the Santaras are the Chola rulers. *The Struggle for Empire*, p. 252.

10. *E.C.*, VIII (1904), Nr. 35, T1. 192, etc.

11. *Ibid.*, Nr. 35.

12. *Ibid.*, T1. 192.

13. *Ibid.*, Nr. 35.

14. *Ibid.*, Nr. 35 and T1. 192.

15. *Ibid.*, T1. 192.

16. *Ibid.*, Nr. 35.

17. The reference to Khara and Dushana in connection with the victory of Jinadatta here seems to be irrelevant as we know very well that they were the brothers of Ravana who were killed by Rama. See *Valmikiramayana, Aranyakanda*, sargas, 26-30.

18. *E.C.*, VIII (1904), Nr. 35.

19. Again this description appears to be purely mythological and has no ground to claim as such, for this city was under the effective sway of the Alupas of South Kanara, *QJMS.*, LVII, p. 28.

20. *E.C.*, VIII (104), T1. 192.

21. *Ibid.*, Nr. 35.

22. *QJMS.*, LVII, p. 32.

23. *E.C.*, VII (1902), Sk. 283.

24. *QJMS.*, LVII, p. 29.

25. *E.C.*, VIII (1904), Nr. 35.

26. *Ibid.*

27. K.V. Ramesh, *op. cit.*, p. 79. f.n. No. 96; Rice : *MCI.*, pp. 138-39.

28. *E.C.*, VIII (1904), Nr. 60.

29. *Ibid.*, VII (1902), Sk. 284.

30. *Ibid.*, Sk. 456.

31. *QJMS.*, LVII, p. 35.

32. *E.C.*, VIII (1904), Nr. Go and *Ibid.*, VII (1902), Sk. 284.

33. *Ibid.*, VIII (1904), Nr. 35.

34. *Ibid.*, VII (1902), Hl. 21-23.

35. *QJMS.*, LVII, pp. 33-34.

36. *E.C.*, VII (1902), Sh. 114.

37. *QJMS.*, LVII, p. 35.

38. *Ibid.*, p. 32.

39. *Ibid.*, p. 35.

40. *E.C.*, VIII (1904), Nr. 35.

41. *Ibid.*, VII (1902), Sk. 53.

42. *QJMS.*, LVII, p. 32, f.n. 18.

43. *E.C.*, VII (1902), Sk. 47. The portion of the numerals of the Saka year seems to be damaged. But on the basis of the name of the year Prabhava this record has been assigned to 1027 A.D. It seems that this record was issued within a month of the release of an earlier record (*E. C.*, VII (1902), Sk. 53) which contains Ashadha in the date portion while this record in question is in the month of sravana of the same year.

44. *E.C.*, VII (1902), Sk. 53.

45. *QJMS.*, LVII, p. 36.

46. *Ibid.*

47. *E.C.*, VIII (1904), Nr. 48.

48. *Ibid.*, Nr. 35.

49. *SII.*, VII, No. 278; K.V. Ramesh : *op. cit.*, p. 106, f.n. No. 27.

50. K.V. Ramesh : *op. cit.*, p. 106.

51. E.C., VIII (1904), Nr. 35.
52. *Ibid.*, VIII (1902), Sk. 195.
53. K.V. Ramesh : *op. cit.*, pp. 103-04.
54. *E.C.*, VIII (1904), Nr. 35.
55. K.V. Ramesh : *op. cit.*, p. 104; *E.C.*, VIII (1904), Nr. 35.
56. *QJMS.*, LVII, p. 36.
57. K.V. Ramesh : *op. cit.*, p. 104; *E.C.*, VIII (1904), Nr. 35.
58. K.V. Ramesh : *op. cit.*, p. 104.
59. *E.C.*, VIII (1904), Nr. 60.
60. *Ibid.*, Nr. 48.
61. *Ibid.*, Nr. 71.
62. *Ibid.*, Nr. 47. This claim has wrongly been attributed to both Virasantara III and his son Bhujabalasantara who did not at all existed. Rice : *MCI.*, p.139; *KTA.*, p.323 and Desai : *MUCK.*, p. 14. Actually Bhujabalasantara is another name of Virasantara. *E.C.*, VIII (1904), Nr. 59.
63. *E.C.*, VIII (1904), Nr. 58.
64. *Ibid.*, No. 70.
65. *Ibid.*, Nr. 35.
66. *Ibid.*, Nr. 47.
67. *Ibid.*, Nr. 35.
68. *Ibid.*, Nr. 37.
69. *Ibid.*, Nr. 35.
70. *Ibid.*, VII (1902), Sk. 62.
71. *Ibid.*, VIII (1904), Nr. 38.
72. *Ibid.*, Nr. 57.
73. *Ibid.*, Nr. 35.
74. *Ibid.*, VII (1902), Sk. 50.
75. *Ibid.*, VIII (1904), Nr. 35.
76. *Ibid.*, and Hisi., p. 348.
77. *E.C.*, VIII (1904), Nr. 35.

78. It is worthy of note in this record that Tailapa II *alias* Bhujabalasantara was not mentioned at the time of the gift offered to *Pamcha - kuta - basadi* by his other brothers along with Chattaladevi. The same is the case with Barmma II also in another inscription. *E.C.*, VIII (1940), Nr. 36. This omission in our opinion is due to the carelessness of the scribe as we do get reference to them in other records; *Ibid.*, Nr. 38.

79. *Ibid.*, Nr. 35.

80. *Ibid.*, Nr. 40.

81. *Ibid.*, Sa. 80.

82. *Ibid.*, Tl. 192.

83. *Ibid.*,Nr. 35.

84. *Ibid.*, Nr. 36.

85. *Ibid.*, Sb. 141.

86. *Ibid.*, Nr. 37.

87. *Ibid.*,

88. *Ibid.*, VI (1901), Kp. 14. This record is actually dated in Saka 1089, Isvara, Vaisakha su. 10, Sunday. The cyclic year Isvara does not fall in this Sake year. Therefore, the Saka year 1079 is appropriate for the date portion of this record and it corresponds to 1157 A.D., April 21.

89. *Ibid.*, VII (1902), Sh. 116; VIII (1904), Sa. 36 and VII (1902), Sk. 38.

90. *Ibid.*, VII (1902), Sk. 46.

91. *Ibid.*, Sh. 116.

92. *Ibid.*, VIII (1904), Sa. 36.

93. *Ibid.*, VII (1902), Sk. 38.

94. *HISI.*, pp. 125-26.

95. *ARSIE.*, 1928-29, No. 526.

96. K.V. Ramesh : *op. cit.*, pp. 118-19.

97. *Ibid.*,

98 *E.C.*, VII (1902), Sk. 103. Sometimes the name of Jagaddevarasa is spelt as Jagadevarasa also.

99 *Ibid.*, VIII (1904), Sa. 159.

100. *Ibid.*, VII (1902), Sk. 103.

101. *Ibid.*,Sk. 103 and VIII (1904), Sa. 159.

102. Careful study of the records of Pattanakudi and Kharipatan belonging to the Silaharas of South Konkan reveal how the latter record differs from the former in giving the genealogical accounts which is much interpolated. Cf. B.R.Gopal *MDSIK.*, I, p. 146.

103. *E.C.*, VIII (1904), Sa. 103.

104. *Ibid.*, Sa. 159.

105. *The Struggle for Empire*, pp. 179 and 199.

106. *E.C.*, VIII (1904), Sa. 28, 91, 92 and 93; *HISI.*, p. 112.

107. *Ibid.*, Sa. 66.

108. *The Struggle for Empire*, p. 180.

109. *MAR.*, 1930, pp. 823-26.

110. *E.C.*, VII (1902), Sk. 103.

111. B.A. Saletore : *History of Tuluva*, pp. 112 ff.

112. K.V. Ramesh : *op. cit.*, pp. 115-16.

113. *E.C.*, VII (1902), Sk. 103 and *Ibid.*, VIII (1904), Sa. 159.

114. *Ibid.*, VIII (1904), Sb. 20.

115. *Ibid.*, Sa. 112.

116. *Ibid.*, Sa. 113.

117. *Ibid.*, Sb. 177, 193 and Sa. 114.

118. *HISI.*, p. 113.

119. *Ibid.*, pp. 125-26.

120. *Shimoga District Gazetteer* (1975), pp. 670-71; *The Struggle for Empire*, p.188.

121. *HISI.*, p. 112.

122. *Shimoga District Gazetteer* (1972), pp. 626-28; *The Struggle for Empire*, p.188.

123. *E.C.*, VIII (1904), Sa. 66.

124. *Ibid.*, Sa. 131.

125. Fleet : *DKD.*, p. 577.

126. *E.C.*, VII (1902), Hl. 27 and 26.

127. Fleet : *op. cit.*, p. 577.

128. *SII.*, XVIII, No. 300.

129. *E.C.*, VIII (1904), Sa. 95.

130. *SII.*, IX, Pt. I, No. 390.

131. *Ibid.*, XVIII, No. 300.

132. *E.C.*, VIII (1904), Sa. 125.

133. Desai : *MUCK.*, p. 50.

134. *E.C.*, VIII (1904), Sa. 125. The Sake year is omitted in the date portion.Other details of the date i.e., Dhatu, *Vaisakha su*.5, Thursday corresponds to1217 A.D., April 13. Hence the saka year omitted should be1139.

135. *E.I.*, V, p. 264; Desai : *op. cit.*, pp. 53-54.

136. Desai : *op. cit.*, pp. 53-54.

137. *Ibid.*, p. 54.

138. *E.C.*, VIII (1904), Sa. 27.

139. *Ibid.*, Sa. 114.

140. *Ibid.*, Sa. 127.

141. *Ibid.*, Sa. 129 and 150.

142. *Ibid.*, Sa. 140.

143. *KUJ.*, VIII (1967), p. 10.

144. *E.C.*, VIII (1904), Sa. 137.

145. *Ibid.*, Sa. 84 and 85.

146. *Ibid.*, VIII (1902), Sk. 312.

147. *The Struggle for Empire*, pp. 194-95.

148. *E.C.*, VIII (1904), Nr. 61, Sa. 31.

149. *Ibid.*, Sa. 45.

150. P.B. Desai : *A. History of Karnataka*, p. 274.

151. *ARSIE.*, 1931-32, No. 262.

152. K.V. Ramesh : *Op. cit.*, p. 140.

153. *SII.*, VIII, No. 247; K.V. Ramesh : *op. cit.*, pp. 186 ff.

154. *ARSIE.*, 1931-32 No. 262

155. *K..V.* Ramesh : op. cit, pp 133-134

156. *JESI.*, VII pp 112 ff
157. *K .V.* Ramesh : op. cit, pp 186ff
158. Genealogy as given in *HISI.*, p. 390.
159. *E.C.*, VIII (1904), Nr. 35, 37 and Tl. 192; *Ibid.*, VI (1901), Kp. 14.
160. *QJMS.*, LVII, p, 30 and f.n. No. 10.
161. *Ibid.*, p. 31 and f.n. No. 14.
162. *Ibid.*, p. 31 and f.n. No. 15.
163. K.V. Ramesh : *A History of South Kanara*, p. 79.
164. *SII.*, VII, No. 294.
165. K.V. Ramesh : *op. cit.*, pp. 93-94.
166. *Ibid.*, p. 104.
167. *Ibid.*, p. 107.
168. M.S. Krishnamurthy : *The Nolambas*, p. 132.
169. *QJMS.*, LVII, p. 31 and f.n. No. 16.
170. *Ibid.*, p. 32 and f.n. No. 17.
171. *E.C.*, VIII (1904), Tl. 192.
172. *Ibid.*, VI (1901), Kp. 14.
173. *SII.*, XVIII, No. 300.

V

THE SINDAS

Three records[1] available at Davanagere, Bhairanamatti and Ranjole Kheni are the main source of information for reconstructing the history of the Sindas in general and of four different families of theirs in particular. In all these three records we find the name of Nidudol Sinda, a mythological figure, who is stated to have married a Kadamba princess from whom he got three sons, whose names are not known according to the Bhairanamatti inscription. It is interesting to know from the Ranjole Kheni record that he had four sons, not three, as stated in the Bhairanamatti inscription, and their names were Prebhusevya, Satyasevya, Jagatsevya and Budhasevya. Further it states that they settled down respectively in Bagadage-desa or nadu, Paliyanda-mandala, Attale-nadu and Ballare-nadu. The members of the Sinda family held sway over several parts of Karnataka as subordinates of the Chalukyas of Kalyana, the Kalachuris and the Yadavas.

The Sindas of Belaguvarti :

The mythical origin of the Sindas is ascertained from some of their epigraphs. The Davanagere inscription states that "From the union of Siva and Sindhu was born a son, to whom Bhava, with affection, gave the name Saindhava with the king of the serpents as his guardians. Saying that unless his son drank tigres' milk he would not become brave, the husband of Gauri out of his goodness created a tigress and drinking her milk the child grew in the world. Moreover, Paramesvara directed the goddess Malati to aid his son in war and gave him a second name of Nidudola Sinda. Being told that Karahata, the *yogapitha*, was his abode, the king took possession of it, driving out the group of kings there by the might of his arm. Thus he became poweful among the kings of the earth, and being constantly praised in the world as brave, generous and of famous origin, he made illustrious the descent of Sinda-vamsa throughout the world."[2] Another record from Bhairanamatti furnishes a slightly different version of the mythical origin of this family. It is stated that, from a desire to behold the earth so belauded by the sons of men, there came from the lower region the serpent-king, Dharanendra and to him there was born at Ahichchatra in the region of the river Sindhu, a son Nidudola Sinda. The serpent-king gave him to the charge of the tigress and on his attaining manhood made him king of the country. Sinda then married a Kadamba princess, and by her had three sons from whom Sinda family was descended.[3]

It is believed from the above statements that the family name of Sinda comes from the union of Siva and Sindhu from whom Nidudola Sinda was born and came to be considered as the founder member of this dynasty. They are said to belong to a Naga family *(Phanirajaramsa)*, possessing the feudatory titles such as *Samadhi-gata-Panchamaha-sabda, Mahamandalesvara*, etc. and were entitled to *Malali* and *turya* instruments. They had the symbols of *Vyaghramriga* and their flag was *Niladhvaja.*[4]

The chiefs of this family describe themselves as the lords of the best of cities, Karahatapura, i.e., Karahad in Satara District, Maharashtra, obviously denoting that they originally had settled at Karahad. Later on they are found ruling over the Bellary - Bidar - Shimoga region of Karnataka contemporaneously with the Silaharas who were administering the region around Karahad in the 10th - 12th centuries. In course of time the Sinda chiefs migrated towards Belaguvarti.[5]

The early history of the Sindavadi-1000 province can be traced back to the last quarter of the 9th centry A.D. An epigraph[6] dated 893-94 A.D. of the reign of Rashtrakuta Akalavarsha Subhatunga Bhatara i.e., Krishna II, (880-915 A.D.) states that *mahasamanta* Kanna, an official of the Rashtrakutas was ruling over the Sindavadi - 1000. This province, on the basis of the findspot of the record i.e., Mamchale (modern Mantralaya) in Yemmiganur Taluk of Kurnool District, Andhra Pradesh, formerly in Alur Taluk of Bellary District, Andhra Pradesh, can be identified with the Sindavadi area of the Ballary region. We also find references to some other Sindavadi provinces comprising the territories of Kisukadu-70, Kelavadi-300 and Harayamgallu - 12, etc. Desai[7] has stated that Karasiga Nanniya Sinda, Jatarasa and Kayavirarasa ruled successively as the earlier members of this branch. But Gopal refutes the former's statement and concludes that they do not belong to the Sinda family at all.[8] The reason for this consideration is that their records fail to attribute any connection with the Sindas of Belaguvarti, though they are referred to as Sindas. His opinion does not hold good because we find that some of the members other than this branch are described in a different fashion in definite terms. As we do not find such variations in these records and they simply refer to them as Sindas, we can infer that there is no harm in considering these members as Sindas belonging to Belaguvarti, though the relationship with the latter is very difficult to make out at present.

Karasiga Nanniya Sinda, who can be better called Karasiga, is said to have been serving during the reign of the Rashtrakuta king Akalavarsha (Krishna III) in 967 A.D. Further it is said that the *mahasamanta* Sudrakayya was administering Kadambaliga - 1000 under the suzerainty of Krishna III. The position of Karasiga is not known.[9] Nanniya has been described as an affectionate, truthful person and quite often it appears as a title.[10] If we take it in the former sense, he may be considered as one who was a beloved of Krishna III. His successor *mahasamanta* Jatarasa was entitled to the honour of *Panchamahasabda.* Gopal does not accept him to be a member of the family of the Sindas of Belaguvarti stating that another chief by name Koralagunda, who was a different member of a Sinda family other than that of Belagutti was adminestering the small tract of Mulugunda - 12 in 994 and 1028 A.D.[11] It is to be noted here that this Jatarasa, unlike the chieftain referred to above, is not given any descriptive epithets and is simply called *mahasamanta* mulgunda Sinda. The interpretation given in this connection by Gopal is not satisfactory as he himself has his reservations about it. Jatarasa was ruling in 992 A.D. over Kadambalinge-1000. His rule might have been for a shorter duration as we find that Koralagunda was adminstering the same district referred to above in 994 A.D.[12]

Mahamandelesvara Kayavirarasa is elsewhere taken to have been ruling in 1061 A.D. as a feudatory of Chalukya Somesvara I.[13] But this is not correct.[14] There is a reference to a local fight during the rule of Kayavirarasa in which Ibhata, son of Biyagopa, fought in a cattle raid, recovered tha cows and probably slew the enemies. The details of this fight are not known because of the worn out condition of the record.[15] It is also known from some other records "that Virasantara and his son Bhujabala had to struggle very hard in order to free their kingdom from those who had no claim to it".[16] Rice is of the opinion that this incident may refer to certain Chalukya princes Bijjarasa and his brother Gonaraja who are stated to have been in full enjoyment of the Santaligenadu in 1042 A.D.[17] However, in the total absence of any evidence in support of Rice's surmise we have to reject his suggestion that there was any dispute between the Chalukyas and the Santaras. Further, it is known from the records[18] that the Santaras were the feudatories of the Chalukyas.

Piriya Chattarasa (Chattarasa I) :

The real history of the Sindas of Belaguvarti starts from the personage of Piriya Chattarasa (i.e., Chattarasa I). A record dated 1164 A.D. furnishes, among the names of the members of the dynasty who ruled in succession, that of Piriya Chattarasa and Dorabbarasi, his wife.[19] Jogarasa and Chattarasa are mentioned as their son and grandson respectively. Two other records of the date of 1180 and 1222 A.D. also testify to this.[20] It is further stated in a record dated 1164 A.D. that Nidudola - Sinda, who seems to be an imaginary and a mythical figure, was ruling over several territories including Karahada - 4000. After him, says the inscription, there ruled quite a few members of his family and, of them, Piriya Chattarasa was a jewel of countless valour. He is considered as the first historical member of this family.[21] He is said to be a victorious and illustrious chief who brought together many districts under one authority.[22] He is also praised in two other records.[23]

Jogarasa (c. 1060-90 A.D.) :

Jogarasa, the son and successor of Piriya Chattarasa is referred to as an young and illustrious ruler.[24] According to Gopal a record from Medur, assignable to 1062-63 A.D. , refers to the rule of Chalukya Trailokyamalla Somesvara I when *Mahamandalesvara,* Chavundarayarasa was the *mahapradhana.* It further states that, while *mahasamanta* Bava Bijjarasa was administering Edavatte - 70, Rettapalle - 70, Magunda - 12 and other areas, Ayyana Jogarasa of the Sinda family, bearing the epithets *Karahata - puravaradhisavara* and *Malatidevilabdha - varaprasada,* was adminstering Masuru - 12, Kunduru - 12, Kalliganuru - 70 divisions, Arakere - 12 and other small territories. the rule of this chief has been fixed between 1060 to 1090 A.D.[25]

Chattarasa II (1090 - 1120 A.D.) :

Chattarasa succeeded his father Jogarasa. He is referred to as the feudatory of Chalukya Vikramaditya VI in 1117 A.D. while the *mahapradhana* Govindarasa was in charge of Banavasi 12000 as the provincial governor. From this record it is apparent that Chattarasa was not only under the control of Govindarasa, but also associated with the adminstration of Edavatte 70- Nadu.[26]

This period witnessed the growing power of the Hoysalas under Vishnuvardhana. He attacked the Pandyas of Uchchangi in 1116 A.D. and defeated them in the battle of Dumme.[27] His general Kamadeva completed the conquest of Uchchangi. Vishnuvardhana is described in 1120 A.D. as "the capturer of Gangavadi, Nolambavadi, Uchchangi and Hanumgal."[28] The absence of the mention of the Sindas in these records, though their territory was very close to the Hoysala capital, shows that the Sindas were very powerful chiefs. Undoubtedly Chattarasa had played a prominent role as *mahamandalaesvara* under the suzerainty of the Kalyana Chalukyas. The *Prbhu* of Hebbala and Sarvvanya Setti, the son of *perggade* Galimayya, are mentioned as the officers of Chattarasa.

Isvaradeva I was the son of Chattarasa II. The absence of his name in all other records of his descendents except a casual reference to him as the father of Machideva and Mallideva[29] obviously denotes that he never ruled. He had three sons, viz. Macharasa, Mallideva and Aiharasa.[30] Macha who is also called as Lakhanripala was the eldest. Mallideva was the second son and Aiharasa, also known as Harasa, was the youngest.[31]

Macharasa (1120-40 A.D.) :

A record from Medur of the reign of Chalukya Vikramadity VI dated in 1113 A.D. refers to Macharasa. We have already seen that his grandfater Chattarasa II was ruling upto 1120 A.D. Therefore it becomes obvious that Macharasa was associated with the administration by Chattarasa II as early as 1113 A.D.[32] A record from Nagavanda dated 1128 A.D. of the reign of Chalukya Bhulokamalla Somesvara III, states that Macharasa was governing Edavatte - 70, Arakare - 12 and another division of Fifty - six.[33] From this it can be deduced that he assumed power independently sometime between 1120 and 1140 A.D.

The name of Macharasa occurs many times in the records of the later members of this family.[34] In one of the inscriptions, he is described as "charging forward on one horse and attacking and dispensing the massed cavalry of the enemies' force', and thus becoming famous.[35] This, in fact, suggests that his position was shaken by the Hoysala predominance because of the decline of the Chalukya influence to the south of Tungabhadra during this period.[36] It is known from a record at Belur[37] that Hoysala Narasimha carried out raids on Banavasi province which included the Belaguvarti principality. After the death of Macharasa, the Sindas became the feudatories of the Hoysalas.[38] He is mentioned as a great soldier who won victories in many battles. Chattaladevi was his senior queen.

Mallideva I (1140 - 55 A.D.) :

Mallideva is known to have succeeded his brother Macharasa who did not leave behind any issues of his own. He is eulogised as *bhuvanakhyata* in an epigraph dated 1222 A.D.[39] Aiharasa seems to have assisted his elder brother Mallideva in administration throughout the latter's reign. He is eulogised as *akhila - danavinodi.*[40] He had a son named Rayarasa.

Isvaradeva II (c. 1155-85 A.D.) :

Mallideva I was succeeded by *Mahamandalesvara* Isvaradeva II, the grandson of Aiharasa, the latter and his son Rayarasa having died before Mallideva I. According to Desai[41] he came to power in 1160 A.D. There is an inscription[42] dated 1158 A.D. of the reign of Kalachuri Bijjala refering to *Mahamandalesvara* Isvaradeva II who was adminstering Edavatte-70. On the evidence of this record, the commencement of his rule can be dated to c. 1155 A.D. His inscription dated 1164 A.D. furnishes an elaborate narration of his coronation full of exaggeration and poetic fancy.[43]

There was much confusion throughout Karanataka during this period due to the political exigencies. Kalachuri Bijjala had defeated the Chalukyas of Kalyana and usurped their kingdom in 1156 A.D. The Hoysalas were becoming more powerful and the Kadambas of Hangal were reluctant to come under the yoke of the Kalachuris. Banavasi - 12000, comprising among other territories Belaguvarti kingdom of the Sindas was being administered by the governor Mayidevarasa under the Kalachuris in 1158 A.D. He was also collecting taxes like *hejjunka* and *vaddaravula.*[44] Another governor, Kesimayya, is also referred to in a record dated c. 1160 A.D. availabel at Belligame.[45] In 1164 A.D. Isvaradeva II, a subordinate of the Kalachuri king Bijjala II, is described as his follower *(anuvarti).* He is further described in 1165 A.D. as the person responsible for the progress *(abhyudaya)* of the victorious kingdom of the Kalachuri king Bijjala. He seems to have added a large portion of territory to his kingdom as far north as Harihara as we find a record of his dated in 1164 A.D. at this place.[46] In the next year i.e. in 1165 A.D. he is stated to have been ruling over several small districts in the Banavasi and Santalige provinces from his camp at Hallavur. The power of the Kadamba king Kirtideva was snatched sway by the Kalachuri ruler as he appears to be the latter's subordinate in 1162 A.D. This event probably enabled Isvaradeva II acquire the Kadamba territories as shown above. Further, he seems to have extended the Western boundary of his kingdom taking advantage of the absence of Kadamba Kirtideva, who was busy in fighting the Santara chief Jagadeva in order to recover some parts of the Hangal region from him.[47]

No doubt, during this fight, the Santaras were defeated by Kirtideva in 1165 A.D. Utilising this opportunity, Isvaradeva was able to acquire the nothern districts of Santalige - 1000.[48] This event led to hostility between these two dynasties viz. the Sindas of Belaguvarti and the Santaras. The latter chiefs, who were at that time subordinates of the Hoysalas, carried out many raids against the Sindas in order to take back their territory. This is proved by the evidences of some of the hero - stones[49] dated 1166, 1172 and 1173 A.D. of the reign of Isvaradeva II. From all the three records we learn that, somhow or other,

Isvaradeva was able to resist the aggression of the Santaras. In some of the records he is consequently described as *Sinda - govinda, Patala - chakravarti* and *Nissankamalla.*[50]

An inscritpion[51] dated 1165 A.D. states that who was ruling over the *kampanas* of Masavuru - 12, Edavatte - 70, Ballave - 70 and Nariyalige - 40 in Banavase - nadu, Male - 70 and Muduhare - 30 in Santalige - 1000, Holaluru - 12 in Mandalinadu, Manujavolalu - 12, Kolliga - 70, Arakere - 12, Branti - 30, Kundur - 70, the Fifty six *(Aivattaru bada),* Attigeri - 12, Padugalu - 12, Arabala - 70 and Kalikatti - 12 in Asendi - nadu, with his capital at Hallavura, Hallur in Hirekerur Taluk of Dharwar District. From this account it is clear that he had extended his territories into Shimoga, Chitradurga and Dharwar Districts and into Ballary District also to some extent. Hallur had become, by this time, one of his capitals as it is described as *rajadhani.* According to this epigraph it would appear that he had extended his own territories and power with the assistance of his father - in - law *(mava)* Allamarasa, who is described as haveing played an important role in the kingdom.[52]

Edevatte - nadu, Ballave (modern Bellary) of the Banavasi - nadu, Maduvalla - 30 and Narinalige - 40 are some of the places stated to be under Isvaradeva's rule in 1172 A.D. when he had fixed his camp at Belaguvarti.[53]

The third record[54] dated 1173 A.D. also refers to a cattle raid. It is very interesting to note in this connection that, inspite of the above disturbance, no hindrance was caused to the rule of Isvaradeva II over the Santalige province.[55] Subsequent to this date, Hoysala Ballala II (1173 - 1220 A.D.) carried expeditions against several chiefs to enhance the glory of his dynasty; the Changalva chief, Kulottungachola Changalva, was defeated in 1173 A.D. at the first instance.[56] Immediately after this event, it seem that Isvaradeva II suffered the same fate as that of the Changalva chief. Because, in a record dated 1175 A.D., he figures as a chief under Todapille - dannayaka who was governing Belaguvarti as an officer of Hoysala Ballala II.[57] His subordination to the Hoysala ruler was however, short lived for a record[58] of the Kalachuri king Rayamurari Sovideva dated 1176 A.D. refers to Isvaradeva II as ruling over Nagarkhanda - 70, as the former's subordinate. The Kalachuri king drove out Hoysala Ballala II from Belaguvarti and obviously reoccupied the reigion around. Isvaradeva II and a minister, Kavanayya by name, are said to have played an important part in the Kalachuri - Hoysala conflict which took place in 1179 A.D.[59] In the course of this war Isvaradeva seems to have recoverd his capital Hallavura - Belaguvarti as he is known to have set himself up there in 1179 A.D.[60] It is further known that he was controlling a number of *nadus* from this capital in 1180 A.D. as a feudatory of the Kalachuri king Sankama (1176 - 81 A.D.). Those *nadus* were : Edavatte - 70, [Nari] valiga - 40, Ballave - 70, the Maduvara - 80, Yadasuleya -

80 in Santalige, the Kolliga - 50, the Arakere - 12, the Manujavolalu - 17, the Attigeri - 12 and Elamberu - 12, etc. His two sons, Pandyadeva and Mallideva are stated to have been ruling over the above *nadus* as governors under his orders.[61]

From the above account we can arrive at the conclusion that he was the most powerul chief among the Sindas whose dynasty i.e., *Sindanvaya* is said to be the cause for the growth of the Kalachuris.[62] He offered several meritorious grants to various gods and goddesses, Brahamanas and institutions. He also had two other sons, viz., Raya and Vijaya.[63]

Mallideva II (1185 - 1205 A.D.) :

Soon after Mallideva II succeeded his father he seems to have faced a threat of invasion from his enemies in 1187 A.D. as Vijayapandya of Uchchangi along with Chatta nripala is stated to have carried out a cattle raid against Nelivarti.[64] During this reign, some major changes took place due to political exegencies.

The Chalukya king Somesvara IV re - established the Chalukyan supremacy in 1184-85 A.D. defeating the Kalachuri ruler Singhanadeva.[65] Naturally, Mallideva switched his allegiance over to Somesvara IV in 1189 A.D.[66] and was administering from Belaguvarti as a *mandalika*. The Kadamba Kamadeva followed his lead and changed his allegiance to Somesvara IV.[67] The period of the rule of Somesvara IV was a short one as the Yadavas in the north and the Hoysalas in the south soon divided among themselves the whole of the Chalukyan empire.[68] A hero - stone of the time of Mallideva II, dated 1195 A.D., refers to the battle of Rattapolli. It does not furnish the name of the overlord. This leads us to believe that Mallideva II might have been ruling independently during this interlude of political chaos probably after the death of Somesvara.[69]

The Hoysalas are said to be the enemies who fought in a battle referred to above.[70] A hero-stone dated 1196 A.D.[71] of the time of the chief refers to a cattle - raid by the soldiers of Umadevi, queen of the Hoyasala king Vira - Ballala II.[72] Another attempt was made probably in 1197 A.D. by the same lady. In both the attacks she was defeated by Mallideva II.[73] He was strong enough to resist enemy attacks many times[74] and successfully continued to rule over his kingdom. However, he seems to have been defeated finally by the Hoysala king Vira - Ballala II as he figures as a feudatory of this ruler in 1192 A.D.[75] Vira - Ballala II had actually made Hallavur one of his camping places which obviously proves that he annexed the Sinda territories that were once under the control of Isvaradeva II and had been inherited by Mallideva II.

Isvaradeva III (1205 - 29 A.D.) :

Mallideva II was succeeded by his son *mahamandalesvara* Isvaradeva III. He figures as a subordinate of the Yadava king Simghana II in 1215 A.D., ruling over the small territory left behind by his father.[76] The actual circumstances which forced him to acknowledge the supremacy of the Yadavas are not known; but the opinion of Desai that "Isvaradeva, though dispossessed of a greater portion of his kingdom, was not without hopes of retrieving the losses his father sustained. He was only waiting for a favourable opportunity which would free him from the intolerable suzerainty of the Hoysala king" is readily acceptable.[77] Some of the hero - stones of the time of Isvaradeva III refer to encounters between him and his enemies in 1215 and 1216 A.D.[78] None of these records give out the identity of the enemies who fought against Isvaradeva III nor do they spell out the results of the fight. However, on the strength of circumstantial evidence the enemies mentioned in the records of Isvaradeva have been identified with the Hoysalas[79] and more specifically with Vira - Ballala II.[80]

Isvaradeva III seems to have lost the confidence of the Yadavas in 1217 A.D. for we find that *mahamandulesvara* Bommidevarasa of Bandanike was placed in charge of Belaguvarti in that year as a subordinate of Singhana. Further, we learn that this Bommideva had bravely opposed Hoysala Ballala when he attacked Belaguvarti and drove him out.[81]

Another record[83] dated in 1218 A.D. refers to the death of Malleyanayaka, a servant of Bommidevarasa referred to above, in a fight when the fort of Belaguvarti was attacked by a *mahamandalesvara.* After analysing the circumstances which brought about the attack on the fort of Belaguvarti, Gopal tentatively concludes that this *mahamandalesvara* is none other than Isvaradeva III.[83] Again in 1219 A.D. he fell upon Abbalur, with an army of 10,000 and a cavalry force of 1000, and captured the cattle when Biragauda of Abbalur, a general of Singhana, fought bravely and vigorously with the enemy who was defeated.[84]

Isvaradeva III attempted a raid on Chikkakeravur (Chikkerur) in 1223 A.D. during which fight Sanneya Soma died while defending the said town.[85] Two other records[86] of the reign of Yadava Singhana of the same date refer to a fight, in which *Nayimda* Bommeyanayka is said to have lost his life. Other details of the fight are not known from these two records owing to their demaged condition. However, Gopal connects the events of these two records with the record referred to above in which Sanneya Soma had lost his life in saving Chikakerevur.[87]

From the above facts it is certain that Isvaradeva III struggled hard throughout his administration fighting superior powers like the Hoysalas and the Yadavas. Despite all these difficulties, he survived till 1222 A.D. for a record dated in the said year mentions him as ruling over some territories.[88] The inclusion of Uchchangi - 30 among these territories makes it clear that he acquired this after the defeat of the Pandyas of Uchchangi by the Hoysalas in 1220 A.D.[89] Chattale was one of his queens. He had three sons viz., Kesava, Sovale and Kalale.

Kesavadeva (1229 - 39 A.D.) :

The first son, Kesavadeva, succeeded him as a feudatory of the Yadavas. His earliest known date falls in 1232 A.D. in which year he was ruling from Belaguvarti. Vankaravuta, the successor of Mayideva - dandanayaka referred to above, seems to have tried to extend the Yadava influence to the south of the Tungabhadra with the support of Isvaradeva III.[90] He was succeeded by Honnabommisetti as the administrator of Banavasinadu in A.D. 1232. Kesevadeva II does not seem to have been on good terms with him as it is recorded that Bamma the general fought on behalf of Kesavadeva against Honnabommisetti, the *malalike* officer of Banavasinadu and a *mandalika* of Singhana II.[91] After this event he might have been driven out by Yadava Singhana as a punishment for having revolted against him. We do not hear anything further about him. On the strength of the information available from the epigraphs of this family, we may conclude that the chiefs of the Sindas of Belguvarti fell into oblivion after him.

Biradeva (1238 - 47 A.D.) :

Kesavadeva II was succeeded by *Mahamandalesvara* Biradeva also known as Harabira.[92] The name of the family to which he belonged is not known. On the basis of the titles borne by him like *murti - narayana* and *vilasa - vallabha* and also his being described as the devotee of the holy feet of god Billesvara which are not akin to those of the Sindas of Belaguvarti, Gopal has rightly doubted whether he was, by extraction, a Sinda at all. Since, however, he is found ruling over Belaguvarti soon after the end of Kesavadeva's rule, Gopal considers him as a local chief who rose to power after the latter's death.[93] He fought with the Yadavas in order to maintain his independence is shown by a record dated A.D. 1239. wherein a reference occurs to the march of the Nayakas of Yadava Singhana (1210 - 47 A.D.) who are said to have captured the fortress of Gutti, burnt tha *nadu* and marched along with their booty openly displayed.[94]

Some of the hero-stones dated 1244, 1245, 1246 and 1247 A.D. bear testimony to the hostility that existed between the Yadava king Singhana, one of the most powerful rulers of his days and Biradeva II.[95] During these attacks the Yadavas seized Kudali (modern Kudligi) and marched against the Sinda capital Belaguvarti on more than one occasion. However, they were repulsed by Biradeva courageously. The last available record of Biradeva is dated Saka 1179 corresponding to 1247 A.D.[96] It also refers to a fight against the Yadava army.[97]

As rightly suggested by Desai,[98] though this hero-stone does not reveal the result of the fight, it may be taken to indicate the total eclipse of the Sindas as a political power. What happened to Biradeva in this fight is not known. Since his records dated beyond 1247 A.D. are not available it may be presumed that he was killed by the Yadava forces ultimately. Thus, at last, the Yadavas succeeded in fainally annexing the traditional territory of the Sindas in 1247 A.D. into their own empire. Certain descendants of the Sinda line, however, seem to have held offices under the adminstration of the Yadavas even after the fall of Biradeva in 1247 A.D.[99]

The genealogy of the Sindas of Belaguvarti[100]

- Piriya Chattarase
  - Ayyana Jogarasa (c 1090 - 1120 A.D.)
    - Isvaradeva I
      - Macharasa(1120 - 40)
      - Mallideva I (1140 - 55)
      - Aiharasa
        - Rayarasa
          - Isvaradeva II (1155 - 85)
            - Pandyadeva
            - Mallideva II (1185-1205)
              - Isvaradeva III (1205 - 29)
                - Kesavadeva (1229 - 39)
            - Raysasa(Rayarasa)
            - Vijayanripala

The Sindas of Bagadage

The descendents of Prabhusevya have come to be called as the Sindas of Bagadage since they ruled over the Bagadage - nadu i.e. Bagadage - 70 consisting of the territories of Kisukadu - 70, Kelavadi - 300 and Nareyambal - 12 - the entire region being known as Sindavadi. There was also another Sindavadi aroung Kurugod in the Ballary District over which the Kurugodu Sindas held their sway. In this connection it is said that, in the beginning, the different regions that came to be called as Sindavadi had their own independent existence and probably came to be clubbed together by the middle of the 11th century.[101] We have only one record furnishing details about this dynasty viz., the Bhairanmatti inscription.[102] This record contains references to the two dates : (1) Saka 911 (wrong for 912) and Vikrita in the reign of Taila II, corresponding to 990 - 91 A.D. (2) Sake 955, Srimukha in the reign of Jagadekamalla Jayasimha II, corresponding to 1033 - 34 A.D. But from an allusion to Somesvara II found in the epigraph, it appears to have been incised on stone later during the reign period of this king (1068 - 76 A.D.)

The Sindas of Bagadage are said to be ruling over the Bagadage region even earlier than the Sindas of Belagutti. Bagadage is identified with Bagalkot in Bijapur District. These members are described as the lords of Bhogavatipura and as governing Ahichchatra. They had the crest of a tiger and belonged to the Naga family. In this epigraph they are eulogised as *Nagavamsodbhava*, *Nagadhvajapratapa* and *Drishtivishakulatilaka*. According to the statement of this inscription Nidudol Sinda was followed by thirty one rulers after whom there was a prince called Sinda. Sinda was succeeded by Kammayyarasa, whose connection with the former is not known. From Sagarabbarasi he had a son named Pulikala, who was a subordinate of Chalukya Taila II in 990 - 91 A.D. His son and successor was Nagaditya (also known as Nagatya or Nagatiyarasa). His mother was Revakabbe. He was a *mahasamanta* and entitled to the *Panchamahasabdas* and to the honour of three golden umbrellas. He made two gifts of land to the god Sindesvara and to a deity of Puradakeri in 1033-34 A.D. His wife was Poleyabbarasi. He was a feudatory of Chalukya Jayasimha II.

Polasinda was the son and successor of Nagaditya. He married Bijjaladevi, whose father is described as *Khandava - mandalesvara.*

Vira Gomka (I) *alias* Banaradityadeva of Bana family is stated to have been ruling over the Gomka - nadu corresponding to some parts of Gulbarga and Chitapur Taluks. He had the epithet *Khandava - mandal - adhisvara* and he can be identified as the father - in - law of Polasinda.[103]

Mahamandalesvara Sevyarasa (c. 1069 - 76 A.D.) was the son and successor of Polasinda. His title obviously denotes that he had risen to the status of *mahamandalesvara*. He was a subordinate of Chalukya Somesvara II (1068 - 76 A.D.).[104]

The Sindas of Erambarage

The epigraphs pertaining to this family do not furnish any information regarding the origin of the chiefs of this branch. However, about the existence of this dynasty, Desai opines that "the Sindas of Erambarage i.e., Yelburga in Raichur District extended their influence during the reign of Chalukya ruler Vikramaditya VI (1076 - 1126 A.D.) and came to be masters of that part of Kuntala, which consequently assumed the name of Sindavadi - *nadu* the early history of which is traced back to the beginning of the 9th centruy A.D."[105] He also states that Sindavadi - nadu of this branch included the districts of Kisukadu - 70, Kelavadi - 300, Bagadage - 70 and Nareyangal - 12.[106] Since Bagadage - 70 figures as the hereditary territory of the Sindas, he further presumes that this family might have been an off shoot of the Sinda family of Bagadage, whose members are known to have ruled prior to the Sindas of Yalburga.[107] According to him, *Mahasamanta* Nagaditya,[108] the illustrious chief of the Bagadage branch who had two wives, Poleyabbarasi being one among them, and was the father of the seven brothers referred to below, was the originator of this family.[109]

As the Bagadage inscription [110] of Nagaditya does not refer to the connection between him and the seven brothers of the Sinda family of Yalburga, the presumption of Desai stands unsubstantiated. Moreover, he does not mention Nagaditya as the father of the seven brothers in his genealogical table.[111] According to the opinion of Panchamukhi, the origin of this family as a ruling power may be placed in or about 1076 A.D., the year of Chalukya Vikramaditya's accession to the throne.[112] While discussing Panchamukhi's view, Gopal asserts that Achugi I was the trusted lieutenant of Vikramaditya VI while the latter was still a prince during the reign of Somesvara II.[113] However, he seems to have accepted the statement of Panchamukhi as he is also of the opinion that the Sindas of Yelburga i.e., Achugi I come into picture as the chieftain of Bagadage under Chalukya Vikramaditya VI.[114]

The genealogical account furnished by the records of this branch refers to the seven brothers viz., Acharasa (Achugi I), Naka, Singa, Dasa, Davana, Chavunda I and Chava.[115]

Achugi I (1076 - 82 A.D.) :

He is the first prince of the family who is described with the significant epithet *"Adimandalika"*.[116] The information about this chief has been gathered from later records as he does not seem to have issued his own records. He is described as endowed with stability equal to that of the mountain Mandara, and as a ruler of outstanding ability in enhancing the glory and the prosperity of the Sinda race;[117] Being of unequalled courage, he attained, in the presence of the Chalukyan king, the pinnacle of greatness among those who sound the trumpet of their firm determination;[118] he was a man of many accomplishments[119] *(nanakalakovidan)*. From this description it is clear that Achugi I started his rule as a chief of the Sindas of Erambarage under the canopy of the Chalukya king Vikramaditya VI (1076 - 1126 A.D.). It is very difficult to know about the predecessors of this chief as we do not get a single reference to them.

The six brothers of Achugi I, referred to above, are said to have discharged thier duties as *nripas*.[120] Naka is described as a weilder of the thunderbolts towards the mountains which were the arrogant and brave hostile kings.[121] Singa and Dasa are also described as abounding with valour and fierce demeanour.[122] As we do not find any attributes (description) for Davana in any records it is doubtful that whether he took any initiative in the adminstration at all. Contrary to this, Chavunda I was distinguished among the brothers. He is stated to have been impetuous in war, the might of his arm having excelled in causing fear to all his enemies.[123] Chava seems to have earned the name Charudatta for his unbounded liberality.[124] It is very intersting to note that though these six brothers of Achugi I were extolled at length no where do we find mention of their rule in succession to Achugi I. The term *nripa* attributed to them, in the light of the above discussion, perhaps simply implies that they were the members of the royal family.[125]

While discussing the genealogy of this family, Panchamukhi points out the mistakes done by Fleet and Barnett in introducing another Singi (II) and in making him the father of Achugi (II), on the basis of the Pattadakal inscription.[126] He also refers to Fleet's indentification of Simga I with *mahamandalesvara* Singannadeva who was governing Kisukadu-70 in 1076 A.D. under Bhuvanaikamalla.[127] Finally he draws the conclusion on the basis of the genealogy furnished in the two Benachametti records dated 1167 and 1187 A.D., that there was only one member called Singa, brother of Achugi I, who never ruled.[128] *Mahamandalesvara* Singannadeva referred to above has not been associated with the Sinda family.[129] On the basis of this epigraph Gopal thinks that the Sindas, at the first instance, were incharge of the Bagadage province only and later both Achugi I and Baramarasa came to hold Kisukadu province also.[130] Panchamukhi further states that "not a single known inscription has described Singa independently except as the father of Acharasa II. This would suggest that he never enjoyed any power".[131] There is a reference to Singa and his queen Kataladevi in an inscription assignable to c. the 12th century A.D. wherein he is described as a subordinate of the Chalukyas.[132] It seems probable that Panchamukhi and Desai were not aware of this record. The Benachamatti inscription of 1167 A.D. reveals for the first time that Perma and Chavunda were his sons from different queens viz., Mahadevi and Chamdaladevi[133] respectively and thus it supplements the information contained in the Ron record dated 1180 A.D.[134]

Baramarasa (1083-1105 A.D.) :

The successor of Achugi I was his son *mahamandalesvara* Barmarasa. The opinion of Desai that Chavunda and his brothers appear to have been acting as regents to Bamma[135] is not justifiable if we consider the limited portion of the entire territory administered by Achugi I and his son Bamma.

He had, according to the Pattadakal record, won the favour of the reigning sovereign, i.e., Vikramaditya VI and received from him a position of honour and rank in the state. His territory comprised Kisukadu - 70 and Nareyamgal - 12.[136] He is described as the lord of the city of Bhogavati in 1085 A.D.[137] His latest available record is dated in 1104 - 05 A.D. Bhulokamalla Permadi of the Savadi inscription dated 1083 A.D. has been identified with Barmarasa. Bhulokamalla and Permadi appear to be his titles. Gopal has clearly shown that Barmarasa was there in 1085 A.D. as a subordinate of Bhulokamalla Somesvara III, a Chalukya prince who might have been associated with his father in administration.[138]

There is a fererence to a *mahamandalesvara* Bammarasa who is said to have got built a temple named Brahamesvara in a record dated 1104-05 A.D. He has been identified with Barmarasa, the son of Achugi I.[139] He appears to have died without issue as otherwise, the Sinda throne would not have been passed on to the descendants of his uncle Sindas. Desai,[140] following the footsteps of Fleet,[141] dealt with in detail, in a separate chapter, the personage of Singa II, who did not at all exist.[142]

Achugi II (1113 - 26 A.D.) :

The Arasibidi inscription dated 1087 A.D. states that *mahamandalesvara* [A] varasa was administering Kisukadu - 70 and Karividi-30 under Vikramaditya VI.[143] Panchamukhi surmises that, at the time of Barmarasa's death, Achugi II, son of Singa, was either a minor or not powerful enough to assert the rights of his family. Subsequently, however, he appears to have acquired possession of his hereditary provinces through the favour of Vikramaditya, which thereafter continued in his line till the end.[144]

A badly damaged inscription[145] dated 1113 A.D. registers the renewal of an original grant by Acharasa, at the request of Aycharaja, the *parggade* of Abbeyagere and others. Acharasa of this record is identified with Achugi II.[146] He has left behind three records[147] dated 1113, 1121-22 and 125-26 A.D. He took a prominent part with his son Permadi[148] in the conquests of his overlord Chalukya Vikramaditya VI by defeating the Pandyas, Hoysalas and other rebels.[149] Taking advantage perhaps of the old age of Vikramaditya VI, the Chalukyan empire was attacked from its four corners, by the Hoysalas from the south, the Kadambas of Goa from the west, the Silaharas of the Konkan from the north and the Pandyas of Uchchangi from the east. Achugi II is said to have courageously fought in these battles and pursued and prevailed against the Hoysalas, took Goa, defeated Lakshma in war, valorously pursued the Pandyas and seized Konkana.[150] The same event is referred to in another record.[151] Desai rightly suggests that the Hoysala opponent in this battle was Vishnuvardhana (1110-52 A.D.).[152] This is evidenced by some of the attacks of the Hoysalas on the Kalyana Chalukyas. Hoysala Vishnuvardhana is said to have invaded Uchchangi and Belvola and he also carried his arms successfully so far to the north to bathe his horses in the Krishna river.[153] The Hoysalas also claim to have inflicted a serious defeat under the leadership of *dandanayaka* Gangaraja in an attack on the army of Vikramaditya VI at Kannegala in A.D. 1117.[154] Having taken the opportunity of the strained relationship between the Kalyana Chalukyas and the Hoysalas, Jayakesin II, the Kadamba chief of Goa, and a subordinate of Chalukya Vikramaditya VI appears to have decleared his independence and thus become his opponent at the battle already referred to. It is surprising to know that Jayakesin II's enmity with the Chalukyan ruler Vikramaditya VI finally ended in a matrimonial alliance as the latter offered his daughter in marriage to Jayakesin II.[155] Tribhuvanamalla - Pandya also called as Irukkuvela was the Pandya opponent. The Pandyas in their epigraphs proclaim that they were the loyal chiefs of the Chalukyas.[156] But we know that they were defeated by the Sinda chiefs.[157] The Pattadakal inscription goes to the extent of stating that the kings of 'Kalinga, Vanga, Maru, Gurjjara, Malava, Chera and Chola were made to accept the supremacy of Vikramaditya VI by the Sinda chief Achugi II.[158] Of course, there may not be much truth in this statement but on the basis of an inscription[159] recording the march of

Vikramaditya VI across the Narmada river and his conquest of kings on the other side of the river, it may be suggested that Achugi II might have been deputed on an expedition against the rival rulers of Malava and Gurjara.

Achugi II had the title *Tribhuvanamalla Kesarin.* This title, according to Desai[160] may have been given to him for the timely service rendered by him to his master while he was in distress. Another title has also been attributed to him viz., *Malavaraari* probably denoting the defeat of the Malavas at his hand.[161] He is said to have been ruling over the Sindavadi - nadu comprising Narayangal - 12, Kelavadi - 300, the Bagadage - 70 and including Kisukadu - 70 acquired by his predecessors.[162] It is evidenced from the above fact that the Sinda family prospered during his rule. Mahadevi is said to have been his queen.[163] We have got two records of his dated 1113[164] and 1125 A.D.[165] He may be taken to have ruled upto 1125-26 A.D. after which no records are available for him.

Permadideva I (1122 (?) - 44 A.D.) :

Achugi II was succeeded by his son Permadideva I. He is known by different names such as Perma, Pemma, Permadi or Hemmadi. The Sinda family commanded much respect and fame during his period.[166] He is described as the very Trinetra (i.e., Siva) in the art of destroying forts, well - versed in the science of arms[167] and skilled in mounting and training restive horses to perfection.[168]

An inscription[169] from Naregal citing an impossible date of 948 A.D. refers to Permadi during the reign of Vikramaditya VI. This record does not refer to any of his exploits. Therefore, it is surmised that this record came into existence some time earlier than the other record[170] and most likely soon after Permadi succeeded his father Achugi II.[171]

The Naregal inscription of the reign of Chalukya Vikramaditya VI, dated Saka 1028 (1104-05 A.D.), traces tha Sinda genealogy down to Permadi I. He is stated to have been governing Kisukadu-70, Kelavadi - 3000 and other districts.[172] Lakshminarayana Rao opines that this record was set up much later than the date mentioned therein, and during the reign period of Permadi.[173] He is stated to have vanquished Kulasekhara, besieged and decapitated Chatta, pursued Jayakesi and seized the royal power of Hoysala Vishnuvardhana. He is also said to have captured the Hoysala king's elephants as well as his treasure - wagons.[174] Jayakesi II, while a prince was once defeated by Achugi II and then by Permadi in about 1122 A.D. Jayakesi II himself was a powerful chief who had succeeded in terrifying the famous Hoysala monarch Vishnuvardhana who was at that time grown into a serious menance to Chalukyan supremacy. Vishnuvardhana, the Hoysala king, plundered Talakadu, attacked Uchchangi, calmly marched by Banavasi, daringly seiged Belvols and sprang forward with joy to the Perdore (i.e., river Krishna) unshaken, and planted his foot on Hanumgal.[175] Parmadideva I, taking cognisance of the situation, drove Vishnuvardhana back to the south of Tungabhadra, plundered Dorasamudra, the capital of the Hoysalas and took Belapura (modern Belur).[176] This information is testified by another fragmentary record from Hanchinal containing eulogy of this Permadi to the effect that he has defeated Jayakesi, the Kadamba, attacked Dorasamudra after driving away Bittiga, the Hoysala and occupied Beluhara, i.e., Belur.[177] He also defeated the friends of the Hoysala ruler, perhaps the Todas and one of the Kongalva chiefs.[178]

We have an inscription[179] of *Mahamandalesvara* Pemmadi, dated in Chalukya Vikrama year 46 corresponding to 1122 A.D. Panchamukhi rightly suggests that he must have ruled conjointly with his father.[180]

The Kodikop inscription of the reign of Chalukya Jagadekamalla II, dated 1144 A.D., describes Permadi and states that he was governing the tracts of Kisukadu - 70, Bagadage - 70, Kelanadu - 300 and Narayamgallu - 12 at that time,[181] from his capital at Erambarage. It does not refer to any achievements of Permadi except stating that he was a firm thunder bolt against the opposing *mandalesas*. Hence, his achievements narrated in both the records[182] must be dated to a period only after 1138 A.D.[183]

Chavunda II (1151 -69 A.D.):

He succeeded his step - brother Permadideva I. He is also called Vira - Chavundarsa. His record dated 1151 A.D. from Arasibidi states that he was governing Kisukadu-70 and other regions as a subordinate of Chalukya Taila III.[184] He seems to have succeeded his step-brother some time between c. 1144 and 1151 A.D., most probably around 1150 A.D. when Hoysala Vishnuvardhana was still ruling.[185] His period is noted for some political changes. The gradual decline of the Chalukyan power paved the way for their subordinates to declare their independence. Kalachuri Bijjala, a subordinate of Chalukya Jagadekamalla II and a *dandanayaka* of Taila III decleared his independence as the former is stated to be ruling over "all the provinces" in 1155 A.D.[186] Taking advantage of an attack of the Kakatiya prince Prola on Taila III from one side he usurped the Chalukyan throne by defeting Taila III. The Beanachamatti record attributes to him the defeat of the Hoysala army and the capture of his elephants. Besides, he is also caredited with having put to flight Kama-nripala of the Pandya family.[187] The event connected with the Hoysalas has already been referred to while dealing with Permadi I. From the account furnished above about the defeat of the Hoysalas by Chavunda II evidently shown that the Hoysala prince must again have risen in vengeance against the declining power of the Chalukyas probably in about 1149 A.D. to assert his independence. Chavunda II, as a faithful subordinate of the Chalukyas checked this aggression on the battle field.[188]

He had three queens viz., Demaladevi, Lakshmidevi and Siriyadevi, of whom the last one was the daughter of the Kalachuri king Bijjala. He begot on Demaladevi, Achugi III and Parmadi II[189] and on Seriyadevi, Vira-Bijjana and Vira - Vikrama.[190] The Hosur record[191] states that Lakshmidevi, was administering Sundi, Hosavur and other places granted by the chief in 1155 A.D. The non - appearance of Siriyadevi during the chiefdom of Chavunda II is noteworthy. It may denote his unhappiness towards his father - in - law. Demaladevi and her son Achugi III are stated to have been governing over the territories sorruonding the ancient capital of Pattadakisuvolal i.e., Pattadakal as the regents of the chief in 1163 A.D.[192] The matrimonial alliance, however, in no way helped Bijjala to take his son - in - law into his confidence as Chavunda II continued his subordination to Chalukyan supremacy till 1163 A.D.

An inscription dated 1165 A.D. registers a gift made on the instructions of *mahamandalesvara* Chavundarasa.[193] The Arasibidi epigraph, dated in 1167 A.D. in the reign of Kalachuri Bijjala, records a gift by Hollarasa, son of Bittarasa.[194] This record seems to suggest that Bijjala had tried to overlook Chavunda and consider another Sinda, of some collateral branch, as the chief of Kisukadu and other territories.[195] But thereafter Chavunda II seems to have accepted the supremacy of Kalachuri Bijjana in whose record he is referred to in 1167 A.D.[196] The Hiremannur record[197] dated 1169 A.D. gives a genealogical account of the Sindas and of Chavunda's exploits. He is stated to have been governing Kisukadu - 70, Bagadage - 70, Nareyangal - 12 and Kelavadi - 300. This epigraph clearly state that he was the son of Chandaladevi while Perma was the son of Mahadevi. According to Panchamukhi, he was holding the reigns of government in conjunction with his sons Achugi III and Permadi II in 1163 A.D.[198]

Vira - Bijjana (1168 - 87 A.D.) and Vira - Vikrama (1169 - 1220 A.D.) :

Chavunda II's rule might have come to an end in 1169 - 70 A.D. for his other two sons, viz. Vira - Bijjana and Vira - Vikrama were ruling over Kisukadu - 70, Bagadage - 70 and Kelavadi - 300 in 1179 A.D.[199] It is very difficult to know under what circumstances these two brothers could manage to hold their sway over the afore said territories after the death of their father. That these two brothers ruled conjointly is evidenced by an inscription dated in 1187 A.D., wherein it is stated that they were ruling together from their capital at Erambarage. This fact is corroborated by other records also. These two brothers have also left behind their own separate records. But this marks no difference in the nature of their joint sway over the territories. Their mother *Pattamahadevi* Siriyadevi seems to have been governing the Sinda territory in 1172 and 1174 A.D. obviously as regent - mother since her two sons were too young *(kumaras)* at that time. Vira - Bijjana's wife was Tripuradevi.[200]

The two brothers are stated to have been governing Kisukadu - 70, the Bagadage - 70, the Nareyangal - 12, Kelavadi - 300 and Kirividi - 30 in 1178 A.D.[201] Kalachuri Ahavamalla had succeeded his brother Sankama in 1181 A.D.[202] The nonmention of any overlord in the Sulebhavi inscription dated 1185 - 86 A.D. of the time of Bijjala and Vikrama makes it clear that they had declared independence during the reign of Ahavamall.[203] Vira - Bijjala's first record[204] is dated in 1173 A.D. He would have assumed power sometime in 1166 A.D. Bijjala's last known record is dated in 1186 A.D. Probably soon after this date he passed away. After this Vikrama or Vikramaditya continued his rule upto 1220 A.D. according to the Kalakappanagudda record.[205] It is presumed that he ruled for over 60 years assuming that he took active part in 1166 - 67 A.D.[206] Great changes had taken place during this period. The position of the Chalukya ruler Somesvara IV was secured for him in 1184-85 A.D. by his *dandanayaka* Brahama who is said to be "a fire of death to the Kalachuris".[207] He is further said to have laid seige to the whole of the earth for the purpose of making the Chalukyas the lords of all the worlds.[208] This fact is further corroborated by some other epigraphs of the Hoysalas.[209]

The circumstances narrated above naturally made Bijjala and Vikrama retransfer their allegiance to the Chalukyas.[210] Which is evident by the fact that a certain Padmadeva, son of *dandanayaka* Brahma, referred to earlier and his maternal uncle Vatsaraja were said to have been jointly ruling the whole of the eastern country, including the Sindavadi province.[211] Between 1189 - 1215 A.D. there prevailed much disturbance for we notice that the two major royal families viz., the Yadavas and the Hoysalas were in constant encounters to seize the Chalukyan territory. Hoysala Vira Ballala seems to have successfully wrested some portion of the territory taken by the Yadava king and he made Bijjala and Vikrama accept his supremacy by defeating them. The Yadavas led an expedition against Hoysala Vira Ballala and were able to get back the portion of land lying to the south of the Krishna and Malaprabha and even extended their arms further south.[212] They even forced Vikrama to change his allegiance to the Yadavas. This is evidenced by a record[213] dated 1220 A.D. of the reign of the Yadava Simghana under whom *mahamandalesvara* Vikramaditya is stated to have been ruling. After this date we do not get any single record belonging to the Sindas of Erambarage. Thus, we notice that *Mahapradhana* Vasudeva - Nayaka ruling over Erambarage under the orders of Yadava Simghana.[214]

Panchamukhi presumes that the Sinda prince Vikrama had passed away between 1220 and 1229 A.D. after which his territory was annexed to the Yadava kingdom, thereby ending the sway of the Sinda chiefs after a glorious career of about 150 years.[215]

The genealogy of the Sindas of Erambarage[216]

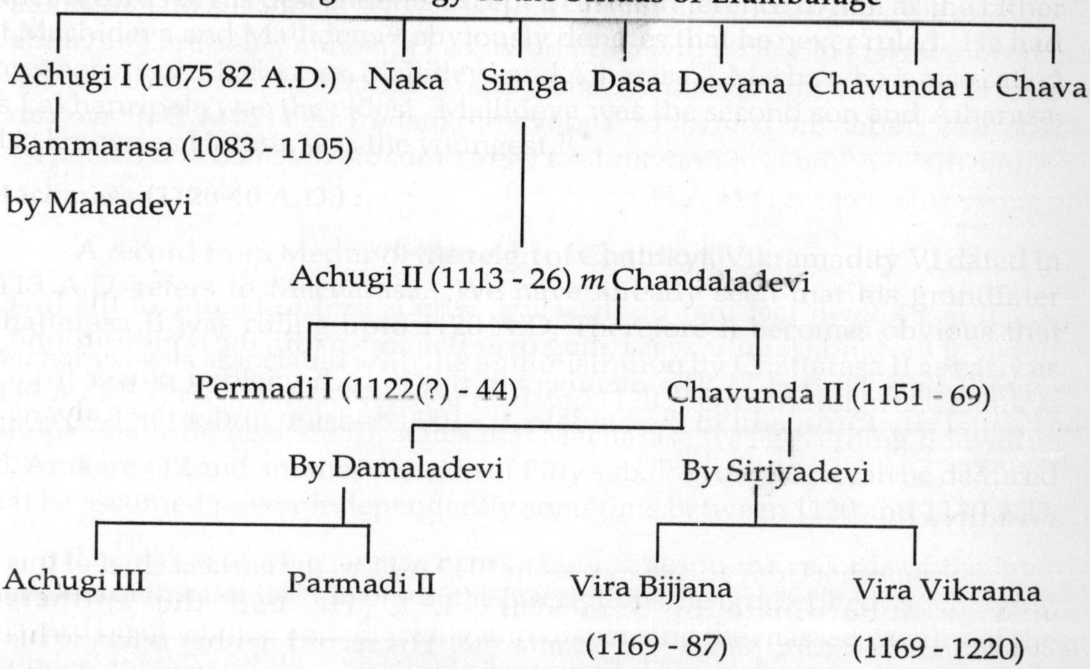

The Sindas of Pratyandaka

The Tidugundi copper plate grant[217] dated 1082 A.D. furnishes some information about this family. Bhima, the first member of this family is described as the lord of the Pratyandaka - 4000 country *(desa)* and as one who was fearless on the battle field. His eldest son *(agra - suta)* was Sindaraja, details about whom are not known. A damaged inscription dated 1048 A.D. mentions a certain chief, whose name is lost, as *mahasamantadhipati* as governing Paliyanda - 4000.[218] Other details about him are not known except that he was a feudatory of Chalukya Somesvara I as he has described himself as *Trailokyamalladeva - pada - pamkaja - bhrumura.*

His son was *mahamandalaesvara* Munja, who bore the epithets *Phanindraiyamsodbhava, Bhogavatipuravarcsvara, Nakula - tilak* and *Sindu - kulu - kamalamarttanda.* He had hold on the Pratyandaka country in 1082 A.D. as a subordinate of Chalukya Vikramaditya VI. He is described as the submarine fire to Gunaka about whom we do not know anything. He is stated to have sold the Vayvada group of 12 villages excluding the village Takkalike to *mahasamanta* Kanna, another feudatory of Vikramaditya VI, who has been identified with Kannakaira II belonging to the Ratta family and who was jointly ruling with his brother Kartavirya II.[219]

A century later, we come to know that Yadava king Bhillama V claims to have defeated a king of Pratyandaka.[220] Pratyandaka is identical with Paliyanda, the head quarters of a 4000 division known as Paliyanda *nalsasira.* Paliyanda itself is identified with Parenda of Osmanabad District in Maharashtra. As this region was under the control of Yadava Singhana I in 1124 A.D.,[221] we can presume that the Sindas of Pratyandaka were probably defeated and ousted by the above ruler before 1124 A.D.

The Sindas of Kurugodu

It is a known fact that Budhasevya, who is said to be one of the first member of the Sinda family, was ruling over Ballare - nadu, the region around present Bellary District.[222] The members of this branch wielded power from the capital city Kurugodu in the Sindavadi - 1000 division under the Kalyana Chalukyas.[223]

Udayaditya :

Mahasamanta Udayaditya figures in 1045 A.D. as the earliest chief of this family, a subordinate of Somesvara I.[224] He had the epithets *Bhogavatipuravaresvara, Kaliyuga - Revanta,* etc. His record neither refers to his family nor to the region over which he ruled. However, he has been assigned to the Sinda family of Kurugodu because the find spot of his record falls in this region.[225] This record also informs us that Trailokyamalla Nanni - Nolamba (Jayasimha III) was ruling over the *nadu.* Moreover, from two inscriptions[226] dated 1046 and 1047 A.D. which refer to the rule of *mahamandalesvara* Gandaradityarasa over Sindavadi - 1000, it is presumed that Udyaditya was not governing Sindavadi province.[227] The status of *mahasamanta* continued upto Chokkarasa.

Bammidevarasa :

He bore the epithets *Bhogavatipuravaresvara, Sindakula - kamala - bhaskara* and *Phanindra - kula - bhushana.* He was ruling over the *agrahara* Tonamkali in Kogali - 500, Nitturu and Basikodu situated in two other divisions of twelve (villages) in 1052 - 53 A.D. During the same period, Trailokyamalla Nanni-nolamba, his superior, was ruling over Kogali - 500, Ballakunda - 300 and Kadambalige - 1000.[228] But it is evident from this inscription that Bammidevarasa had ruled over 12 villages though he was not associated with the administration of Sindavadi province.[229] It is however difficult to say how he was connected with Udayaditya.

Chokkarasa :

We hear about a Chokkarasa after a lapse of nearly 40 years as holding the office of *mannaya* in 1091-92 A.D. He was a feudatory of Piriya Ketaladevi,[230] the queen of Vikramaditya VI.

Bacharasa :

Again there is a gap of four decades after the rule of Chokkarasa. Bacharasa, also known as Bachibhupa, was governing Sindavadi - 1000 in 1132 A.D. under *yuvaraja* Taila (III) in the reign of Bhulokamalla. He was endowed with the epithet of *mahamandalesvara* which clearly indicates his improved feudatory status. In this connection it can be noticed here that his predecessors had the title of *mahasamanta* only. It furnishes the genealogical account of his family and further it refers to a place Guttikallu as his capital. He is stated to have granted the village Ittage in Garuje - 70 a sub - division of Adavani - 500 in Sindavadi - 1000 to god Karekanthesvara of Tumbula. His valour is also eulogised.[231]

Another record from the same place, which was issued immediately after two years of the above record dated either in 1133 or 1134 A.D., mentions Trailokyamalla Mallidevamaharaja as ruling over Sindavadi province.[232] What happend to Bacharasa in the meanwhile is however difficult to ascertain in the present state of our knowledge.

Rachamallarasa I:

He was a *mahamandalesvara* and a subordinate of Chalukya Jagadekamalla II in 1141 A.D.[233] This inscription refers to a gift offered jointly by this chief and Kumara Kesiyanna nayaka, his own subordinate, to Nirvannideva of Mulugunda. It is doubted whether he ruled over any division.[234] But it is certain that he was adminstering some region in the Sindavadi province which included Ballare as he is associated with this place in the present record. In a record[235] of the same suzerain dated 1147 A.D. Irmadi Bhimarasa and Rachamalla, two brothers, who were administering over Ballakunde-nadu are mentioned. The former is eulogised as *Phani - vamsa - kamala - dinapa, Phani - vamsa - kumuda - chandra, Phani - vamsa - lalata - tilaka* and *Sindakulatilaka.* There might have been a Bhima I about whom we do not know as this inscripiton refers to Irumadi Bhima i.e., Bhima II. Rachamalla mentioned in this epigraph is identical with Rachamallarasa of Ballare.[236] It is evident from an inscription[237] of 1173 A.D. that this Rachamalla I was ruling over the city of Kurugodu in Ballakunde – nadu. Two records from Kurugodu dated 1173 and 1181 A.D. respectively in the reign of Chalukya Somesvara IV refer to these Sinda chiefs. The first part of the inscription of 1173 A.D. furnishes the genealogy. Here, Rachamalla is described as *Bhogindravamsodbhava.*

Desai thought that the date of the first of these two records is misleading and incorrect[239] and has suggested that Rachamalla I died sometime between 1146 and 1169 A.D. thinking that Rachamalla II might have passed away in 1181 A.D. But Gopal is tempted to identify Rachamalla of this epigraph with Rachamallarasa of Ballare viz., Rachamalla I of 1141 A.D.[240] and prasumes that he continued his chieftainship from Kurugodu till at least 1173 A.D., the date of the present record. His presumption holds good for we find Rachamalla II continuing his rule ove Kurugodu upto 1195 A.D.[241]

Rachamalla II :

The second part of the above record, dated 1181 A.D., refers to him. An incomplete and undated record inscribed on the second face of the slab mentions that a temple was constructed in memory of the departed soul of Rachamalla I.[242]

The rule of Rachamalla, obviously Rachamalla II, over Kurugodu as a subordinate of Kalachuri Sovideva and Sankama respectively is recorded during 1176 and 1177 A.D.[243] His own record[244] dated 1195 A.D. states that he was the son of Irungola and grandson of Rachamalla I. From this fact it would appear that Rachamalla II, who was able to rule for over 20 years, succeeded his grandfather.[245] In this connection it may be surmised that Irungola, said to be the father of Rachamalla II, did not rule at all, a surmise further fortified by the non - availability of his records.

Another family of the Sindas, designated as Sindas of Renjeru, whose epigraphs are spread over in Bidar District, Karnataka has been dealt with in detail by Gopal.[246]

REFERENCES

1. *EC.*, XI (1903), Dg. 43; *Ep. Ind.*, III, p. 235 and B.R. Gopal : *MDSIK.*, I, p. 87.

2. *EC.*, XI (1903), Dg. 43; *ARIE*, 1958-59, No. B. 556.

3. *Ep. Ind.*, III, p. 235.

4. *EC.*, VII (1902), Hl. 20, 50 and Sk. 316; *Ibid.*, XI (1903), Dg. 43.
5. Gopal : *op. cit.*, I, p. 95.
6. *SII.*, IX, Pt. I, No. 55.
7. Desai : *MUCK.*, pp. 8-15.
8. Gopal *: op. cit.*, pp. 95-96.
9. *EC.*, XI (1903), Hk. 23.
10. Gopal *: op. cit.*, p. 95.
11. *Ibid.*, p. 96.
12. *Ibid.*,
13. Desai *: op. cit.*, p. 14.
14. Gopal *: op. cit.*, p. 96.
15. *EC.*, VII (1902), Sk. 69.
16. *Ibid.*, VIII (1904), Nr. 47 and 59.
17. Rice : *MCI.*, p. 139.
18. *EC.*, VIII (1904), Nr. 47 and 59.
19. *Ibid.*, Xi (1903), Dr. 43.
20. *Ibid.*, VII (1902), Hl. 20 and 50.
21. Gopal *: op. cit.*, p. 96.
22. *EC.*, XI (1903), Dg. 43.
23. *Ibid.*, VII (1902), Hl. 20 and 50.
24. *Ibid.*, XI (1903), Dg. 43; VII (1902), Hl. 20 and 50.
25. Gopal *: op. cit.*, pp. 97-99.
26. *Ibid.*, VII (1902), Sk. 316.
27. *Ibid.*, VI (1901), Cm. 99.
28. *Ibid.*, V (1902), Cm. 212, VI, (1901), Tk. 76.
29. *Ibid.*, VII (1902), Hl. 45.
30. *Ibid.*, Hl. 25 and 45.
31. *Ibid.*, Hl. 20 and 50; XI (1903), Dg. 43.

32. Gopal : *Op cit.*, pp. 98-99.
33. *Ibid.*, pp. 97-98.
34. *EC.*, XI (1903), Dg. 43; VII (1902), Hl. 20, 25 and 50.
35. *Ibid.*, VII (1902), Hl. 20.
36. Desai : *op. cit.*, p. 25
37. *EC.*, V (1902), El. 193.
38. *Ibid.*, VII (1902), Hl. 98.
39. *Ibid.*, Hl. 20.
40. *Ibid.*, XI (1903), Dg. 43.
41. Desai : *op. cit.*, p. 28.
42. *ARIE.*, 1958-59, No. B. 571.
43. *EC.*, XI (1903), Dg. 43.
44. *Ibid.*, VII (1902), Sk. 190.
45 *Ibid.*, Sk. 146.
46 *Ibid.*, XI (1903), Dg. 43.
47 Desai : *op. cit.*, pp. 28-30.
48 Fleet : *IKD*, p. 577.
49 *EC.*, VII (1902), Hl. 98, 27 and 26.
50. *Ibid.*, Hl. 26.
51. Gopal B.R. : *op. cit.*, pp. 28-30
52. *Ibid.*, p. 100.
53. *EC.*, VII (1902), Hl. 27.
54. *Ibid.*, Hl. 26.
55. Fleet : *DKD.*, p. 577.
56. *EC.*, VII (1902), Hl. 20.
57. *Ibid.*, Hl. 45.
58. *Ibid.*, Sk. 206.
59. *Ibid.*, VI (1901), Mg. 33; Desai : *op. cit.*, p. 36.

60. *ARIE.*, 1960-61, No. B. 545.
61. *EC.*, VII (1902), Hl. 50.
62. *Ibid.*, VI (1901), Mg. 33.
63. *Ibid.*, VII (1902), Hl. 20.
64. *Ibid.*, Hl. 35.
65. Fleet : *DKD.*, p. 646.
66. *EC.*, VII (1902), Hl. 46.
67. *Ibid.*, VIII (1904), Sb. 179.
68. *IA.*, II, p. 299.
69. *EC.*, VII (1902), Hl. 51.
70. Desai *: op. cit.*, pp. 41-42.
71. *EC.*, VII (1902), Hl. 37.
72. Desai *: op. cit.*, pp. 41-42
73. *EC.*, VII (1902), Hl. 28.
74. *Ibid.*, Hl. 28.
75. *Ibid.*, Sk. 315.
76. *Ibid.*, Hl. 44.
77. Desai *: op. cit.*, p. 49.
78. *EC.*, VII (1902), Hl. 41, 42 and 44.
79. Desai *: op. cit.*, pp. 50 - 52.
80. *EC.*, VII (1902), Hl. 48.
81. *ARIE.*, 1958-59, No. B 572.
82. *Ibid.*, No. B 611.
83. Gopal *: op. cit.*, pp. 103-04.
84. *EC.*, V (1902), p. 263.
85. *ARIE.*, 1957-58, B. 248.
86. *Ibid.*, Nos. 239 and 241.
87. *Ibid.*, No. 248; Gopal *: op. cit.*, p. 104.

88. *EC.*, VII (102), Hl. 20.
89. *Ibid.*, XI (1903), Hk. 56.
90. *Ibid.*, VII (1902), Hl. 20.
91. *Ibid.*, Hl. 43.
92. Desai : *op. cit.*, p. 58.
93. Gopal : *op. cit.*, p. 106.
94. *EC.*, VIII (1904), Sb. 319.
95. *Ibid.*, VII (1902), Hl. 49, 54, 56 and 58.
96. *Ibid.*, Hl. 55; The date 1247 A.D. has been arrived at on the basis of the cyclic year Plavanga given in this record. Otherwise the Saka 1179 corresponds to 1257 A.D.
97. *Ibid.*,
98. Desai : *op. cit.*, p. 61.
99. *EC.*, VIII (1904), Sb. 209, 291 and 295.
100. Genealogy as given by Gopal : *op. cit.*, p. 105.
101. *Ibid.*, p. 107.
102. *Ep. Ind.*, III, pp. 230 ff.
103. *Ibid.*, XXXVIII, pp. 236 ff.
104. *Ibid.*, III, p. 230 ff.
105. Desai : *op. cit.*, pp. 67-68.
106. *Ibid.*, p. 67.
107. *Ibid.*, p. 69.
108. *The Struggle for Empire*, p. 167; *Ep. Ind.*, III, p. 230 ff.
109. Desai : *op. cit.*, pp. 69-71.?
110. *Ep. Ind.*, III, p. 230 ff.
111. Desai : *op. cit.*, p. 116.
112. *Ep. Ind.*, XX, p. 111.
113. Gopal : *op. cit.*, p. 110.
114. *Ibid.*, p. 109.

115. *Ep. Ind.*, XX, p. 109 ff.

116. *Ibid.*,

117. *JBBRAS.*, XI, p. 269.

118. *Ibid.*, p. 233.

119. *Ibid.*,

120. *Ibid.*,

121. *Ibid.*, p. 269.

122. *Ibid.*,

123. *Ibid.*, p. 233.

124. *Ibid.*, p. 269.

125. Desai : *op. cit.*, p. 74.

126. *Ep. Ind.*, XX, pp. 112 ff.; Desai also has done the same mistake, see Desai :*op. cit.*, p. 77.

127. *SII.*, XI, Pt. I, No. 117.

128. *Ep. Ind.*, XX, pp. 110 ff.

129. Gopal : *op. cit.*, p. 111.

130. *Ibid.*,

131. *Ep. Ind.*, XX, p. 112, f.n. No. 1.

132. *SII.*, XV, No. 92.

133. *Ep. Ind.*, XX, p. 110.

134. *Ibid.*, XIX, p. 227.

135. Desai : *op. cit.*, p. 74.

136. *Ep. Ind.*, XX, p. 112.

137. *SII.*, XI, Pt. II, No. 179; f.n. No. 21.

138. Gopal : *op. cit.*, p. 111.

139. *Ibid.*, p. 112.

140. Desai : *op. cit.*, p. 77.

141. Fleet : *DKD.*, p. 574.

142. *Ep.* Ind., XX, pp. 111-12.

143. *Ibid.*, p. 112.

144. *Ibid.*,

145. *SII.*, XI, Pt. II, No. 163.

146. Gopal : *op. cit.*, p. 112

147. *SII.*, XI, Pt. II, No. 163; *JBBRAS.*, XI, p. 247; *SII.*, XI, Pt. II, No. 176.

148. Gopal : *op. cit.*, p. 112.

149. *Ep. Ind.*, XX, p. 112.

150. *JBBRAS.*, XI, p. 235; Desai : *op. cit.*, p. 80; *HISI.*, p. 96; *Ep. Ind.*, IX, p. 256.

151. *JBBRAS.*, XI, p. 244.

152. Desai : *op. cit.*, p. 80.

153. *IA.*, ii, p. 302.

154. *HISI.*, pp. 95-96.

155. *Ep. Ind.*, XIII, p. 311.

156. *EC.*, XI (1903), Dg. 139.

157. *Ibid.*, Dg. 90.

158. *JABBRAS.*, XI, p. 269.

159. Fleet : *IKD.*, p. 452.

160. Desai : *op. cit.*, p. 83.

161. *Ibid.*,

162. Fleet : *DKD.*, p. 452.

163. *JBBRAS.*, XI, pp. 234-35.

164. *SII.*, XI, Pt. II, No. 163.

165. *Ibid.*, No. 176.

166. *JBBRAS.*, XI, p 233

167. *Ibid.*, p. 236.

168. *Ibid.*, pp. 235, 245.

169. *SII.*, XI, Pt. II, No. 119.

170. *Ibid.*, No. 155.

171. Gopal : *op. cit.*, p. 113.

172. *SII.*, XI, Pt. II, No. 155.

173. Vide *Bom. Gaz.*, I, Pt. II, p. 575, f.n. No. 3; *Ep. Ind.*, XX, p. 114; *SII.*, XI, Pt. II, No. 155 and introduction , p. iv.

174. *Ep. Ind.*, XX, p. 112.

175. *EC.*, VI (1901), Kd. 69.

176. *JBBRAS.*, XI, p. 244.

177. *KI.*, V, No. 72.

178. Desai : *op. cit.*, p. 90; *EC.*, VI (1901) Cn. 83.

179. *SII.*, XV, No. 83.

180. *EC.*, XX, p. 112, f.n. No. 5.

181. *SII.*, XV, Nos. 28 and 42.

182. *Ibid.*, XI, Pt. II, No. 155 and *KI.*, V, No. 72.

183. Gopal : *Op. cit.*, p. 113.

184. *SII.*, XV, No. 47; *Ep. Ind.*, XX, p. 112.

185. Gopal : *op. cit.*, p. 114.

186. Rice : *Mys. Ins.*, p. 100.

187. *Ep. Ind.*, XX, p. 112 and f.n. No. 8.

188. *Ibid.*, p. 112.

189. Not Permadi III as given by Panchamukhi, *Ibid.*, p. 111.

190. *Ibid.*, p. 111.

191. *SII.*, XV, No. 236.

192. *JBBRAS.*, XI, p. 272; Fleet : *DKD.*, p. 576.

193. *SII.*, XV, No. 237.

194. *Ibid.*, No. 108.

195. Gopal : *op. cit.*, p. 115.

196. *Ep. Ind.*, XX, p. 113.

197. *SII.*, XV, No. 238.

198. *Ep. Ind.*, XX, p. 113; According to Gopal his two sons are not heard of

after 1163 A.D. Gopal : *op. cit.*, p. 115. But Achugi III seems to have been serving under Somesvara IV till 1194 A.D., *SII.*, XX, No. 74.

199. *Ep. Ind.*, XX, p. 113.
200. *Ibid.*,
201. *SII.*, XV, Nos. 134 and 142; *ARTE.*, 1927 - 28, B.K. No. 32.
202. Fleet : *DKD.*, p. 488.
203. *SII.*, XV, No. 242.
204. *Ibid.*, No. 240.
205. *Ibid.*, No. 165.
206. Gopal : *op. cit.*, p. 117.
207. *Ep. Ind.*, XX, p. 113.
208. Fleet : *DKD.*, p. 464.
209. *Mysore Gazetteer*, Pt. II, p. 859.
210. *SII.*, XV, No. 77.
211. *MAR.*, 1916, No. 555.
212. *Ep. Ind.*, XX, p. 114.
213. *SII.*, XV, No. 165.
214. *ARIE.*, 1926-27, B.K. No. 200; *Ep. Ind.*, XX, p. 114.
215. *Ep. Ind.*, XX, p. 114.
216. Genealogy as given by Gopal : *Op. cit.*, p. 116.
217. *Ep. Ind.*, III, pp. 306 ff.
218. *SII.*, IX, Pt. I, No. 108.
219. Fleet : *DKD.*, pp. 553-54.
220. Gopal : *op. cit.*, p. 123.
221. S.H. Ritti : *The Seunas*, pp. 72-73.
222. B.R. Gopal : *op. cit.*, p. 89.
223. *Ibid.*, p. 124.
224. *SII.*, IX, Pt. I, No. 100; Desai : *op. cit*, pp. 119 ff.

225. Gopal : *op. cit.*, p. 124.

226. *SII.*, IX, Pt. I, Nos. 102 and 105.

227. Gopal : *op. cit.*, p. 125.

228. *SII.*, IX, Pt. I, No. 109.

229. Gopal : *op. cit.*, p. 125.

230. *SII.*, IX, Pt. I, No. 159.

231. *Ibid.*, No. 226.

232. *Ibid.*, No. 228.

233. *Ibid.*, No. 235.

234. Gopal : *op. cit.*, p. 126.

235. *SII.*, IX, Pt. I, No. 249.

236. *Ibid.*, No. 235.

237. *Ep. Ind.*, XIV, pp. 270 ff.

238. *Ibid.*, pp. 370 ff.

239. Desai : *op. cit.*, p. 121.

240. *SII.*, IX, Pt. I, No. 235.

241. *Ibid.*, No. 322.

242. The death of Rachamalla II is referred to wrongly in this connection, cf. Gopal : *op. cit.*, p. 127.

243. *SII.*, IX, Pt. I, Nox. 296-97.

244. *Ibid.*, No. 322.

245. Gopal : *op. cit.*, p. 128.

246. *Ibid.*, p. 117.

VI

THE RATTAS

Though more than one family of Rattas are known to Karnataka history, the one which came into existence during the rule of the Rashtrakuta Krishna II[1] and continued their sway till the rule of the Chalukya Taila II on some parts of the Kundi province with Sugandhavarti (modern Saundatti) as their capital. They may be designated as the 'early Rattas of Saundatti' in view of its comparative antiquity.[2] Fleet takes the expression *'Baisanvaya - saroja - vana - marttanda'*[3] to mean that Santivarma overthrew some members of that family.[4] Whereas Desai states that those chiefs of the family which rose to prominence under the rule of Krishna III[5] and ruled over some parts of the Kundi province including Sugandhavarti were of the Baisa family.[6] If the reading *Baisanvaya* is corrected to *Jainanvaya* then it gives a clear picture of this dynasty denoting that they were of Jaina persuation. This is supported by the mention that the early Ratta chief Prithvirama was the disciple of Indrakirtisvamin of Mailapatirtha and Kareyagana.[7]

The Early Rattas of Saundatti

The history of the early Rattas can be known from some of their records.[8] According to the genealogy furnished in one of the records[9] dated 875-76 A.D., Merada figures as the first member of thier family. Further details are not known about him. He was succeeded by his son Prithvirama, who is stated to be a disciple of Indrakirtisvamin who in turn was the disciple of Gunakirti - munisvara. The latter again was the disciple of Mullabhatta of Mailapatirtha and Kareya - gana. Prithvirama was patronised and invested with the position and authority of a feudatory status by the confirment of the title *mahasamanta* by the Rashtrakuta monarch Krishna II.[10]

Prithvirama is stated to have constructed a *Jinendra - bhavana* for which he made a grant of eighteen *nivarttanas* of land.[11] Pittuga, his successor, has been credited with the defeat of Ajavarman (?) whose identity cannot be made out.[12] His wife was Nijiyabbarasi.

Pittuga was succeeded by his son *mahasamanta* Santivarman. An epigraph[13] of the reign of Chalukya Taila II dated 980 A.D. refers to him and states that he had built a Jaina *basadi* at Sugandhavartti and made a grant of 150 *mattars* of land to it. The gift was entrusted to Bahubali - bhattaraka. Nijiyabbarasi, his mother, had also granted 150 *mattars* of land to the same Jaina basadi. With the help of the genealogical account and dates of the chiefs provided in an epigraph[14] the period of each chief can be fixed as follows:

Narada 840-65 A.D.

Prithvirama 865-900 A.D.

Pittuga *m* Nijayabbarasi 900-50 A.D.

Santivarman *m* Chandikabbe 950-85 A.D.

Fleet opines that Kartavirya I rose against Santivarma and eventually appropriated the entire Kundi province from that person[15] on the basis of an inscription which states that Kartavirya I, the later Ratta chief of Saundatti and Belgaum had fixed the boundaries of the Kundi country[16] (*Kuhundidesayaghatam sadhitam tena bhudhuja).*

Desai,[17] on the other hand, states that there was no hostility between Santivarma and Kartavirya I as stated by Fleet and opines that the former was holding charge of Sugandhavarti during this time while Kartavirya I was ruling from his capital Sogal situated in Belgaum District in 980 A.D.[18]

We agree with the opinion of Fleet and would further like to state that Santivarman's rule was eclipsed gradually due to the growing power of Kartavirya I under the supremacy of Chalukya Taila II.

The Later Rattas of Saundatti and Belgaum

The early epigraphs belonging to this branch do not give any information about the origion of these chiefs. But the later records of the 13th century trace the origin of this family to the Rashtrakutas.[19] Bhandarkar feels that the Rashtrakuta family was the main branch of the race of Kshatriyas named Rattas who gave their name to the country of Maharashtra.[20] C.V. Vaidya agrees with the evidence of the later records[21] and Desai states that the Rattas belonged to the same clan as the Rashtrakutas, though their claim of being actually descended from Krishna III can no longer be accepted.[22] In spite of the accounts furnished in their later epigraphs and opinions expressed by various scholars, it is very difficult to associate the Rattas with the Rashtrakutas who had the appellation Ratta.[23] We have arrived at this conclusion after considering the evidence of the early records which are likely to be more authentic than the later ones.

We on our part feel that the word *Ratta* has been derived from the Sanskrit term *Rashtra* and may be the same as *Rashtrika* designating officials of the *Rashtra,* which is normally a bigger unit than a *vishaya.*

The Rattas are known after the names of their two capitals viz., Saundatti and Belgaum. Hence they are called as the Rattas of Saundatti and Belgaum. The chiefs of this family are stated to have ruled over the Kundi province, comprising parts of Belgaum District and the Terdal division in the former Sangli state now merged in Kolhapur District[24]. They were entitled to the honour of *Panchamahasabda',* were heralded in the public by the sounds of the musical instruments *trivali,* had the *Sindhura - lanchhana* and carried the *Suvarna -garuda - dhvaja.*[25]

Nanna, who is referred to as *Kantheyabharada* Nannapayya,[26] was the earliest member of this family. His son Kartavirya I, also known as Katta and described as *Bhujabala Chakravarti,* was a subordinate of Chalukya Taila II (973-97 A.D.). He seems to have been the real founder of this family as he is stated to have fixed the boundaries of the Kundi *(Kuhundi)* province.[27] His two sons viz., Davari or Dayima and Kannakaira I also knwon as Kanna succeeded him as administrators of the Kundi province.[28] Eraga, the son and the successor of Kannakaira I bore titles such as *Ratta - narayana* and *Ratta - marttanda.*[29] He was serving under Jagadekamalla I in 1041 A.D. Ankarasa succeeded his elder brother Eraga in 1048 A.D. The succession of Ankarasa to the Ratta throne immediately after Erega shows probably that Sena I, son of the latter was an infant at that time. Ankarasa was a *mahasamanta* of Trailokyamalla i.e., Somesvara I (1043-68 A.D.). Till now we know that Kartavirya I had his sway over Kundi province without any capital. But during the rule of Ankarasa, Sugandhavartti (modern Saundatti in Parasgad Taluk of Belgaum District) became the capital of the Rattas. By this evidence, Ankarasa seems to have established the rule of the Rattas on a firm basis.[30] He was succeded by his nephew Sena I, also known as Kalasena, who continued his subordination to both Somesvara I (1043-68 A.D.) and Somesvara II (1068 - 76 A.D.) Mailaladevi was his wife.[31]

Kannakaira (Kanna) II (1083-87 A.D.)

His son *mahasamanta* Kannakaira II, also called Kanna, was ruling under the supremacy of Vikramaditya VI in 1083 A.D.[32] Kannakaira is stated to have purchased the Vayvade group of 12 villages from Munja, a chief of the Sindas of Pratyandaka in 1082 A.D.[33]

Kartavirya II (1087-1100 A.D.)

Kartavirya II succeeded Kanna and rose to the status of *mahamandalesvara.*[34] An inscription[35] of the reign of Chalukya Bhuvanaikamalla (Somesvara II) describes him as the lord of Lattalurapura *(Lattalurppuravaresvara)* and contains the genealogical account of his family. He, in conjunction with his wife Bhagaladevi, renewed a gift of land in 1087 A.D. formerly made by *mahasamanta* Ankarasa, his grandfather's brother.[36] His subordinate Gonka was entrusted with the administration of Teridala-12,[37]

An inscription[38] dated 1098 A.D. (?) gives the genealogy of the Ratta family and states that *mahamandalesvara* Kartavirya II was a subordinate of Vikramaditya VI. It refers to a temple of Jinendra built by Kalasena (i.e., Sena I). Further it refers to another gift of land by Sena II to the same temple. It also refers to a gift of land made by Kannakaira II, to his guru Kanakaprabha Siddhantadeva. We learn from this record that Kartavirya continued to serve under Chalukyan supremacy even on that date.[39] His son Sena II is described in this record as *mandalikagraganya* which definitely denotes that he was officially sharing with his father the burden of administration.

Sena II (1100 - 30 A.D.) :

Kartavirya II was eventually succeeded by his son *mahamandalesvara* Sena II, probably in 1100 A.D. He and *dandanayaka* Chamunda seem to have been entrusted with the charge of the Kundi province in 1121 A.D. under Jayakarna, the son of Vikramaditya VI, who had some hold over the central parts of his father's dominions.[40] Sena II seems to have been a powerful feudatory as his qualities are extolled at length in an inscripiton.[41] Lakshmidevi was his wife.[42]

Ankideva, a *mahasamanta* referred to in an inscription of 1129 A.D., is said to have belonged to the Ratta family.[43] But he does not seem to have been actively associated with the administration of the Kundi province as none of the available epigraphs reveal his place in that family. Moreover, by this period, the Ratta chiefs had risen to the status of *mahamandalesvaras*. Desai, therefore, rightly concludes that he was a Ratta scion who must have been either a minor feudatory or a high official of Chalukya Somesvara III (1126-38 A.D.).[44]

Kartavirya III (1162-90 A.D.):

A new era begins in the annalas of the Ratta family with the accession of Kartavirya III. He receives high praise obviously because he had enhanced the power of the Rattas as a subordinate of Jagadekamalla II (1138-55 A.D.). The event of the succession of Taila III in 1151 A.D. to the Chalukyan throne and his defeat at the hands of Kalachuri Bijjala in or about 1162 A.D. marks an important turning point in South Indian history. It had its bearing on the fortunes of the Ratta family also. At the end of this turmoil, which some chiefs continued as the adherents of Taila III, a few others switched over their allegiance to Kalachuri Bijjala,[45] who had appropriated from the Chalukyas the paramount epithets[46] and titles such as *samastabhubanasraya sri - prithvi-vallabha, maharajadhiraja - paramesvara parama - bhattaraka*[47] in the flush of his victory over Taila III. Kartavirya III did not lag behind in taking advantage of the events of the period and declared his independence for we see that he was ruling from Nesarige in 1162 A.D. without making any reference to his suzerain or to his own subordination.[48] However, he was deprived of his independent status soon as he appears as a subordinate of Kalachuri Bijjala in 1165 A.D.[49]

According to above inscription, Kalana who was ruling from his capital at Valavada, was a subordinate of Silahara Vijayaditya. He got constructed the Neminatha *basadi* at Ekkasambuge situated in Koravalli gampanadu of Kundi province. Ekkasambuge is the same as modern Eksambi in Chikkodi Taluk, Belgaum District. Further it records a gift of land, a house site for a *danasala,* garden etc., by Kartavirya III for worship, offerings etc., at the *basadi* referred to above. From the mention of Kalana as a subordinate of Silahara Vijayaditya it may be presumed that Vijayaditya was commanding a better position than the Rattas under that supremacy of Kalachuri Bijjala and that he had been made their overlord by imperial writ.

The attribution of the title *Chakravarti* beside *mahamandalesvara* in Konnur record,[50] the date of which is lost but which is assignable to Kattama obviously Kartavirya III tempts us to surmise that the Rattas had once again attained independent status some time after 1165 A.D. taking advantage of the Kalachuri-Hoysala dispute over the possession of the southern provinces. His rule as an independent chief was, however, short lived for we hear that *dandanayaka* Bhayideva was ruling over the Kundi province in 1187 A.D. after obtaining that province from Somesvara IV as a reward for defeating certain enemies in a battle.[51]

Though the enemies with whom Bhayideva fought is not referred to in this record, on the strength of the name of the province which was awarded to him, we may safely conclude that the Rattas were among them. Padmaladevi, also known as Padmavati, was the of Kartavirya III and she is described as a woman of great beauty, and possessed many accomplishments.[52]

Lakshmideva I (1190-1210 A.D.) :

The dates furnished by the record belonging to Kartavirya III's son and successor Lakshmideva I do not fit in with the known chronological history of the Rattas. His Honnikeri record[53] consists of two dates viz., 1209 and 1257 A.D. In this connection, Fleet opines that "the first date of this record, however, overlaps, and is not easily reconcileable with the earlier dates of his sons Kartavirya IV and Mallikarjuna".[54] As the first date of this record definitely refers to the rule of Lakshmideva I from Venugrama, we presume that he might have jointly ruled with his two sons during this date.

Let us turn our attention to the events which are significant from the point of view of the political conditions of this period. On one hand, the Chalukyas of Kalyana and the Kalachuris had lost their kingdoms and, on the other, the Yadavas had been renderd powerless. The only dominant power of the day was that of the Hoysalas despite tha reverses which they had suffered at the hands of the Yadavas. The dispute between these two major political parties i.e., the Yadavas and the Hoysalas, continued unabated for acquiring the southern provinces. It this melee Chalukya Somesvara IV in his distress, took shelter with the Kadambas of Goa.[55]

Consequent on these developments Lakshmideva I ended his subservience to the Chalukyas and declared his independence. This is proved by his Honnikeri record referred to above as it does not mention any sovereign. Another important event during the rule of Lakshmideva I is the shifting of the Ratta capital *(rajadhani)* from Saundatti to Venugrama i.e., Belgaum as may be gathered from the Honnikeri inscription.[56] During the early part of 12th century A.D. Belgaum as the chief town of a group of villages known as the Venugrama - Velugrama - 70,[57] was under the administration of the Goa Kadambas.[58]

From the above fact we can arrive at the conclusion that Lakshmideva I had come to possess the territories of the Kadambas of Goa which included Venugrama i.e., Belgaum. This Venugrama continued as the capital of the Rattas till the end of their rule. Chandrikadevi, also known as Chandaladevi, was the wife of Lakshmideva I. She is stated to have been the daughter of a person named Raja belonging to a family of *mahamandalesvaras*. Her father belonged to the clan of Yaduvamsa, whose members were lords of the Hagaratage District. He had the hereditary title "supreme lord of Kupanapura" i.e., modern Koppal, Raichur District.[59]

Kartavirya IV (1199-1219 A.D.) and Mallikarjuna (1199 - 1210 A.D.) :

Kartavirya IV and Mallikarjuna succeeded their father Lakshmideva I.[60] An inscription[61] of Kartavirya IV dated 1199 A.D. states that he is said to have been protecting the 84 *(mahajanas)* of Iskhugrama i.e., Belgaum from his *nelevidu* (capital) at Venugrama. Soon after his accession, he drafted his younger brother Mallikarjuna to assist him in the affairs of administration. Another record[62] dated 1204 A.D. informs us that Kartavirya IV was enjoying the *samrajya* from Venugrama in conjunction with his brother who is spoken of as the *yuvaraja*. This fact is also alluded to by a third record[63] dated 1208 A.D.

It appears that Kartavirya IV tried to recover some parts of the Kundi country which were lost during the reign of Kartavirya III to the Silaharas. This is confirmed by his Bhoj copper plate dated 1208 A.D. wherein it is stated that he recovered the Koravalli Kampana.[64] His benevolence to religious institutions can be known from his records dated 1201, 1202 and 1202-03 A.D. respectively.[65]

The records of this family dated after 1210 A.D. do not refer to Mallikarjuna. Therefore, it is presumed that his death had occurred sometime before that date. Consequently Kartavirya, who had enjoyed the assistance of his brother in his administration all along, had to shoulder responsibility single handed.

Yadava Singhana, the successor of Jaitugi I, defeated Bhoja II, the Silahara chief of Karad, about 1213 A.D.[66] The non-appearance of the above monarch in the Ratta province after his conquest of Silahara Bhoja possibly indicates that Kartavirya IV was too powerful to be challenged.[67] Echaladevi and Madevi (Mahadevi) were the two wives of Kartavirya IV.[68] It is presumed [69] that the former was the daughter of the Silahara Bhoja II who was styled *Paschima - Chakravarti*.[70] How far it is true is difficult to make out. Kartavirya ruled till 1219 A.D.[71]

Lakshmideva II (1219-38 A.D.) :

Mahamandalesvara Lakshmideva II, son of Kartavirya IV and Madevi (Mahadevi) succeeded to the throne in 1219 A.D.[72] He bore tha title *Boppanasinga*.[73] The power of the Rattas began to decay during his rule. The prevalance of a record of Yadava Singhana II dated 1222 A.D. at Manoli is sufficient to prove that some eastern portions of the territory belonging to the Rattas had by then fallen into the hands of the Yadavas.[74]

An inscription of Lakshmideva II dated 1228 A.D.[75] furnishes the genealogy of both the Rattas and Kesiraja, *prabhu* of Kolara and states that Lakshmideva II was governing the Sugandhavartti-12 division (findspot of the record is Saundatti) from Venugrama. Lakshmideva II lost his hold over the Kundi country after this date as we find Nallasetti governing the same country from Venugrama under Yadava Krishna.[76] A record[77] dated 1236 A.D. registers a grant of land, house and (site for) haystock*(banambe)* made by Lakshmideva's queen Lalitadevi at Mattivada which was under her administration.

Prior to 1237 - 38 A.D. he was deprived of some of his teritories as it was disposed off to an official of Yadava Singhana.[78]

The genealogy of the later Rattas of Saundatti and Belgaum

Nanna
- Kartavirya I
  - Davari (Dayima)
  - Kannakaira (Kanna) I
    - Erega (1041 A.D.)
      - Sena (Kalasena) I *m.* Mailaladevi
        - Kannakaire (Kanna) II (1083-87)
        - Kartavirya II (1087 - 1100) *m.* Bhagaladevi
          - Sena II (1110-30) *m.* Lakshmidevi
            - Kartavirya III *m.* Padmaladevi (1162-1190)
              - Lakshmideva I *m.* Chandrikadevi (1190 - 1210)
                - Kartavirya IV (1199 - 1219)
                  - Lakshmideva II (1219 - 33)
                - Mallikarjjuna(1199-1210):
    - Ankarasa (1048)

Feudatories Under The Rattas of Saundatti and Belgaum

In the last chapter we saw how the Rattas played a very significant role as the feudatories of the Chalukyas of Kalyana, the Kalachuris and the Yadavas. Some chiefs, who can be designated as local governors having control over some allotted subdivisions and villages were serving under the Rattas. It is very difficult to know the history of these local chiefs as their epigraphs are very few and do not throw much light on their political history. While we gather stray names and dates of such chiefs from inscriptions, it is not possible to fix the duration of their reigns or to furnish a cogent history for them.

The Yaduvamsa of Hagaratage :

The very name itself indicates that the origin of these chiefs from the Yaduvamsa and their administration over Hagaratage - nadu - 300 extending over parts of the Belgaum and Bijapur Districts. They had the title of *Kupanapuravaradhisvara.*[79] Desai[80] identifies Kupanapura with Kopananagara referred to in *Kavirajamarga*[81] and says that it was their original home. Usually it is the practice of the Indian rulers to call as the lords of some place which would naturally be their original capital. Considering this aspect, Kupanapura cannot be considered as their original home as felt by Desai. At the same time, when they come into historical limelight, we sea no tangible connection between them and Kupanapura for they had by then made Hagaratage as their chief town.

Brahma, the son of Rebbe, seems to be the founder member of this branch as he is referred to as the supporter of his race.[82] His successor was Raja I whose daughter Chandaladevi or Chandrikadevi was given in marriage to Lakshmideva I, the chief of the Ratta family.[83] Raja II, the last known member of this family, was the contemporary of the Ratta chief Kartavirya IV.[84]

The Prabhus of Kolara :

The members of this branch claim their descent from the lineage of Vasishtha.[85] Madiraja (I), an early member of this family, was a *Prabhu* and held control over Kolara, identical with Korti - Kolhar on the banks of the Krishna river.[86] Madiraja II succeeded his father Bhutanatha. He was a contemporary of Kartavirya IV. There is an elaborate description about his martial activities. Desai's opinion regarding his participation with Ratta Kartavirya IV in a war against the Yadava Singhana may not hold good as no single inscripition belonging to either family refers to this aspect. On the contrary, description of his war - like acts may be related to the internal fights between him and his own brothers in which he is stated to have been killed ultimately.[87] He was succeeded by his elder sister Bijayavve. What had happened to his other brother who fought with him is not known. Later on it appears that the administration of Kolara passed on to Gauri, daughter of Madiraja I, who had been given in marriage to Mallikarjuna of the Banihatti family. On that occasion Kolara was given as dowry, thereby ending the administration of *Prabhus* of Kolara.

The chiefs of Banihatti :

Members of this branch are stated to have belonged to *Samasigakula*, a branch of the Induvamsa, which had originated from Atri, a renowned sage. There were born in that family many brahmanas one among them gaining for the family its feudal status.[88] From the above narration it is clear that the chiefs of this family belonged to the brahmana community.

Rudrabhatta, who was a poet figures as the first member of this family. His excellence in composing poems fetched a reward of eighteen villages including Banihatti, which was considered the chief town, from a certain Kanna, who has been identified with his namesake, the first member of the Ratta family, i.e., Kanna I. Banihatti is situated near Jamukhandi in Bijapur District. Subsequently Sridhara I, son of Kalideva, seems to have been entrusted with the administration of the eighteen villages acquired previously by his grandfather Rudrabhatta. Sridhara II succeeded his father Mahadeva and grandfather Kalideva. He is said to have been killed in a battle that took place between him and the people of Ganasarovara, at Holavara. The two places referred to in this connection cannot be identified in the present state of our knowledge. The reason for the battle is also not known.

Mahadevanayaka, son and successor of Sridhara II, continued his enmity with the people of Ganasarovara who were responsible for his father's death. It is proved by the fact that he destroyed his enemies and reestablished the status of his family. He is also stated to have regained his father's property by purchase. In this task, he was assisted by a king who is supposed to be a Ratta chief.[89] Out of his three sons, Mallikarjuna succeeded as ruler of Banihatti.[90] It has already been stated that he married Gauri, the daughter of Madiraja II of the *Prabhus* of Kolara and got Kolara as dowry. This matrimonial alliance enabled him to make Kolara his family residence.[91] He rose to a position of a counsellor under Munichandradeva, the chief minister who was administering over Sugandhavartti - 12 during the reign of Lakshmideva II, the Ratta chief. He was succeeded by one of his sons Kesiraja or Kesavaraja who seems to have been a saint more than a chief as he was more interested in religious activities.[92] The last ruler of this family was Madiraja, the son of Kesiraja.

The family of Halleyarus :

Nothing is known about its origin. But this family is said to belong to the Balatkara - gana. Balatkara - gana significantly contributed a chain of Jaina pontiffs who were stated to be the preceptors of these chiefs at Kondanuru a Jaina centre at that time. Kondanuru has been identified with Konur in Gokak Taluk of Belgaum District. The above account clearly shows that the members of this family were Jainas by faith. They enjoyed the position of headmen of a circle of villages under the chieftainship of Sena I, the Ratta feudatory. Soriganka was the first chief of this family. He is stated to have been a contemporary of Sena II.

Nidhiyama - Nayaka was the son of Gamanda. He obtained the position of the *prabhu* of Kondanuru in about 1085 A.D. while Ratta Kannakaira II was ruling over the Kundi province. Kalideva and Baladeva were his two sons. Nothing further is known about this family after Nidhiyama - nayaka.

The Nayakas of Nesarige :

These chiefs had their administration over a circle of six villages having Nesarige (in Belgaum District) for its chief town. They had six *gaundas* as headmen of the six villages under their control.

Habbana or Habbaya nayaka was the first member of this branch and on him Chalukya Somesvara IV (1184-1200 A.D.) conferred the rank of *Nayaka*. His valiant features are described at length. He is credited with the defeat of Konkanigas. Desai supposed that the Konkanigas were none but some minor chiefs serving under the Kadambas of Goa,[93] who had by that time transferred their allegiance to the Hoysalas.[94] The non - mention of a Ratta chief in an inscription dated 1187 A.D. of the time of Habbayanayaka indicates that he was under the direct control of Somesvara IV.[95] Soon after the death of Somesvara Iv, Habbayanayaka once again accepted the supremcy of the Rattas[96] under Kartavirya IV. Bachya - Nayaka and Biraya - Nayaka were the two sons

REFERENCES

1. *SII.*, XX, No. 13.
2. *Ibid.*, No. 18.
3. *Ibid.*, line No. 8.
4. Fleet : *DKD.*, p. 550.
5. Desai, seems to have followed Fleet and treated Krishna referred to i n an inscription dated 875 - 76 A.D. as Krishna III Cf. Fleet *op. cit.*, p. 411, f.n. No. 1. But the above record belongs to Akalavarsha (Krishna II). According to B. R. Gopal *SII.*, XX, No. 13.
6. Desai : *MUCK.*, p. 150.
7. *SII.*, XX, No. 13.

8. *Ibid.*, XX, Nos. 13, 18 and 247; *Ep. Ind.*,XIII, p. 15 ff.

9. *SII.*, XX, No. 13.

10. Fleet treats Krishna II as Krishna III stating that the date given in this record i.e., 875-76 A.D. (*SII.*, XX, No. 13) was not authentic as far as Prithvirama's period is concerned. Ignoring this date for the above said reason he places the date of Prithivirama somewhere about 940 A.D. and attributes this record to Krishna III. Fleet : *op. cit.*, p 552; For further details about the fixation of the date of 940 A.D. for Prithvirama, see Fleet : *op. cit.*, p. 411, f.n. No. 1.

11. *SII.*, XX, No. 13.

12. *Ibid.*, No. 18.

13. *Ibid.*, No. 18.

14. *Ibid.*,

15. Fleet : *DKD.*, p. 553.

16. *SII.*, XX, No. 62.

17. Desai : *op. cit.*, pp. 152 and 156.

18. *Ep. Ind.*, Vol. XVI, p. 7 ff.

19. Fleet : *JBBRAS.*, X, p. 251; *I.A.*, XXXII, p. 217.

20. Bhandarkar : *Early History of the Dekkan*, p. 62.

21. C.V. Vaidya : *History of Mediaeval Hindu India*, III, p. 288.

22. Desai : *op. cit.*, p. 143.

23. *Ep. Ind.*, V, pp. 188 - 97 ff. and plate.

24. *SII.*, XVIII, Introduction, p. XXV.

25. Fleet : *op. cit.*, X, pp. 217 ff; *IA.*, XIX, p. 243.

26. *Ep. Ind.*, XVI, p. 8; *SII.*, XX, Nos. 50, 62 and 247.

27. *SII.*, XX, No. 62.

28. Fleet : *op. cit.*, pp. 217-18.

29. *SII.*, XI, Pt. I, No. 74; *IA.*, XIX, p. 165 ff.

30. *SII.*, XX, No. 247.

31. Fleet : *op. cit.*, X, p. 201.

32. *Ep. Ind.*, III, p. 306 ff.

33. *Ibid.*,
34. *SII.*, XX, No. 62.
35. *Ibid.*, XX, No. 50.
36. *Ibid.*, No. 247.
37. *IA.*, XIV, p. 24.
38. *SII.*, XX, No. 62.
39. The rule of Kartavirya II according to Desai comes to an end in 1094 A.D. Desai *op. cit.*, p. 197.
40. *DKD.*, p. 455.
41. *Ep. Ind.*, XIII, p. 15 ff.
42 Fleet : *op. cit.*, X, p. 229.
43. *DKD.*, p. 555.
44. Desai : *op. cit.*, p. 172.
45. *DKD.*, pp. 460-61.
46. *Ibid.*, p. 462.
47. Rice : *Mys. Ins.*, p. 92.
48. *DKD.*, p. 555.
49. *ARIE.*, 1959-60, App. B.No. 395; *MAR.*, 1916, pp. 48-50.
50. Fleet : *op. cit.*, X, p. 229.
51. *IA.*, XIV, p. 26.
52. Fleet : *op. cit.*, X, p. 229.
53. *IA.*, XXXII, p. 217 ff.
54. Fleet : *DKD.*, p. 556.
55. *Struggle for Empire*, p. 185.
56. *IA.*, XXXII, p. 217 ff.
57. Desai : *op. cit.*, p. 180.
58. Mores : *Kadambakula*, p. 192.
59. Fleet : *op. cit.*, X, pp. 232-33, 235.
60. Fleet : *op.cit.*, p. 230; *Ep. Ind.*, XIII, pp. 115 ff..; and *IA.*, XXIX, p. 280.

61. *ARIE.*, 1960-61, App. B.No. 388; *KI.*, II, p. 115 ff. and *IA.*, XXIX, p. 280.

62. *Ep. Ind.*, XIII, p. 15 ff.

63. *IA.*, XIX, p. 248.

64. *Ibid.*, pp. 242-43.

65. *ARIE.*, 1955-56, App. B.No. 151; 1940 - 41, No. BK 10 and 1961-62, App. B.No. 483.

66. P.B. Desai : *A History of Karnataka* (1970), p. 230.

67. Desai : *op. cit.*, p. 187.

68. Fleet : *op. cit.*, X, p. 231, 273.

69. Desai : *op. cit.*, p. 192.

70. *IKD.*, p. 549.

71. *ARIE.*, 1951-52, App. B.No. 41; Fleet : *op. cit.*, X, p. 240 ff.

72. *ARIE.*, 1940-41, App. B.No. 6 ; *SII.*, XX, No. 248; *KI.*, I, No. 32. pp. 75-76.

73. Fleet : *Op. cit.*, X, p. 282.

74. *DKD.*, p. 558.

75. *SII.*, XX, No. 248; Fleet *Op. cit.*, X, p. 260 ff.

76. *Struggle for Empire*, p. 192.

77. *ARIE.*, 1942-43, App. B. No. 9.

78. Fleet : *DKD.*, p. 558.

79. *JBBRAS.*, X, p. 235.

80. Desai : *Op. cit.*, p. 201.

81. *Kavirajamarga*, I, p. 6, verse 37.

82. Fleet : *op. cit.*, p. 232.

83. *JBBARAS.*, X, p. 233.

84. Desai : *op. cit.*, p. 203.

85. *EC.*, VI, Cm. 137.

86. Desai : *op. cit.*, p. 204.

87. *JBBRAS.*, X, p. 277.

88. *Ibid.*, p. 275.

89. Desai *: op. cit.,* p. 209.
90. *Ibid.,*
91. *Ibid.,* p. 210.
92. *Ibid.,*
93. *Ibid.,* p. 216.
94. Rice : *Mys. Inss.,* p. 119.
95. Desai *Op. cit.,* p. 217.
96. *Ibid.,* p. 253.
97. Desai *: op. cit.,* p. 219.

VII

THE CHANGALVAS

In this chapter an attempt is made to trace the early history of the Chángalvas down to the 13th century. Such an attempt is confronted with impediments with regard to the genealogy and chronology as one attempts to elicit information from inscriptions which are either fragmentary or damaged.[1]

The Changalvas claim their origin from a king named Changalva, who seems to be a fictitious or an imaginary person,[2] and a resident of Dvaravati. He is said to have defeated Bijjala, a Kalachurya king who supplanted the Chalukyas and assumed paramount titles. They also claim to be descendents of the Yadavas[3] and of the Lunar race[4] and in conformity with this claim, as already pointed out, they mention that Dvaravati was their original capital. It is not known how far we can rely on this Puranic or mythological ancestry.

Turning our attention to the epithets and titles they bore we see that they had conventional titles such as *mahamandalesvara, mahamandalika* and *mandalesvara,* denoting their feudatory or subordinate position to the imperial power of the day and also their restricted power over the region of their rule. This family seems to have carved out its kingdom in the region bounded by the Kaveri on one side and the mountains of Coorg on the other. Thus it was sandwiched between its Hoysala neighbours on one side and the Kadambas on the other side of the plains and this principality came to be known as Changa-nadu.[5]

Nannichangalva alias Rajendrachola Nannichangalra

(Beginning of the 11th century to 1085 A.D.)

Barring the mythological founder, Changalva, we come across Nannichangalva the first historical personality of this dynasty. It is unfortunate that we do not know when he actually commenced his rule. Even the inscription[6] which mentions this chief is not dated. But it is assigned to the commencement of 11th century on palaeographical grounds. Under these circumstances, we can only infer that his rule had commenced prior to 1024 A.D. as will be explained later. The above undated inscription states that he ratified and confirmed a grant made earlier by the Ganga king Marasimha (61 - 74 A.D.) who is said to have renovated one of the *basadis* at Hanasoge on the occasion of the above grant. Therefore, it is evident that Nannichangalva and Marasimha, in point of time, were not far removed as the last known date of the Ganga king Marasimha was 974 A.D.

A bird's eye view of the political situation of the period is provided here. The Hoysalas and the Kalyana Chalukyas were the two conflicting major powers for securing control over their respective borders.

The then Kalyana Chalukya emperor, probably Jayasimha II (1015 - 43 A.D.), seems to have sent a general *(dandanayaka)* in or about 1024 A.D. as surmised by Derrett to enlarge his sphere of influence in the south under the command of Mallideva. The latter seems to have won some laurels in containing the Changalva chief along with others and extracted tributes and ended his triumphal march over the Hoysalas. The campaign was decisive in character but, at the same time, it did not root out the Changalvas altogether. For we notice that the Changalva's aggressive raid eastwards against the Chola territory north of the modern city of Mysore. This aggressive campaign against the Cholas bears testimony to two important factors : (1) The Changalvas were once again able to consolidate their power and influence within a span of 12 years after the attack of Mallideva; and (2) their attempt to set themselves free from the Chola yoke.[7]

The Chola prefix viz., *Rajendra* has given rise to some conjectures and surmises by scholars. A fact which cannot be denied in this connection is that the Chola prefix definitely shows the subservient position of the Changalvas and also the adoption of the name of the overlord and contextually we cannot ignore the fact that the Changalvas were defeated by the crown prince Rajendra.[8] Rice categorically asserts that the Changalvas were subdued during their initial days.[9] Contrary to these views another scholar is of the opinion that there was no need for the Changalvas to rise against their overlord the Cholas unless their territorial interests were jeopardised.[10] But whatever may be the views expressed whether it is a revolt of rebellion or occasional bickerings, one thing is certain that the Changalvas never had any independent status and even if it were so, it was only shortliverd. However, the hostility that existed between the Cholas and the Changalvas, proving the latter's non - subjugation till 1037 A.D. is well attested to by the following records of the Changalvas. A damaged inscription[11] dated 1033 A.D. mentions the death of an individual in a fight with the Changalvas during the reign of the Chola king Rajendrachola I (1012 - 44 A.D.). A herostone[12] dated 1034 A.D. refers to the death of Binjavuniradeva in a fight with a Changalva - nayaka (name not given) while the latter was passing through the kingdom of Rajendrachola to Padikabe. Two other hero - stones,[13] both dated in 23rd (1036 A.D.) regnal years of Rajendrachola I, record details of the cattle - raid conducted by a Changalva, who bore the titla *Tigularmari* (obviously a metathesis of the word *Tigularmari*), along with his younger brother. The ascription of the title *Tigularmari* to the Changalva chief in an inscription of his overlord is not easy to explain. M.H. Krishna has identified the Changalva mentioned in these two records with Nannichangalva[14] while B.R. Gopal endorses the view of M.H. Krishna and further elobarates that Nannichangalva was no other than Virarajendra - Nannichangalva[15] and Rajendrachola - Changalva,[16] basing his conclusion on the titles found in some other records. He also concludes from the titles mentioned in the above records that these two records might be posterior to the Ankanathapur record which is dated in 1037 A.D.[17]

The Changalvas and the Kongalvas were two neighbouring minor powers. Though they were the feudatories of the Cholas, they were frequently at logger - heads with each other because of their desire to augment their fortunes and power. Their trials of strength can be gleaned from the inscriptions of this period.

An inscription[18] dated 1079 A.D. refers to tha attack of the Changalvas on the Kongalvas at Saligame (i.e., modern Saligrama). The continued hostility is well evidenced by an inscription[19] of 1105 A.D. from which we derive the conclusion that hostility lasted at least upto 1105 A.D. In the period between these two events of 1079 and 1105 A.D. the Changalvas appear to have lied low in a state of inaction. Derrett rightly believes that "the pressure from the Chalukyas of Kalyana caused a decline of the Changalvas in about 1080 A.D. followed by a temporary revival between about 1090 and 1094 A.D. before the Changalvas and the Kongalvas slid into oblivion".[20] The last known date of Nannichola changalva is 1079 A.D. It may not be wrong if we surmise that his reign lasted upto 1085 A.D. taking into consideration the eclipse and decline of the Changalvas as pointed out above.

Kulottunga Chola Changalva Odeyaditya (1091 - 1145 A.D.) :

Kulottungachola Changalva Odeyatya (a mistake for Odeyaditya), as his name indicates, was a feudatory of the Chola king Kulottunga Chola I.[21] He was the first chief to assume the feudal title *Mahamandalesvara.* During this period one can notice the ascendency of the imperial powers, the Cholas and the Hoysalas. The Hoysalas were no match to the bureaucratic Cholas and they did not want to poke their nose directly into the affairs of the Chola sovereign. Instead of that thety tried to attack the Changalvas who were the political dependents of the Cholas and this resulted in their attack on them in 1104 A.D.[22] The Changalvas could not face the combat singly and they sought the assistance of the neighbouring power, the Kongalvas, probably patching up their differences so as to defend their position against the aggressive attacks of the Hoysalas. We do not know at present whether the Cholas helped them in this hour of distress. The indecisive victory perhaps drove the Changalvas to bide for a better opportunity to take revenge against the Hoysalas. In this endeavour they did not meet with any success, as we find a certain Punisa, a Hoysala *dandanayaka,* defeating the coalition army of the Changalvas and the Kongalvas in or about 1120 A.D. This victory of his *dandanayaka* was perhaps the reason why Vishnuvardhana adopted the lofty title at a later date in A.D. 1130. According to which he was a submarine fire to the ocean of the forces of the Changalva chief.[23] The term 'ocean' implies the Changalva had built up a huge force consisting mostly of allied forces, such as the Kongalvas and others.

The second encounter with the Hoysalas was during the reign of Vishnuvardhana in 1124 A.D.[24] and in this battle the hill chiefs seem to have rendered considerable help to the Changalvas against the Hoysalas. Inspite of this, the Changalvas could not turn the tide of the battle and the adoption of the title in 1130 A.D. is an indication that the victory was already achieved by that time over the Changalvas.

The Hoysala king Narasimha I (1152 - 73 A.D.), as claimed by an inscription,[25] killed a Changalva chief in a battle fought sometime before 1145 A.D. and acquired as war booty elephants, horses and royal jewels. The victim of the battle, though his name has not been given, was, perhaps, Kulottungachola Changalva Odeyaditya who stormed Bannegavadi during the reign of Hoysala Narasimha I.[26] The reason for this fight seems to be the frequent trouble which the Hoysalas were experiencing from the Changalvas. In tracing the cause and course of the battle Derrett gives a vivid account of the political background. He says that the Changalva seems to have raised an army and taking advantage of Hoysala Narasimha's pre - occupations elsewhere harassed him. In the later part of 1145 A.D. an expedition was fitted out to deal with this menace and it found itself involved against a general insurrection in Bayal - nad and along the whole length of the southern frontier which had even in previous years been sufficiently troublesome to Hoysala Vishnuvardhana himself. The confederacy of the Changalvas was resisted by Govideva of Huliyuru with remarkable distinction. In 1155 A.D. the general Bokimayya conquered the Changalva territory, displayed the superiority of the royal forces, and putting down the Changalvas, reestablished order.[27]

Available inscriptions do not throw much light on the political history of the period between 1150 and 1171 A.D. But it is evident from the study of the inscriptions bearing dates covering this period that this period was a chaotic one. This can be illustrated with a few examples. In 1150 A.D. the Vira - kongalva seems to have driven out a certain Changalva chief.[28] In another instance, a cattleraid at Hanasoge by the Nayakas of Konganadu in 1163-64 A.D. is recorded[29] and thirdly a certain Changalva chief is said to have been taken prisoner in 1171 A.D. by Sovideva, the Kadamba governor of Banavasi.[30] In all these three instances it is not possible to identify the Changalva chief who met reverses at the hands of the victors.

Kulottunga Chola Changalva (1172 - 87 A.D.) :

Mahamandalesvara Kulottungachola Changalva, who came to the throne in 1172 A.D., seems to have straightened the fortunes of his house.[31] We have already stated that between 1150 - 71 A.D. the Changalvas had some setbacks. His two inscriptions[32] dated 1174 A.D. refer to the rule of this chief and his mention in these records as Bhujabala - Changalva is probably indicative of the fact that he rebuilt the fortunes of his house by the prowess of his arms *(bhujabala).*

A Hoysala inscription[33] of 1174 A.D., of the time of Ballala II (1174 - 1220 A.D.), refers to the hostility between the Hoysalas and the Changalvas. In giving details, it records that the Changalva chief Pemmavirarasa repulsed Bettarasa dannayaka, the Hoysala general, who seems to have killed Mahadeva, probably the predecessor of the Changalva chief. Pammavirarasa has been identified as Kulottunga - Chola - Changalva.[34]

Derrett attributes the reason for the failure on the part of the Hoysalas to imprint their victory over the Changalvas as due to the prevalent disorder in the Hoysala kingdom in 1174-75 A.D. during the reign of Ballala II. He aptly observes that the Changalvas and the Kongalvas were restless, inimical and disloyal to the imperial throne. Ballala II had to "pay a price for assuming his crown by force in controlling the very instruments through which he had come to power".[35]

From the available scanty materials one has to study the political history of this period with caution and care. While reconstructiong the political history from the skeletal remains of the epigraphical sources we are confronted with the shifting allegiances of the minor powers or their subjugations by the imperial powers. To put it in other words, in 1175 A.D. we come across the Changalva chiefs who were serving under the Hoysala monarch Ballala II in the Coorg region.[36] In 1177 A.D. the same Changalva chiefs had to be compelled to pay homage to the Hoysala monarch.[7] Further the name of the Changalva chiefs has not been mentioned in the above two records. Derrett opines that there was an internal disgreement between Narasimha and Ballala in containing the Kalachuris in the north. During this period the Changalvas incurred the displeasure of the Hoysalas. In consequence of this Ballala II overran and plundered the hilly country in the west, including Changa - nadu, with a considerable force.[38] The hostility never ended here. In 1179 A.D. Ballala II, who was away from his capital, felt the threat of the Changalvas. On his way back to his capital, Ballala II crossed swords with the Changalvas near Hosavidu. The outcome of the battle seems to be the rooting out of the Changalvas. The Changalva warrior who lost his life has been taken as one of the Changalva subjects and not the chief himself.[39] As a result of this, we do not get any inscription for a period of 26 years after 1179 A.D. and subsequently the simple epigraph which we come across is followed by a gap of 34 years and thus upto 1239 A.D. nothing is heard of the Changalvas. Even the reign period of Kulottunga Chola Changalva lasted only upto 1187 A.D. Therefore from 1187 to 1239 A.D. there was a gap of more than five decades for which we have no information on the Changalvas.

A damaged record[40] which has been assigned to 1250 A.D. mentions a Changalva as holding the office of *desimukhya.* The name of this Changalva chief is, however, not known to us.

Somadeva and Boppadeva (1252 A.D.) :

These two chiefs seem to have jointly ruled as *mahamandalesvaras* from their capital Srirangapattana to the south of the Kaveri near Siddapura.[41] As a clear reference is made in the epigraph to the Hoysala king Somesvara (1233 - 67 A.D.) it is evident they were his subordinates. Unfortunately, except in this record, we do not get any information partaining to these chiefs.

Mallideva (1280 A.D.) and Hariharadeva (1280 - 96 A.D.):

These two chiefs seem to have succeeded Somadeva and Boppadeva and their earliest known date is 1280 A.D. Mallideva had adopted the Chola appellation Kuottunga Chola besides the feudal epithet *mahamandalesvara.* Thus he styles himself *mahamandalesvara* Kulottunga Chola Vira Changalva.[42]

Hariharadeva who ruled jointly with his father at the commencement, later on continued his independent rule till 1296 A.D. He was also adopting the Chola appellation *Choladeva* like his father.[43] It is surprising to note that the Changalvas, inspite of their rise and fall, did not forget their impeiral masters viz., the Cholas. It is very interesting to note that the imperial Cholas had ceased to exist by 1279 A.D.[44] But Mallideva and Hariharadeva continued to pay obeisance to the Chola house as late as 1296 A.D. It is stated that these two members did not belong to this family as published texts of the inscriptions do not so indicate.[45] This is not proper. The very feudal epithet that they bore as other members of this family is itself sufficient to establish that they really belonged to the Changalva family. In the absence of Hariharadeva's records after 1296 A.D. the span of his rule over Changanad cannot be known with certainty.

For the subsequent period, we do get the mention of a couple of names associated with the family name Changalva. For instance, a certain Munivaraditya is referred to twice,[46] once in association with the family name Changalva in a damaged and fragmentary record. As one of the two records does not relate him with the Changalvas, it is clear that he cannot be a Changalva.[47] Tribhuvanamalla, referred to in an undated record,[48] seems to be a Changalva chief. But he cannot be identified with any known ruler of this dynasty as the record is very fragmentary. Annadani - arasu, who is stated to have been a member of the Changalvas, is referred to in connection with the construction of the sluice of a tank at Dobbamalale. His record was wrongly assigned to 1106 A.D. by Rice, whereas it is assignable only to the 15th century.[49] He too could not be considered as one of the members of the Changalvas merely on the ground that Annadani - Mallikarjuna was the tutelary deity of the Changalvas.

From the available records, it can be concluded that Harihara was the last effective chief of the family. The later Changalvas continued their loyalty and subordination upto 1544 A.D. to the respective imperial powers of the day in the midst of the great political changes that Changa - nadu had witnessed in the course of its long chequered history.[50]

REFERENCES

1. *E.C.*, I (1972), Introduction, p. XV.
2. *Ibid.*, IV (1898), Introduction, p. 16.
3. *Ibid.*, V (1976), Kn. 25.
4. *Ibid.*, IV (1975), pp. 132.
5. Derrett. *The Hoysalas* (1957), p. 13.

6. *E.C.*, V (1976), Kn 24.
7. Derrett : *op. cit.*, p. 19-20; *E.C.*, V (1976), My. 113 - 14.
8. *E.C.*, III (1974), p. 108, f.n. No. 3.
9. *Coorg Ins.*, I, p. 13.
10. *E.C.*, I (1972), Introduction, p. 15.
11. *Ibid.*, V (1976), Kn. 113.
12. *Ibid.*, Kn. 85.
13. *Ibid.*, My. 113-14.
14. *MAR.*, 1944, pp. 58 ff.
15. *E.C.*, V (1976), Kn. 21.
16. *Ibid.*, Kn. 20.
17. *Ibid.*, III (1974), Hk. 7.
18. *Ibid.*, V (1976), Kn. 66.
19. *Ibid.*, Kn. 67.
20. Derrett : *op. cit.*, p. 33.
21. *E.C.*, IV (1975), Introduction p. cxxx; pp. 137.
22. *E.C.*, V (1901), Hn. 162.
23. Derret : *op.cit.*, pp. 47-48.
24. *E.C.*, V (1901), B1. 178.
25. *Ibid.*, VII (1979), Ng. 64; Introduction, p. zcvi.
26. *Ibid.*, IV (1975), Hs. 33.
27. Derrett : *op. cit.*, pp. 71-72.
28. *E.C.*, XV (1943), Hn. 130, p. 153; *MAR.*, 1913, p. 23.
29. *E.C.*, V (1976), Kn. 44.
30. *Ibid.*, VII (1902), Sb. 345.
31. *Ibid.*, IV (1975), pp. 12.
32. *Ibid.*, pp. 14-15.
33. *Ibid.*, pp. 118.

34. *Ibid.*, IV (1975), Introduction, p. cxxx; *contra., Ibid.*, V (1976), Intro. p. cvi.
35. Derrett : *op. cit.*, p. 81; *E.C.*, VII (1902), Hl. 20.
36. *E.C.*, I (1972), Cg. 93, 42.
37. *Ibid.*, V (1901), Bl. 86.
38. Derrett : *op. cit.*, p. 78; *E.C.*, V (1901), Bl. 86.
39. *Ibid* pp. 41-42.
40. *E.C.*, V (1901), Bl, 88.
41. *E.C.*, V (1901), Ag. 53.
42. *Ibid.*, Bl. 89.
43. *Ibid.*, I (1972), Introduction, p. xv.
44. *Struggle for Empire* (1957), p. 248.
45. B.R. Gopal : *MDSIK.*, I, p. 172.
46. *E.C.*, I (1972), Cg. 36, 95.
47. B.R. Gopal : *op. cit.*, p. 173.
48. *E.C.*, I (1972), Cg. 97.
49. *Ibid.*, Cg. 88.
50. *Ibid.*, Introduction, p. xv.

VIII

THE KONGALVAS

The main source of information of the political history of the Kongalvas are some hero-stone inscriptions which are either mostly mutilated or fragmentary, making it difficult to arrive at a coherent and connected political history of the Kongalvas with precision and accuracy.[1]

The country of Konganad, which was once held and administered by the Ganga prince Ereyappa in the 9th century A.D., comprised the modern Arakalgud Taluk and the adjoining 7000-country (*Elu savira sime)* lying to the north of Coorg and round about Malambi. This Konganad, also known as Kongunad - 8000, lay watered by the rivers Hemavati and Kaveri.[2] The Hoysalas on the hills and the Kadambas on the plains were their neighbours. The Kongalvas inherited this principality as a fief for the feudal services rendered to their erstwhile overlords, the Cholas, when the Gangas went into oblivion.

Rice traces the origin of these chiefs from the Alupas of South Kanara depending on the suffix *Al.* which means to rule.[3] However, there is no evidence to prove epigraphically or historically their connection with the Alupas. The only possible explantion which seems to be nearer the truth is that they were the rulers of Kongunad and hence came to be known as *Kongu + alva.*

TheKongalvas are known to have flourished even as early as 6th century A.D. as evidenced by the Gudnapur inscripiton[4] of Ravivarman probably as a feudatory under the Kadambas. Beyond this, due to the absence of any other epigraphical reference to their existence either during the period of the Kadambas as well as subsequent to them, it is not possible to get any connected history of them till we come to the end of 10th century A.D.

The conquest of Gangavadi at the close of 10th century was an important event in the annals of the Chola as well as Kongalva history. Rajaraja the great uprooted the Gangas and triumphantly marched into the Karnataka country. Manija, probably the first member of the Kongalva family appears to have assisted greatly the Chola emperor in the battle of Panasoge fought in about 1004 A.D. to which date the commencement of the rule of the Kongalvas is generally attributed. The Chola emperor, pleased with the valuable services rendered by Manija, directed his son, the crown - prince, and military general Panchavan-maharaya[5] to confer the title *"Kahatriya-sikhamani Kongalva"* on Manija and gave him Malavvi[6] (modern Malambi) as a fief. The Kongalvas who thus earned the favour of the Cholas began to assume Chola styles and titles which probably irked their neighbours, the Changalvas.

The Kongalvas, as the vassals of the imperial Chola rulers, maintained cordiality and friendship with the latter. On the contrary, they had occasional encounters with their neighbours, the Changalvas. The fall of the Chola empire was perhaps the reason for the Kongalvas to seek shelter under the suzerainty of the Hoysalas later on.

Rajendrachola I Kongalva (1020 - 55 A.D.) :

It was already pointed out that the first member of this dynasty was Manija who is assumed to have held sway from 1005 to 1020 A.D.[7] Manija was succeeded by his son Rajendrachola probably in 1020 A.D. His record dated 1022 A.D., which is damaged, appears to state that Nripakama had encountered Kannama and that Jogayya, the Hoysala general rescued his overlord and killed Kannama, himself dying the process.[8] B.R. Gopal does not consider Nripakama as a Hoysala king inspite of the fact that he is refferred to as Nripakama Poysala.[9] But he considers, as we shall see later, Tribhuvanamalla Ballala Poysaladeva as Ballala I.[10] In the same manner Nripakama Poysala referred to in this record was undoubtedly a Hoysala monarch (1022 - 47 A.D.), whose attack on Banavasi, the Kadamba capital and its neighbour Rajendrapura definitely shows that he ultimately overran the Kongalva kingdom.[11] Another inscription[12] dated 1026 A.D. refers to an attack of Rajendra Kongalva I on a Poysala, who is described as *Munda Poysala*. The exact connotation of the word *munda* has eluded the historians.[13] We do not know in what sense *munda* has been used as an adjective in this record. Out of the three records[14] of his period, the last one mentions an encounter in which Kogillanayanka lost his life on behalf of Rajendrachola Kongalva. We do not get any epigraphs for a period of nearly 32 years. During this period, i.e., in about 1120 A.D., we hear that the Kongalvas intervened in some campaign hoping to cause embarrassment to the Hoysala *dannayaka* named Punisa, due to which the Hoysala king at a later date is described as "a wild fire in the forest" that is the Kongalvas.[15] An inscription[16] dated 1058 A.D. registers grants by Rajendrachola Kongalva to a *basadi* built by his father whose name is not stated in the record. Pochabbarasi is described as the mother of Rajadhiraja in this record. She is said to have granted villages and lands to Gunasena-pandita. Similar information[17] is given in another record also. Rajadhiraja Kongalva, following in the footsteps of his parents, also donated some gifts to a *basadi* to which Gunasena-pandita referred to above belonged.[18]

Rajadhiraja Kongalva (c. 1055-65 A.D.) :

It is evident from the abovce three records that Rajadhiraja Kongalva was the son of Rajendrachola Kongalva I and Pochabbarasi. He seems to have succeeded his father in c. 1055 A.D. His mother was still living in 1058 A.D. in which year she offers some grants to her preceptor Gunasena - pandita, whose death took place before 1064 A.D.[19]

Rajendraprithvi Kongalva (c. 1065 - 1100 A.D.)

He appears in a record[20] dated 1066 A.D. as the ruling chief. A fragmentary epigraph belonging to c. 11th century A.D.[21] refers to some consecration by Rugmini (mistake for Rukmini) - mahadevi. Another record dated 1390 A.D.[22] incidentally refers to the consecration of a *basadi* by Rajadhiraja for the merit of his mother Pochabbarasi. In this connection, it also further refers to Rukminidevi who seems to have constructed a shrine *(dehara).* As Rajadhiraja and Rukminidevi are mentioned together it may not be wrong to suppose that they were husband and wife.[23] Rajendraprithvi Kongalva is eulogised in 1079-80 A.D. as *Orayur - puravaresvara* and *Survavamsasikshamani.*[24] A hero-stone[25] refers to the rule of a certain Rajendrachola - Kongalva and seems to record the death of his chief queen Padmaladevi. Since the record is dated in 1077 A.D. this ruler has been identified with Rajendraprithvi Kongalva.[26] Another undated record[27] also mentions the death of a queen of Prithvi Kongalva who is obviously the same as Rajendraprithvi Kongalva. Some of the epigraphs belonging to his reign dated 1070,[28] 1091,[29] and 1094 A.D.[30] refer to some grants offered by this chief to the god Vira - Siddehesvara (Mahadeva), Adityadeva and Pollesvara. During the reign of Tribhuvanamalla Kongalva, in 1079 A.D.[31] an attack on Saligame by the Changalvas is referred to. In this encounter Trailokya-setti and Belutu-setti fought against the Changalvas and lost their life.

Tribhuvanamalla Kongalva (c. 1100-20 A.D.) :

An inscription[32] dated 1104-05 A.D. belonging to the reign of Tribhuvanamalla Kongalva refers to an attack made by the Changalvas on Saligame. In this attack, Masayya son of Trailokya-setti fought against the enemies and fell. Trailokya-setti referred to above may be identified with the deceased hero of the same name,[33] mentioned in an encounter fought earlier in 1079 A.D. at the same place.[34] The ruling king Tribhuvanamalla Kongalva of the present record, according to B.R. Gopal, is probably different from Rajendraprithvi Kongalva. Therefore, he is taken to be son and successor of Rajendra II.[35] An inscription[36] assignable to c. 1104 A.D. refers to a raid by Tribhuvanamalla Ballala Poysaladeva, obviously Ballala I (1100-10 A.D.), upon the Kongalva. Tribhuvanamalla Kongalva commenced his rule possibly almost at the same time when Ballala I commenced his rule. Further it is stated that Ballala I started defeating small chiefs like the Kongalvas as he had the desire of becoming an independent ruler[37] as is also evidenced by the above record. The Gubbi epigraph[38] refers to a ruler *mahamandalesvara, adataraditya* Tribhuvanamallachola Kongalva. He has been identified with Tribhuvanamalla Kongalva[39] who also assumed the title *Adataraditya*.

It is interesting to note in this connection that two chiefs of this family bear the title *Tribhuvanamalla.* Rice has stated that Tribhuvanamalla is the name borne by Rajendraprithvi Kongalva.[40] Another scholar[41] who had earlier denied that this was neither a name nor a title afterwards changed his opinion while reviewing the inscriptions of Tribhuvanamalla Kongalva and there again he had expressed doubts about the change of allegiance of the Kongalvas.[42] Ultimately he came to the view that the Kongalvas took the title *Tribhuvanamalla* probably to appease the Chalukyas after realising the declining influence of the Cholas in the southern Karnataka region.[43] Thus, the statement made by Rice gains in strength from the above narration. The reason for changing the names of these chiefs is well furnished by Derrett.[44]

Vira Kongalva (c. 1120 - 45 A.D.) :

The Holenarasipura inscription[45] records the construction of Satyavakya Jainalya by this chief. The preceptor, Prabhachandra - siddhantadeva of this record has been identified with his name sake in the Sravanabelgola epigraph and on that basis this record is assigned to c. 1120 A.D.[46] The identification of Duddamallarasa of Ankanathapura inscription,[47] who is said to have been camping at Hennegadanga with Vira Kongalva is said to be Molate in 1128 - 29 A.D.[48] He seems to have continued his rule till 1145 A.D.

Vira Dudda Kongalva (Virachola Kongalva) (c. 1145 - 80 A.D.) :

In his records he is referred to as *mahamandalesvara Tribhuvanamalla* Vira Dudda Kongalva. His three records are dated 1171, 1175 and 1177 A.D. The first record dated 1171 A.D.[49] mentions that he was ruling from Molate, when Hoysala Narasimha I attacked the camp and destroyed it. Tammadiya Rudra, at the instance of Kongalvadeva, fought in the battle and lost his life. From this record it is clear that the Hoysalas tried to capture the territories of the Kongalvas. Molate became the capital of the Kongalvas during his period. The Kongalvas appear to have lost their hold over parts of their possessions after the encounter referred to above. Another epigraph[50] dated 1175 A.D. refers to him as Virachola Kongalva. Padumaladevi and Somaladevi, in whose presence the chief offered the gift in this record, are identified as the wife and daughter of Hoysala Ballala II.[51] The non-mention of the Hoysalas as their supreme lords and also the absence of royal titles in the case of the aforesaid ladies tempt us not to consider them as the queen and the daughter of Ballala II.[52] An inscription[53] dated 1177 A.D. once again refers to the rule of Vira Dudda Kongalva.

Rajendra Billa Kongalva (1213 A.D.) :

He is the last known member of this family. He is stated to have been ruling from the capital Molate in 1212 A.D.[54] He had the titles *Malerajaraja, Malaparoluganda,* etc. which were common to the Hoysalas. From the adoption of the above attributes, which are akin to those of the Hoysalas, we can infer that, by this period, the Kongalvas had been defeated and forced to accept the suzerainty of the Hoysalas. What happened to the members of this family after Rajendra Billa Kongalva is difficult to asscertain. Other members referred to in some of the epigraphs, the proper dates of which are not known but have been assigned to this dynesty by Rice, are as follows:

Badiva Kongalva[55] and *Maharajendra.*[56] These two persons cannot be identified with any known member of this family as we do not get necessary information from their records. In addition to the above, a certain chief whose name is not known but who is probably associated with the term *Kongakshitipati,*[57] a Kongalva chief whose name once again is not known but who is stated to be a *Yama* (god of death) to the Kadamba family,[58] and a certain Kongalva chief (?) referred to in connection with some battle against a Changalva chief [59] could not be connected with this lineage for want of sufficient data.

The genealogical tables furnished by the scholars are given below:

Table 1[60]

Rajendrachola Kongalva (1026 A.D.)
|
Rajadhiraja (mother Pochabbarasi)
|
Rajendra II (1058 A.D.)
|
succeeded by
|
Rajendra Prithuvi Kongalva (1066 - 1100 A.D.)
(Adataraditya ; Tribhuvanamalla - chola Kongalva)
|
Virachola Kongalva (1176 A.D.)

Table 2[61]

Rajendrachola (known date 1026 A.D.)
|
Rajadhiraja
|
(Rajendrachola II *m.* Pochabbarasi (1058 A.D.)
|
Rajadhiraja II *m.* Rukminidevi
|
Rajendra Prithuvi Kongalva *m.* Padmaladevi (1070, 1077 A.D.)
|
Virachola Kongalva (1175 A.D.)

Table 3[62]

Manija (c. 1005 - 20)
|
Rajendrachola Kongalva (c. 102 - 55)
|
Rajadhiraja Kongalva (c. 1055 - 65)
|
Rajendra Prithivi Kongalva
|
(Rajendrachola Kongalva) c. 1065-1100)
|
Tribhuvanamalla Kongalva (c. 1100 - 20)
|
Vira Kongalva (c. 1120-45)
|
Vira Dudda Kongalva (Virachola Kongalva) (c. 1145 - 80)
|
Rajendra Billa Kongalva (1213 A.D.)

REFERENCES

1. *E.C.*, I (1972), Introduction, p. 13.
2. *KTA.*, (1968), p. 408; Derrett, *The Hoysalas*, (1957), p. 13; *E.C.*, I. 1972,Introduction, p. xviii.
3. *E.C.*, V (1902), Introduction, p. VIII.
4. *Srikanthika*, pp. 61-72.
5. contra.*K.TA.*, p. 408.
6. *E.C.*, I (1972), Cg. 65.
7. B.R. Gopal, *MDSIK.*, I, p. 180.
8. *E.C.*, V (1902), Mj. 43.
9. B.R. Gopal *op. cit.*, I, p. 178.
10. *E.C.*, V (1902), Hn. 162.

11. *Ibid.*, VI (1901), Mg. 19.
12. *Ibid.*, V (1902), Ag. 76.
13. *Ibid.*, Introduction, p. vi; Derrett, *op. cit.*, p. 21, and Coelho *Hoysalavamsa*, p. 27.
14. *E.C.*, V (1902), Hn. 131, 64 and Ag. 75.
15. Derrett : *op. cit.*, p. 47.
16. *E.C.*, I (1972), No. 72.
17. *Ibid.*, No. 68.
18. *Ibid.*, No. 69.
19. *Ibid.*, No. 71.
20. *Ibid.*, V (1902), Ag. 93.
21. *Ibid.*, I (1972), No. 70.
22. *Ibid.*, No. 75.
23. B.R. Gopal : *op. cit.*, p. 181.
24. *Ibid.*,
25. *E.C.*, I (1972), No. 81
26. B.R. Gopal : *op. cit.*, p. 181.
27. *E.C.*, I (1972), No. 73.
28. *Ibid.*, Nos. 48-49.
29. *Ibid.*, V (1902), Ag. 94.
30. *Ibid.*, Ag. 95.
31. *Ibid.*, (1976), Kn. 66.
32. *Ibid.*, Kn. 67.
33. B.R. Gopal : *op. cit.*, p. 180.
34. *E.C.*, V (1976), Kn. 66.
35. B.R. Gopal : *op cit.*, p. 182.
36. *E.C.*, V (1902), Hn. 162.
37. B.R. Gopal : *op.cit.*, p. 182.
38. *E.C.*, V (1902), Hn. 16.

39. B.R. Gopal : *op. cit.*, p. 183.
40. *E.C.*, V (1902), Introduction, p. VII.
41. *Ibid.*, I (1972), Introduction, p. xiv.
42. *Ibid.*, V (1976), Introduction, p. cvi.
43. B.R. Gopal : *op. cit.*, p. 182.
44. Derret : *op cit.*, 1957, p. 33.
45. *E.C.*, V (1902), Hn. 7.
46. *Manavika Karnataka*, III, No. 2, p. 13.
47. *E.C.*, V (1902), Hn. 56.
48. B.R. Gopal : *op. cit.*, p. 183.
49. *E.C.*, V (1902), Hn. 90.
50. *Ibid.*, I (1972), No. 89.
51. Rice : *Coorg Ins.*, p. 18.
52. *E.C.*, I (1972), Introduction, p. xiv; B.R. Gopal : *op. cit.*, p. 184.
53. *E.C.*, V (1902), Hn. 91.
54. *Ibid.*, Ag. 35.
55. *Ibid.*, Ag. 63; B.R. Gopal : *op. cit.*, p. 178; *Manavika Karnataka*, III, No. 2, p. 8.
56. *E.C.*, V (1902), Mj. 59.
57. *Ibid.*, V (1976), Kn. 86.
58. *Ibid.*, XV (1943), Hn. 64.
59. *Ibid.*, Hn. 130.
60. *Ibid.*, I (1886), Introduction, pp. 17-18.
61. *Ibid.*, I (1972), Introduction, p. XIV.
62. B.R. Gopal : *op. cit.*, p. 184.

IX

THE KADAMBAS

The Kadambas of Karadikallu

The territory of these chieftains who are known as Kadambas seems to have comprised Lingsugur Taluk of Raichur District which included Karadikallu and Navali as we find that many records belonging to them were spread over this region. The division ruled by these chiefs is known as the Karadikallu. It is interesting to note that this division is referred to as Karadikallu - 300[1] as well as Karadikallu - 400.[2] Credit goes to Desai who noticed the existence of this royal family for the first time.[3] They possessed titles such as *Kadambarabharana* and *Banavasipuravaresvara*. The latter title seems to be conventional. They also had other titles like *Toredadiya Bhima* probably associating them with the river Krishna, an association further confirmed by the epithet *Krishnanady - Ubhaya - tata - rajahamsa.* From these two epthets it can be ascertained that this family was adminstering a region which spread on either banks of the river i.e., Navali on the eastern bank of the Krishna, and the Bijapur District forming a part of the other bank.[4]

Bacharasa (1033 A.D.) :

It is surmised that Bacharasa who had the title *Banavasipuravaresvara* and was holding the office of *manneya* under Chalukya Jagadekamalla I (1015 - 43 A.D.) in 1033 A.D. was a predecessor and most likely the father of Nagavarma. This surmise is based on the fact that both the above members enjoyed the office of *manneya.*[5]

Nagavarmarasa (1066, 1077 A.D.) :

Nagavarmarasa who was also bolding the office of *manneya* as he is called *manneya* Nagavarmarasa in a record[6] dated 1066 A.D. is stated to have been the earliest member of this branch. The Hyderabad Museum inscription[7] alludes to this fact. This record is dated in the first year of the reign of Chalukya Vikramaditya VI i.e., 1077 A.D. It states that when Tribhuvanamalla Vira Nolamba Pallavapermanadi, identical with the Chalukya prince Jayasimha III, was administering Karadikal - 400, *mahamandalesvara* Nagavarmarasa was holding the hereditary fief of the village Tamgola as *mannevasamya (tamma Kadambanvaya vamsada Tangola).* The title attributed to him in this record evidently indicates that he was elevated from his position of *manneya*[8] in 1066 A.D. to the better status of *mahamandalesvara* after a decade i.e., in 1077 A.D. There is a gap of 35 years between the rule of Nagavarmarasa, who probably ended his rule in 1077 A.D. and that of Bhutarasa who commenced his in 1113 A.D.

An attempt has been made in this connection to fill up this gap by bringing a Kadamba chief Singarasa[9] considering him as the son (?) and successor of Nagavarmarasa and the father (?) and predecessor of Bhutarasa. Further, it is also suggested that Madhavattiyarasa was the younger of the sons of Singarasa as he is described as *Singanankakara.*[10] As we do not get further details about Singarasa referred to above, from the epigraphs pertaining to this family, it is very difficult to consider him as one of the members of this family in the present state of our knowledge.

Bhutarasa (1113, 1119 A.D.) :

Mahamandalesvara Bhutarasa is referred to in two records dated 1113[11] and 1119 A.D.[12] He is stated to have installed a golden *kalasa* on the temple of Jadeyasankaradeva at Navile, consecrated Traipurushadeva on the bank of the Krishna and made a grant of the village Muttage in Karadikallu - 3000 for worship and offerings in the temple.[13]

Madhevattiyarasa (1124, 1135 A.D.) :

Mahamandalesvara Madhvattiyarasa is referred to in an epigraph[14] dated 1124 A.D. He is considered as the successor of Bhutarasa as there is only a gap of 5 years between them.[15] According to this record while Abbaladevi, queen of Vikramaditya VI, was ruling over the village named Linga perhaps the findspot of the record i.e., Lingsugur situated in Karadikal - 400 as her *bhatta - grama* (personal fief) in 1124 A.D., Madhavattiyarasa made a grant of land to god Kalidevasvara. He continued his subordination to Bhulokamalla Somesvara III (1126 - 38 A.D.) as he is stated to have consercrated Jalasayanadeva in 1135 A.D. near the Traipurusha temple which was earlier consecrated by Bhutarasa.[16]

Again there prevails a gap of nearly 56 years after the last known date of Madhavattiyarasa in 1135 A.D. During this period, the Kadambas had lost their hold over Karadikal - 400 for some unknown reason. This fact is made known from an inscription[17] of the reign of the Yadava king Bhillama V dated 1191 A.D. which states tha Malaya - nayaka, the chief minister of Bajjarasa III, of the Kadamba lineage, reestablished the rule of the Kadambas which was in abeyance for some time and found delight in seeeing that Bajjarasa III was in possession of the kingdom. From this account it is presumed that Bajjarasa III commenced his administration of the territory in c. 1185 A.D.[18] Further, this record furnishes the genealogy of the Kadambas (obviously Kadambas) who wielded their power over Karadikal - 400. They had similar titles as the ones borne by the chiefs referred to earlier. However, the connection between them is not known. The chiefs mentioned are as follows :

Bajjarasa I
|
Kacharasa I
|
Bajjarasa II *m.* Bachaladevi
|
Kacharasa II *m.* Sajjaladevi
|
Bajjarasa III *m.* Holladevi

If, as already stated, Bajjarasa III started his rule in c. 1185 A.D. then there would be a gap of about 50 years between Madhavattiyarasa and Bajjarasa III. The first four members referred to in their pedigree will have to be accommodated in this gap of 50 years. Bajjarasa III is said to have ruled till 1215 A.D. as a subordinate of Yadava Singahana[19] (c. 1210 - 47 A.D.). And, according to the availabe epigraphs of this family, Bajjarasa III appears to have been the last ruler in this lineage.

The Kadambas of Nurumbada

The chiefs of this branch were administering the area around Rattihalli/ Rattapalli - 70 division and Itagi / Ittage - 30 division known as Nurumbada in the 11th - 12th centuries. Both the above places are situated in Dharwar District. The banner of this family consisted of Hanuman figure *(sakha - charendra - dhvaja)*. They are described as the worshippears of Kadambasvara in whose honour a temple was constructed at Rattihalli.

Two records available at Rattihalli,[20] dated 1174 and 1235 A.D., belonging to Kalachuri Rayamurari Sovideva and Yadava Singhana II respectively give the pedigree of this family as follows :

Biradeva I — Ketarasa I

Ketarasa I
|
Namarasa
|
Ketarasa II *m.* Attimabbe

Polakesi — Permadi — Ranaki Ranaka — Biradeva II *m.*Bachaladevi — Bammarasa — Mallideva

Biradeva II *m.*Bachaladevi
|
Ketarasa III *m.* Kanchaladevi

Laliyadevi

Doraladevi

Garuda Pandya *m* Bachaladevi — Virapandya

Biradeva I :

Biradeva I is the earliest member of this family who is referred to in the Kanvi Siddageri inscription[21] which though it refers itself to the time of Chalukya Jayasimha II (1015 - 43 A.D.) is to be assigned to 1174 A.D. This assignment is justified both by its palaeography and by its mention of *mahamandalesvara* Pandyadevarasa who is identical with the king of the same name referred to in the Rattihalli record[22] dated 1174 A.D. of the reign of Kalachuri Rayamurari Sovideva.[23]

According to the Kanvi Siddageri epigraph,[24] Biradeva I obtained the authority to rule over the group of 100 villages from king Jayasimha as a reward for defeating the enemy and capturing the royal elephant which was presented to his sovereign. Very little is known about Ketarasa I and his son Namarasa. Ketarasa II's wife was Attimabbe known as Attiyabbe[25] from whom he had three sons viz., Biradeva II, Bammarasa and Mallideva. He also had three sons named Polakesi, Permadi and Ranaka from another wife.[26]

Biradeva II:

Among the brothers it is known that Biradeva II wedded Bachaladevi who was the daughter of Gutta I of the guttas of Guttavolal, i.e., Guttal in Haveri Taluk, Dharwar District. Biradeva II seems to have served under Chalukya Vikramaditya VI (1076 - 1126 A.D.) and Somesvara III (1126-38 A.D.)

Ketarasa III :

An inscription[28] from Rattihalli which is undated but belongs to the reign of Chalukya Jagadekamalla II (1138 - 55 A.D.) furnishes the genealogy of *mahamandalesvara* Ketarasa III. It is evident from the above account that he was also subordinate of the Chalukyas. Further, in this record, his *mahapradhanas*, the three brothers Rayarasa, *sandhivigrahi* Malla and *Mantri* Sovana or Soma, who were sons of Bhaskara and Malikavve, are referred to.

Ketarasa III had three wives. Kanchaladevi is stated to be the eldest. It is difficult to ascertain to which family she belonged. Laliyadevi, another wife, is said to be the daughter of Mallideva of the Gutta family whose sister Bachaladevi had been given in marriage to Biradeva II as pointed out above. The third wife, Doraladevi, was perhaps, the daughter of Isvaradeva I of the Sindas of Balagutti.[29]

Mahamandalesvara Pandyarasa and Virapandya :

Pandyarasa, same as Garuda Pandya, and Virapandya, two brothers succeeded their father Ketarasa III. Pandyadevarasa renewed a gift of land which was earlier donated by Biradeva I.[30] They are stated to have been forced to come under the sway of Kalachuri Rayamurari Sovideva.[31] Afterwards they accepted the supremacy of Yadava Singhana II.[32]

Mahamandalesvara Pandyarasa married Bachaladevi, daughter of Vikramaditya I of the Gutta lineage. The rule of this dynasty over Nurumbada seems to have ceased after Virapandya as we do not hear anything about this family thereafter.

REFERENCES

1. *ARIE.*, 1958 - 59, App. B, No. 711.

2. *HAS.*, 18, No. 9.

3. *Ibid.*, No. 18. *A Corpus of Inscriptions in the Kannada Districts of Hyderabad State; IHQ.*, XXXIV, pp. 167-69 and S.H. Ritti, *The Sevunas*, pp. 310-20.

4. B.R. Gopal : *MDSIK.*, I, p. 70.

5. *ARIE.*, 1958-59, App. B.No. 714.

6. *Ibid.*,
7. *HAS.*, 18, Ins. No. 6.
8. *ARIE.*, 1958-59, App. B. No. 714.
9. *Ibid.*, No. 687.
10. *HAS.*, 18, No. 9; B.R. Gopal : *op. cit.*, p. 72.
11. *HAS.*, 18, p. 18; *IHQ.*, XXXIV, p. 168.
12. *ARIE.*, 1958-59, App. B. No. 711.
13. *Ibid.*,
14. *HAS.*, 18, No. 9.
15. B.R. Gopal : *op. cit.*, p. 71.
16. *ARIE.*, 1958-59, App. B. No. 711.
17. *HAS.*, 18, Ins. No. 16.
18. B.R. Gopal : *op. cit.*, p. 73.
19. *HAS.*, 18, Ins. No. 17.
20. *KI.*, VI, Nos. 37 and 44.
21. *Ibid.*, No. 7.
22. *Ibid.*, No. 37.
23. B.R. Gopal : *op. cit.*, I, p. 67.
24. *KI.*, VI, No. 7.
25. *Ibid.*,
26. B.R. Gopal : *op. cit.*, p. 69.
27. *Ibid.*,
28. *KI.*, VI, No. 31.
29. S.H. Ritti : *The Sevunas*, p. 318.
30. *KI.*, VI, No. 7.
31. *Ibid.*, No. 37.
32. *Ibid.*, No. 44.

X

THE HAIHAYAS OF ARALU - 300

The chiefs of this branch are described as the lords of the city of Mahishmati *(mahishmati-puravaradhisvara).* But details regarding the origin of this family are not known. They ruled over the Aralu - 300 division as *mahamandalesvaras.* This subdivision comprised the region in and around modern Aralur situated in Sedam Taluk, Gulbarga District.

The first member of this branch is Recharasa who makes his appearance in 1038 A.D. as a subordinate of Chalukya Jagadekamalla II.[1] He was succeeded by Bijjarasa I in 1051 A.D.[2] Bacharasa was the successor of Bijjarasa I. His record,[3] dated 1071 A.D., unlike those of his predecessors, does not refer to his overlords which in turn is an indication that his rule was of an independent nature. Whether his independence was due to the quarrel between Somesvara II and Vikramaditya VI is not known. Kalabbarasi, the wife of Bacharasa according to this record,[4] offered a gift of 300 *mattars* of land to the god Lokesvara of Ingulige (i.e., modern Ingalagi, Chitapur Taluk, Gulbarga District).

Mahamandalesvara Anemarasa was the successor of Bacharasa. He appears in 1096 A.D. as the subordinate of Chalukya Vikramaditya VI.[5] It may be remembered here that Bacharasa his predecessor had ruled as an independent chief. A place- name Palla-karate is referred to in this record in connection with the donations made to the god Brahmesvara of that place by the chief. This Pallakarate is identical withits namesake Halkatta, the findspot of the record. Another record[6] from Kammarawadi belonging to Anemarasa dated 1104 A.D. records the gift of land etc. to the gods Mulasthanadeva and Somanatha by the chief.

Bijjarasa II was succeeded by Lokaditya in c. 1147 A.D. He figures as a subordinate of Bammanayya who bore a string of important designations such as *Mahapradhana, Senadhipati, Kaditaverggade, Kannadasandh....ivisrahi* and *Piriyadandanayaka*. Bammanayya was a feudatory of Chalukya Jagadekamalla II[7].

Anemarasa II, the younger brother of Lokaditya, succeeded to the Haihaya chieftaincy as a subordinate of Chalukya Taila II in 1158 A.D. His record[8] refers to a gift of land etc. to the god Bijjesvara evidently after the name of Bijjarasa II at Pallakarande (obviously Halkatta) in Aralu - 300, by this chief for conducting services such as *snana, naivedya, chaitra - pavitra,* etc. to the deity. Anemarasa II had two sons viz., Bijjarasa III and Yecharasa.

Bijjarasa III succeeded his father in 1209 A.D. He is stated to be a subordinate of Yadava Singhana.[9] His subservience to the Yadavas is obviously due to the changed political circumstances in that particular period. The Yadavas had succeeded in establishing their kingdom on firm basis by this time. The general tendency of the feudatories was to change their allegiance to the powerful kings of their days. Bijjarasa III was not an exception to this. He accepted the supremacy of the Yadavas as by then the rule of the Chalukyas had become a closed chapter. Bijjarasa III and his wife Siriyadevi conjointly made a gift to the god Lokesvara.[10]

An inscription dated 1212 A.D. of the time of the Yadava Singhana refers to Kacharasa as the son of Yacharasa and states that he was ruling over Aralu - 300. Further it records some gifts made by him to the god Yechesvara, obviously so named after his father.[11] A doubt has been expressed about the succession of Yacharasa to the Haihaya chiefdom.[12] There was only a gap of hardly three years between the rule of the two chiefs as the last record[13] of Bijjarasa III is dated in 1209 A.D. and the first record[14] of Kacharasa is dated in 1212 A.D. There will not be much scope for the rule of any other incumbent within this short span of 3 years. Therefore, it is surmised that Yecharasa the younger brother of Bijjarasa III and the father of Kacharasa may not have ruled. His description as *mahamandalesvara* in an inscription[15] of his son Kacharasa may at the most mean that he actively assisted his elder brother in the administration. In this connection we fully agree with Narasimha Murthy's contention that the god Yechesvara, to whom Kacharasa offered some gifts in 1212 A.D., may have been so named and installed in memory of his deceased father.

Kacharasa was succeeded by *mahamandalesvara* Bijjarasa IV in 1221 A.D. He was also a subordinate of Yadava Singhana.[16] According to the availabe epigraphs, he is the last known chiefs of this family.

The Haihayas of Morata - 300 :

The chiefs of this family with the same dynastic appellation of 'Haihaya' also claim to be lords of the city of Mahishmati *(Mahishmatipuravaradhisvara).* These chiefs are stated to have ruled over the division *(nadu)* of Morata - 300 (comprising the present Manvi Taluk of Raichur District) as *mahamandalesvaras.*

Revarsa, the earlist known chief of this family, is described as "the submarine fire to the ocean which is Mummuni of Konkan *(Mummunikonkaniga - jaladhi - vadavanala),* the subject of admiration to the Panadya *(Pandyakutuhala)* and a terror to the city of Dhara *(Dharanagarabhayamkara)".* He bore the title *"Muvadi - ganda".* He was governing the province of Ededore - 2000 in 1052 A.D. as a subordinate of Chalukya Trailokyamalla i.e., Somesvara I.[17] The political conditions of this period can be gleaned from the description of Revarsa as quoted above. He might have adopted all these titles after successfully assisting his master in some of his wars as it is stated that Somesvara I, together with his generals and Ravarasa, invaded North Konkana and overthrew Mummuni, the chief of that province. Revarsa is also known as Vanniya - Revan[18] who fled away when Chola Rajendra II rallied his forces with great skill against Somesvara I.

Again, in 1054 A.D., he is described as 'the submarine fire to the ocean of Mummuni Konkaniga'. In the same year he appears to have gained control over some parts of the Lingsugur Taluk as he is stated to have granted a supplementary grant of land and *manneya samya* of the villages, Karadikal and Kudalige situated in Kembavi - 24 and of Nagaravura situated in Sagara -300 to the god Malibesvara which was installed by Maliyabbarasi, his wife.[19]

There is a gap of nearly 75 years between the rule of Revarsa and that of Ghattidevarasa. That, for some unknown reason, the members of this family had gone into oblivion for over 75 years after the rule of Revarsa is evidenced from the non - availability of their records during this period. Anyhow, in this gap of 75 years, we notice the rule of a local family of 'Ahihayas', another form of Haihaya, in the Gulbarga District.[20] Ghattidevarasa figures in an inscription[21] dated 1139 A.D. as the chief of this Haihaya family after a lapse of nearly 75 years. He was governing from his headquarters at Morata,[22] which was a fortified town,[23] in 1148 - 49 A.D. As we do not get earlier reference to this fort it is evident from this record that the fort mentioned herein must have been constructed during his reign.

Narasimha Murthy has rightly surmised that Hallarasa, the successor of Ghattidevarasa, was ruling in between 1148-49 and 1178 A.D.[24] An inscription,[25] assignable to 12th century A.D., which is of course effeaced, refers to the rule of Hullavarasa (apparently Hallarasa). His record states that Malhat, the capital of the Morata - 300 division housed an educational institution *(Ghatikasthana)*. He had a queen bearing the name Rekaladevi,

Mallidevarasa I was the successor of Hallarasa. In an inscription[26] dated 1178 A.D. he figures as a subordinate of Kalachuri Sankama. From this we can deduce that the power of the Chalukyas had weakened by then. Therefore Mallideva, to safeguard his position, appears to have accepted the supremacy of Kalachuri Sankama who at that time was a powerful king. His subordination to Sankama did not, however, last long, for the subsequent transfer of his allegiance to the Chalukya Somesvara IV is attested to by his two records[27] dated 1190 and 1191 A.D. His attitude of changing allegince twice within a short span of 12 years shows the prevalence of the political instability in this period. The reason for this is well known. Much disturbance prevailed during this period because of the constant crossing of swords between the major powers such as the Chalukyas, the Kalachuris, the Hoysalas and the Yadavas for supremacy.

Taking advantage of these circumstances, Mallideva seems to have subsequently declared his independence as his record[28] dated 1196 A.D. does not mention any overlord. He is stated to have killed Bijja of Modeganur and to have defeated a certain Hadiga and a general of Bhillama. Under what circumstances he killed Bijja and defeated Hadiga is not known. From the mention of this incident in his record we can presume that an encounter between him and some other chief may have taken place. It is not possible to identify the first two members referred to in this inscription. Narasimha Murthy is of the opinion that the general of Bhillama mentioned in this connection was one who had taken upon himself the task of expanding the Sevuna kingdom.[29]

Mailugideva of Manuve figuring in a record[30] of 1191 A.D. belonging to the rule of Chalukya Somesvara IV has been identified with this Mallidevarasa I. He is said to have camped at Ayyana Sirivura i.e., modern Sirvara in 1196 A.D. His chief queen was Makaladevi. He had three sons viz., Allahulideva, Hallagadeva and Bairugideva.[31] It was doubted earlier whether any of the three sons of Mallideva I had ruled over the chiefdom of Morata - 300 after their father.[32] But we have now a record[33] assignable to the 13th century wherein he is referred to as *mahamandalesvara kumara* Allahulideva, which increases the possibiity of his having succeeded his father.

Nothing definite can be said about the rule of his two brothers viz., Hallagadeva and Bairugideva because of the paucity of their records. According to the available epigraphs Mallideva II ascended the Haihaya throne in 1217 A.D. as a subordinate of the Yadava Singhana. At this time he was administering from Ayyana - Sirivura[34] (modern Sirvara). No records of this family dated beyond 1217 A.D. have as yet been discovered. In conclusion, it can be said that both the Haihaya families came into existence during the rule of the Chalukya Jagadekamalla II. Chiefs of this family served as *mahamandalesvaras* from the beginning to the end, successively under the Chalukyas, the Kalachuris and the Yadavas. Among the chiefs of both the families, the notables were Bacharasa and Mallidevarasa I as they had gained enough power to enjoy independent status.

REFERENCE

1. *ARTE.*, 1959 - 60, No. B. 444.
2. *Ibid.*, 1958 - 59, No. B. 623.
3. *Ibid.*, 1959 - 60, No. B. 439.
4. *Ibid.*,
5. *Ibid.*, No. B. 431.
6. *Ibid.*, 1960 - 61, No. B. 505.
7. *Ibid.*, 1959 - 60, No. B. 440.
8. *Ibid.*, No. B. 431.
9. *Ibid.*, No. B. 437.
10. A.V. Narasimha Murthy : *The Sevunas of Devagiri*, p. 216.
11. *ARIE.*, 1959 - 60, No. B. 432.
12. A.V. Narasimha Murthy : *op. cit.*, p. 216.
13. *ARIE.*, 1959 - 60, No. B. 437.
14. *Ibid.*, No. B. 432.
15. *Ibid.*,
16. *Ibid.*, 1960-61, No. B. 506.

17. *Ibid.*, 1953 - 54, No. B. 256; *HAS.*, 18, No. 5.
18. *The Struggle for Empire*, pp. 171 and 169.
19. *ARIE.*, 1958 - 59, No. B. 644; *Ep. Ind.*, XII, pp. 291 - 93; *The Struggle for Empire*, p. 167.
20. *Ep. Ind.*, XII, p. 292.
21. *ARIE.*, 1960 - 61, No. B. 558.
22. *Ibid.*, No. B. 553.
23. *Ibid.*, No. B 559.
24. A.V. Narasimha Murthy : *op. cit.*, p. 214.
25. *ARIE.*, 1960-61, No. B. 554.
26. *Ibid.*, No. 556.
27. *Ibid.*, 1953-54, No. B. 258; *Ibid.*, 1961 - 62, No. b. 560.
28. *Ibid.*, 1960-61, No. B. 557.
29. A.V. Narasimha Murthy : *op. cit.*, p. 214.
30. *ARIE.*, 1961 - 62, No. B, 560.
31. *Ibid.*, 1960 - 61, No. B. 557; cf. *Ibid.*, Introduction, p. 30.
32. A.V. Narasimha Murthy : *op. cit.*, p. 214.
33. *ARIE.*, 1961 - 62, No. B. 559.
34. *Ibid.*, 1957 - 58, No. B. 380.

XI

THE NIDUGAL CHOLAS

The appellation 'Chola' adopted by some feudatory rulers of Karnataka needs some explantion. Some feudatories assuming the title *Chola - maharaja* ruled over a small tract between Hemavati and Nidugal with Penjeru of Henjeru as their capital from 8th to 12th centuries. The provenance of their inscriptions is roughly spread over the modern districts of Tumkur, Chitradurga and Bellary. Of the members of this dynasty, noteworthy personges are Chola Dhananjaya Eriga ruling Alavadi - 600 under the Gangas[1] and his contemporary Cholika Muttarasa ruling from Kandakotta,[2] both claiming the dynastic appellation Chola Maharaja. However, the exact relationship between these chiefs and the Imperial Cholas is yet to be established beyond doubt. In other words, it is not known with certainty whether they were an off - shoot of the imperial Cholas. The decline of the Chola - Maharajas paved the way for the advent of the Nidugal Cholas at the end of the 11th century.

The members of this new line of Cholas, styling themselves as the Nidga Cholas, are said to be the descendants of the mythical Karikalachola,[3] professing their allegiance to the Chalukyas of Kalyana, the supreme sovereign power of the day. These chiefs had their capital, first at Henjeru (modern Hemavati in Madakasira Taluk, Anantapur District, Andhra Pradesh) and later shifted to Nidugal in Tumkur District due to political exigencies. The place Nidugal became part and parcel of their nomenclature in history and they are better known as Nidugal chiefs.

In general, the epigraphical sources over that the Nidugal Cholas belong to the Solar race (Ina - vamsa), tracing their origin to Kasyapagotra. Their tall claim that they were descendants of Karikala Chola *(Karikala - chola -*

kulambaradyumani) and their title *Uraivur - purvaradhisvara* no doubt reminds us of the renowned king of the remote past of that name and the ancient Chola capital Uraiyur near Tiruchchirappalli. This political perquisite had probably emboldened them to. call themselves as *mahamandalesvaras* with the special privelege of *pamchamahasabda.* In addition to these, some of the titles borne by them, viz. *Nigalankamalla, Aruvattaru - mamdalikara talegomda - ganda* imply their mastery over the territories they ruled or overran or the martial valour with which they beheaded the 66 chieftains of their times. The genealogical references as gleaned from the later inscriptions of the members of the dynasty reveal that the first scion of this house was Jata and the last one was Ganesvara with the epithat *mahamandalesvara.* As pointed out earlier, Jata is known only from the inscriptions of his successors. His son Brahma Bhogendra is also known to us from similar sources.

Mangi (1079 -1109 A.D.) :

The genealogical position of Mangi as the third member of this dynasty is suggested by two inscriptions dated 1079[4] and 1083 A.D.,[5] which give his name as Mangarasa and Iriva - Mangarasa and imply his Chola affiliations by epithets such as *Uraiyurpuravaradhisvara.* He is also endowed with the title *Mahamandalesvara* and probably occupied a feudatory status under the Chalukyas of Kalyana and more particularly under the king Tribhuvanamalladeva i.e., Vikramaditya II. There are two other inscriptions of the king Vikramaditya VI dated 1092[6] and 1109[7] in which Cholamaharaja Ghateyana and Gateyanka are referred to. The diction of the texts prompts us to assign these records to Mangi on the evidence that his political jurisdiction over the Kaneyakallu - 300 District clinches beyond doubt the possibility of Mangi being the subordinate of Vikramaditya VI.

Mangarasa was succeeded by Bichi and Govinda about whom practcally nothing is known. They are shady figures in the genealogical list.

Irungola I (1125 - 43 A.D.) :

Mahamandalesvara Irungola I was the son and successor of Govinda born to Mahadevi.[8] His earlier record[9] dated in Chalukya Vikrama year 48 (= 1125 A.D.), showing his subservient position, refers to his rule from Gondavadi, the chief town of Kaniyakallu - 300. Gondavadi might have been christened after his father Govinda as a mark of respect and reverence or the place might have been the principal city of government under Govinda. His subordinate Aiharasa is also mentioned in the record cited above as ruling over Bangicheru - 30, a place situated to the south of Kaneyakallu. A demaged record[10] from

Kasavagondanahalli refers to Irungola and his rule. Rice has assigned this record to 1106 A.D. the date being doubtful. But this can be attributed to his period as it seems to mention his rule over Govindavadi. Another damaged inscription[11] of the 18th century A.D. refers to his grants for the repairs of Mallikarjuna temple. An inscription[12] dated 1128 A.D. which affirms his rule over Rodda - 300, Sire - 300, Haruve - 300, Kaniyakallu - 300 and Sindavadi - 1000 not only gives a fair idea about his territorial possessions but also the nuclear position occupied by Nidugal by its proximity. Thus, Irungola successfully exercised direct control over his principalities as a feudatory of Chalukya Trailokyamalladeva (Somesvara III - 1126 - 38 A.D.). The two officials who figure in his records are *mahaprabhu* Erakamanagamunda[13] and *mahapradhana* and *Senadhipati* Ketanaverggade.[14] His wife Alpadevi whose virtues are eulogised in an undated inscription[15] of Jagadekamalla II (1138 - 55 A.D.) from Hemavati, is presumed according to K.V. Ramesh as one who had hailed from the Alupal house, on the basis of the etymology of the name. He is also of the opinion that she was perhaps either the sister or the daughter of Kavi Alupendra[16] (1110 - 60 A.D.) Her religious leanings towards Jainism, her charitable disposition in protecting a ruined Jaina temple and her being the lay disciple of the Kanur-gana of Konda - kundanvaya find mention in an inscription.[17] Irungola issued an order in 1134 A.D., to the *Mahapradhana* Garuda-setti to make certain gifts for the service of the god Bhimesvaradeva and for the feeding of ascetics.[18] He is also said to have caused the construction of the Kesava temple along with others and made grants of land for the service of the same god in 1140 A.D.[19] Irungola's record[20] dated 1143 A.D. incidentally refers to the death of Ganganaverggada and his follower in an onslaught *(dhali)*. On the evidence of this record it can be presumed that death of Irungola I might have occurred subsequent to 1143 A.D. i.e., the date of the present record. The upper limit of this chiefs' reign was hitherto believed to be 1140 A.D.[21] But from this, it can be inferred that his rule extended atleast upto 1143 A.D. We do not know anything about the adversary whom the deceased heroes Ganganaverggade and his follower encountered nor do we know the venue of the battle in which they met their fatal end. There are, however some evidences to show that the reign of Irungola was cut short probably after this battle. An inscription[22] dated 1162 A.D., provides an indirect reference to the effect that Irungola's pride was broken by Uttamachola, a subordinate of the Hoysala king Narasimha I (1152 - 73 A.D.). We may not be far from the truth if we infer that the quelling of the pride was nothing but the annihilation of Irungolachola. In this context, we may have to study an inscription[23] belonging to Hoysala Narasimha I (1152 - 73 A.D.) dated 1159 A.D. which eulogises Vishnuvardhana (1110 - 52 A.D.) and describes the defeat of Irungola at his hands. As this record is later in point of time i.e., 16 years after the known date of Irungolachola I, we have to be cautious in our utilisation of this record. However, the possibility of his defeat at the hands of Vishunuvardhana is not to be summarily rejected. As a passing remark, we may refer to another Hoysala record[24] dated 1176 A.D. of the time of Narasimha I which informs us that Irungola was a lay disciple of Nayakirit Siddhanthadeva.

Mallideva (1147 - 85 A.D.) :

Irungola's successor Vira - Nonamba Mallideva[25] was a loyal subordinate under the Chalukyas commencing from Jagadekamalla II and ending with Somesvara IV. His initial year seems to be 1147 A.D. We have already stated that his father died sometime around 1143 A.D. We have no means of knowing epigraphically what had happened between 1143 and 1147 A.D. and whether Mallideva succeeded to the throne smoothly without any resistance. His record[26] dated 1147 A.D. asserts that Henjeru was his capital and in the same year he made a royal gift to the god Ramesvara set up by Ramadeva in Sirevolal of Sira - nadu after laving the feet of Udyoga - Rama - pandita. In the same record his queen Ballidevi who was looking after the Siruvolal tank also made some gifts after laving the feet of Tejorasi - pandita. In this connection two records deserve mention here as they refer to Mallideva. The dates of these records are of doubtful nature. Rice however, assigned these two records to 1108[27] and c. 1110 A.D.[28] respectively. The dates given by this scholar seem to be wrong as they overlap with the reign of his father and they are too early to be ascribed to Mallideva, as we know Irungola's reign lasted upto 1143 A.D. Namana, who was a *Tantrapala* seems to have served his father also as he figures in a few records dated c. 1150[29] and 1169 A.D.[30] wherein he is eulogised at length. He seems to have confirmed gifts and grants which were formerly bequeathed by Irungola I, to the Nagesvara temple at Nidugal.

Mallideva was said to be ruling from Hiriya ... loka in 1160 A.D.,[31] the name of the place not being available in full on account of the damaged nature of the record. His record[32] dated in 1162 A.D. mentions his rule over Siranadu from the capital Henjeru. It registers the grant of land for the service of the god Desisvaradeva set up in Henjeru by Periyaluva - setti, son of Alahiya - Manavala and Andamme of Akuru hailing from interior Rajaraja - valanadu of the Chola country. Another inscription,[33] also of doubtful date but belonging to the same chief, mentions some Desi merchants and their munificient gifts. It is evident from these two inscriptions that there was excellent trade relationship between the Chola country and Karnataka in those days. The community dealt in several commercial commodities boosting inter - state economics. Besides Ballidevi, of whom a reference was made earlier, Lakamadevi[34] ans Sitadevi[35] were two other queens of Mallideva. Lakamadevi is said to be the crowned consort of the king. She had made some grants to a temple at Arasiyakere. Sitadevi was also not lagging behind in making gifts to temples and Nonambesvara, which is described as the *Ghatikasthana* of Henjerupattana, received her patronage in the form of gifts. The record[36] of Mallideva dated 1168 A.D. is politically important. This was a period of stress and strain for the house of the Chalukyas of Kalyana. A study of the political history of those days reveals that the Chalukyas of Kalyana were unseated from power by the Kalachuris. It is interesting to note that, in this inscription of 1168 A.D. Mallideva refers to the Chalukya Chakravarti (probably Taila III) as his overlord though the latter's reign had actually ended in 1162 - 63 A.D. Obviously his professing allegiance to the Chalukya throne was either a matter of convenience or was merely symbolic. Progressively and consistently a tradition came into vogue among the feudatories of the Kalyana Chalukyas of adopting imperial titles and epithets by way of showing their allegiance to their masters both in times of peril and prosperity. This is a characteristic feature which one can notice in almost all the royal feudatory families of the imperial dynasties of Karnataka. It also clearly points to the independent status of Mallideva and to his taking advantage of the political exigencies of the period. An inscription,[37] from Hemavati, dated in the 2nd regnal year, Vyaya of Tribhuvanachakravartin Kulottunga mentions Mallideva with the title *Uraiyur puravaradhisvara.* As a rule, the Nidugal Cholas used to claim the Karikala lineage in their inscriptions. The absence of this aspect in this present inscription is noteworthy. The 2nd year (Vyaya) quoted corresponds to 1165 A.D. and therefore it becomes more difficult for us to assign this record to Kulottunga III (1178 - 1218 A.D.) as his initial year is 1178 A.D. i.e., 13 years posterior to this record. Under this circumstance, we may not be able to identify Kulottunga of this record. Further, by this year Bijjala's usurpation of the Chalukya throne was complete and Mallideva had attained independent power. The Govindavada inscription[38] of his reign as a subordinate of the Chalukya king Tribhuvanamalladeva (?), dated 1169 A.D., records the gift by the chief of the village Santarane and of lands etc., for the service of the god Nilakanthesvaradeva for whom a temple was built by his father

In 1176 A.D.[39] *mahaprabhu* Mallayaka Gandaya granted some lands with the approval of the chief Mallideva. Another record[40] dated 1179 A.D., wherein Mallideve and the queen Lakmadevi are highly praised, states that they constructed five temples for five gods at Maleyanur in Sira - nadu and granted some lands etc., for the service of the gods. Once again it is interesting to note that though the Kalachuryas were the then actual rulers of the Chalukya dominions, still the Chalukyas are stated to be ruling. There is another record[41] dated in the cyclic year Sarvari which corresponds to 1180 A.D. and mentions some grants to the mercantile community. His rule over Henjeru continued upto 1185 A.D. as evidenced by Patasivaram record[42] which may perhaps be the last dated record of his reign. The significant fact is that Mallideva seems to have accepted the overlordship of Chalukya Somesvara IV (1181 - 89 A.D.) the last Chalukya ruler. His allegiance was of the nature of personal rather than political loyalty. In this record he is also named as Tribhuvanamalla - Bhogadeva. In another record[43] he styles himself as Piriya - Bhoga.

A damaged inscription,[44] the date of which is lost, but which belongs to the reign of *mahamandalesvara* Trailokyamalladeva, refers to his subordinate *mahapradhana Heggade* Attimayya who is stated to have consecrated the god Kesavadeva in Pushpagiri and made provision for the worship of the god. Where ever there is absence of any mention of his overlord, it has to be presumed that his rule was virtually an independent one so as to reconcile the varied conflicting statements.

Bommadeva (1186 - 85 A.D.) :

Mahamandalesvara Bommadeva succeeded his father Malideva.[45] His initial record[46] dated in 1186 A.D. during the reign of the Chalukya king Somesvara (IV) refers to his rule over Henjeru. Another of his records[47] attracted the attention of the scholars with regard to its date Saka 1057 (1135 A.D.) which could not be taken as genuine as it yields a much earlier date for his accession. Perhaps, without the knowledge of his initial record dated 1186 A.D. referred to above, Rice ascribed this record to 1190 A.D. keeping in his mind the rule of his predecessor which ended in 1185 A.D. and thus allowing a reasonable gap of 5 years for the latter to commence his reign. The inscription which is now under study also provides a reference to his sway over Henjerupattana wherein his queen (name not preserved) made some arrangements for the repair and maintenance of a temple. From other sources we come to know that Bachaladevi[48] was the name of his queen. Similarly his governance over Govindavadi is established by an epigraph[49] assignable to 1195 A.D. It also shows that he was a feudatory, like his father, under Somesvara IV.[50] An interregnum of nearly 30 years can be noticed between the last known date of Bomma and the accession of his successor *Mahamandalesvara* Irungola II. By way of justification one can ascribe this feature to the fact that Ballala II (1173 - 1220 A.D.) had encamped at Nidugaldurga in 1218 A.D.[51] clearly indicating that the Nidugal chiefs were relegated to the background and Hoysala influence was the upper most in this region for a considerable number of years.

Irungola II (1225 - 77 A.D.) :

Born to Bachaladevi,[52] Irungola II[53] ruling at Nidugal-pattana in 1225 A.D., was credited to have had a high degree of proficiency in archery and use of arms.[54] He had epithets like *Tribhuvanamalla, Nissanka-Pratapa-Chakravarti* and *Viradanavamurari.*[55] His benevolence to Jainism is well attested to by many grants made by him and recorded[56] (1232 A.D.) in a number of inscriptions.

Inscriptions dated in 1248,[57] 1249[58] and 1256 A.D.[59] record details of his grants made for various religious purposes. From a study of these epigraphs we are able to elicit information regarding the areas and places in which he wielded political influence and among them mention may be made of the Nidugal fort,[60] Abbinavolalu[61] and Kambadahole.[62] The mention of the *Nanadesis, Mahavadda-vyavaharis, Mummuridandas* in his records goes to show that he wielded considerable influence with these powerful mercantile bodies too. A record[63] of 1260 A.D. says that he was ruling over Gundanahalli. His son Tripurantakadeva figures in a record[64] dated 1262 A.D. as ruling over Haniyadurga (modern Brahamagiri). This inscription is of great importance as it conveys for the first time the name of his son who is not at all found in any of the genealogical accounts of this dynasty. A hero-stone from Tumkur is also of great importance for our present study. As has been pointed out earlier, the overbearing power of the Hoysalas was being felt even before his accession to the throne. Probably this state of affairs viz., the hostility between the Hoysalas and these chiefs continued even during 1269 A.D. These hostilities which took an ugly turn in the form of cattle raids resulted in the death of loyal subordinates of both the sides. The present hero - stone inscription[65] dated in 1269 A.D. belongs to the reign of the Hoysala king Narasimha III (1254 - 92 A.D.). It eulogises the bravery of Appeyanayaka who was in the service of the *Mahapradhana.* Chikkaketayya *damnayaka,* the feudatory of the Hoysala king, defended Anebiddasariya-nadu (a corrupt form of Anebidda - Arasiya - nadu) when Irungola II made incursions and succeeded in driving out the intruder and fell a victim. Further, Irungola II's alliance with the Sevunas is a significant one. A record[66] of Narasimha III dated 1276 A.D. registers a formidable invasion of the Sevunas against the Hoysalas which, according to the Hoysala accounts was repelled. Our interest in this record lies in the participation of Irungola II on the side of Sevunas which indicates the enmity nourished by these two powers for more than four decades. Inspite of their superior political and military powers it appears that the Hoysalas could not dislodge Irungola II as evidenced by a record[67] dated 1277 A.D. according to which he was then ruling over

Nidugal. This appears to be the last known date for this chief. This inscription, which refers to the construction of a Jaina - basadi in stone from *Upana* to *stupi*, is not of any political importance to our study. Unfortunately we do not know anything about the immediate successors of Irungola II.

As a result, it is difficult to fill up the gap between the last year of Irungola II and the first known date of his remote successor Ganesvara. The period roughly covers 15 years i.e., 1277 - 92 A.D. However, a reference is made to Vira Bomma the successor of Irungola II and predecessor of Ganesvara. It is well established from the genealogical list[68] that Ganesvara's father was the son of Irungola II. Unfortunately we do not get any records of this chief Vira Bomma and we are under duress to attribute the long period of paucity of records of these chiefs to protracted political trouble and turmoil in the region. In support of our view, we have a Hoysala record[69] of Vira Narasimha III dated 1285 A.D. which contains a claim that he had broken the pride of Nidugal, thereby showing the mastery of the Hoysalas, who kept these chiefs under subjugation to a great extent.

Ganesvara (1292 A.D.) :

The presence of Ganesvaradeva's record dated 1292 A.D.,[70] through which his *dandanayaka* Baichaya granted Mareyur situated to the south of Nidugal to lord Somanatha of Nidugal clearly shows that Ganesvara had regained control of his capital Nidugal. A second record[71] bearing the same date i.e. 1292 A.D. is a significant one. This mutilated record being a hero - stone naturally gives rise to the presumption that there was clash and combat between two parties the details of which are unfortunately not easily made out. From the diction it can be understood that it was an offensive attack on Hulukunte by *Savanta* Rayanayaka, son of Kudalur Dadugeyanayaka; it describes his heroic fight with opposing forces and also records the sacrifice of his life along with his retinue. The phrase *Prathama rajya* in this record immediately following the date portion may indicate the first year of Ganesvara's accession. We have no evidence at present to tell for how many years his rule had lasted. The growing power of Ballala III and the total absence of Ganesvara's records after 1292 A.D. probably indicate the ascendency of the Hoysala power which spelt the death knell of the Nidugal Cholas and brought about the end of Ganesvara's reign in its very first year.

From the genealogical references, we understand that Ganesvara was the last member of this dynasty and probably after him no Nidugal chief of note had ruled. However, a few members professing Nidugal Chola descent figure in some sporadic inscriptions. The period of their rule and their exact dates are conjectural. However, from the point of view of their connection with Nidugal, they are discussed below though their genealogical positions are nowhere stated and are open to correction. Whatever little information we get from the inscriptions are either insufficient or defective in dating. The so called record of Govinda II is not an exception to this. His record[72] is dated actually in Saka 1121 i.e., 1199 A.D. Rice has assigned this record to 1207 A.D. Under the present circumstances, it is not possible to reconcile the date mentioned in the record and the date suggested by Rice. It simply refers to him as the foremost of the Solar race. Likewise his son Irungola is referred to as ruling over Heddore.[73] The same record further states that Bamma who is described as *Nigalankamalla* was the son of Bhoga and Bijjaladevi. We know next to nothing about his father Bhoga, who is said to be the successor of Irungola and Govinda. And thus, we are at our wit's end to know the exact position of these line of kings. Bamma's reign seems to have marked the consolidation of his territory in the realm of defence. He is said to have protected Bodda, Kaniyaka Siru - nadu, Umbalige of Madiyamanadu, Lunka, Nasumbu, Nonambavadi and Ramadi. It further records that an impregnable line of fortification connecting the fort of Haniya and Nidugal was constructed by the king's minister Bicha as a protective measure to ward off enemy attacks. All his four sons viz., Bijjana, Baira, Irungola and Bavantiga, according to an inscription,[74] unitedly gave some gift to *Rajaguru* Devendraguru. A solitary record[75] refers to *Mahamandalesvara* Perumaladeva. Rice has assigned this record to 1285 A.D. In the absence of any other evidence this chief cannot be identified.

In conclusion, mention may be made of some chiefs who ruled after the Nidugal Cholas as *Mahamandalesvaras* adopting titles such as *Cholamaharaja,* etc. The exact relationship of these chiefs with the main line of the Nidugal Cholas is not known. In this connection, a few inscriptions deserve mention. The Doddabanagere inscription[76] dated 1337 A.D., acquaints us with a certain Bairarasa and his two sons. Another record[77] dated 1393 A.D. mentions *Mahamandalesvara* Virachola and the installation of god Nandikesvara by Lakshmibaiavve. The last record[78] dated 1481 A.D. mentions Ramaparajadeva and his grant at Rantevolalu.

Genealogy of the Nidugal Cholas

E.C., XII (1904), Pg. 50

Jata
|
Brahma Bhogendra
|
Kalimangi
|
Bichi
|
Govinda *m.* Mahadevi
|
Irungola I
|
Piriya Bhoga
|
(Mallideva)
|
Brahma (Bomma) *m.* Bachale
|
Irungola II

E.C., XII (1904), Pg. 53.

Manu
|
Karikalachola
|
Mangi
|
Babbedeva
|
Govinda
|
Irungola I
|
Mallideva
|
Brahma
|
Irungola II Vira (?) Bomma
|
Ganesa
|
(Ganesvara)

REFERENCES

1. *E.C.*, XII (1904), Mi. 92-94; 97, 100-01.
2. *Ibid.*, Mi. 94-96.
3. *Ibid.*, Pg. 35, 50, 53, 79; Si. 7.
4. *SII.*, IX, Pt. I, No. 146.
5. *Ibid.*, No. 152.
6. *Ibid.*, No. 161.
7. *Ibid.*, No. 179.
8. *E.C.*, XII (1904), Pg. 43.
9. *SII.*, IX, Pt. I, No. 209.
10. *E.C.*, XI (1903), Cl. 16.
11. *SII.*, IX, Pt. I, No. 709.

12. *E.C.*, XII (1904), Si. 7.
13. *Ibid.*,
14. *SII.*, IX, Pt. I, No. 233.
15. *E.C.*, XII (1904), Si. 25; *SII.*, VI, No. 555.
16. K.V. Ramesh : *A. History of South Kanara* (1970), pp. 114 - 15.
17. *ARSIE.*, 1917, No. c. 20.
18. *SII.*, IX, Pt. I, No. 229.
19. *Ibid.*, No. 234.
20. *ARSIE.*, 1913, No. c. 85.
21. K.V. Ramesh : *op. cit.*, pp. 114 - 15.
22. *E.C.*, XII (1904), Tp. 61.
23. *Ibid.*, II (1973), No. 481.
24. *Ibid.*, No. 73.
25. *Ibid.*, XII (1904), Pg. 43.
26. *Ibid.*, XI (1903), Cl. 21.
27. *Ibid.*, Cl. 43.
28. *Ibid.*, Hr. 30. .
29. *Ibid.*, XII (104), Pg. 43.
30. *SII.*, IX, Pt. I, No. 270.
31. *E.C.*, XI (1903), Si. 40.
32. *SII.*, IX, Pt. I, No. c. 16.
33. *ABSIE.*, 1917, No. c. 16.
34. *E.C.*, XII (1904), Pg. 35.
35. *Ibid.*, Si. 23; *SII.*, VI, No. 557.
36. *E.C.*, XII (1904), Si. 23.
37. *ARSIE.*, 1899, No. 117.
38. *SII.*, IX, Pt. I, No. 269.
39. *E.C.*, XII (1904), Pg. 79.

40. *SII.*, IX, Pt. I, No. 273.

41. *ARSIE.*, 1913, No. C 84.

42. *SII.*, IX, Pt. I, No. 278.

43. *E.C.*, XII (1904), Pg. 50; *ARSIE.*, 1917, No. c. 34.

44. *SII.*, IX, Pt. I, No. 283.

45. *E.C.*, XII (1904), pg. 50.

46. *SII.*, IX, Pt. I, No. 280.

47. *E.C.*, XII (1904), Si. 30.

48. *Ibid.*, Pg. 50.

49. *Ibid.*, Si 37; *ARSIE.*, 1917, No. C. 8.

50. *SII.*, IX, Pt. I, No. 298.

51. *E.C.*, V (1902), Hn. 61.

52. *Ibid.*, XII (1904), Pg. 50.

53. *ARSIE.*, 1917, No. C. 34.

54. *E.C.*, XII (1904), Pg. 50.

55. *Ibid.*, Pg. 32.

56. *Ibid.*, Pg. 52.

57. *Ibid.*, Pg. 50.

58. *ARSIE.*, 1913, No. C. 89.

59. *E.C.*, XII (1904), Si. 11.

60. *Ibid.*, Pg. 50.

61. *Ibid.*, XI (103), Hr. 37.

62. *ARSIE.*, 1913, No. C. 89.

63. *E.C.*, XII (1904), Pg. 14.

64. *Ibid.*, Si. 34.

65. *Ibid.*, Tm. 49.

66. *Ibid.*, V (1902), Bl. 164 and 165.

67. *Ibid.*, XII (1904), Si. 32; *ARSIE.*, 1917, No. c. 40.

68. *E.C.*, XII (1904), Pg. 53.

69. *Ibid.*, V (1902), Ak. 151.

70. *Ibid.*, XII (1904), Pg. 53.

71. *Ibid.*, Si. 60.

72. *Ibid.*, XI (1903), Mk. 23.

73. *Ibid.*, Mk. 20.

74. *Ibid.*, Mk. 24.

75. *Ibid.*, XII (1904), Pg. 47.

76. *Ibid.*, Si. 8.

77. *Ibid.*, Si. 105.

78. *Ibid.*, Mi. 1.

XII
THE PANDYAS OF UCHCHANGI

The Pandyas of Uchchangi claim their descent from the Yadavas of the unar race.[1] Their titles are 'the Lord of Kanchipura' (*Kanchipuravaradhisvara*) Champion in cutting on both sides (*parichchedi-ganda*) and 'defeater of the esigns of Rajigachola' i.e., Kulottunge I (*Rujuigucholamanoharanga*), etc.

Mangaya also known as Adityadeva and described as an ornament of ie Yadavakula is the earliest known member of the family. He was succeeded y his son Pandya who receives high praise in the genealogical account.[2] His on was Chediraja Pandya[3] who is credited with victory over the Chedi or Dahala ountry. He was a subordinate of Chalukya Somesvara I. Desai states that he as the real founder of the family.[4] But it is not correct. Whether the title *arichchedi-ganda* denotes the defeat of the Chedi king Karna is very difficult to scertain. Chediraja was called *Pandya* on account of his great partiality for the andya country (*Pandya avani virachita sthirapakshapatah Pandya-Khyayaiva udrudham bhudirudhimapa*).[5] Irukkapala, according to Desai, was his successor.[6] ut the genealogy of the Pandyas as known from the epigraphs does not refer him as the successor of Chediraja but, instead, gives the name of his son and iccessor as Palmanda or Palatta-Pandya.

almanda-Pandya (Palatta-Pandya) (1070-80 A.D.):

He was the first mahamandalesvara of his family and also bore the title igal amkamalla. He seems to be the real founder of the family as he was ling over the Nolambavadi-32000 province in 1079 A.D. as a subordinate of halukya Vikramaditya VI.[8] He is stated to have secured their kingdoms to oth the Chalukyas and the Chola kings (*Chalukya-Chola narapalakayo arajya\svarajyadam vijayate yudhi yasva 'sauryam*).[9] Nolambavadi-32000 over which the Pandya chiefs held sway was a large tract in which were included parts of the present Shimoga, Chitradurga, Bellary and Anantapur Districts.[10] Some of the feudatories of the Chalukyas other than the Pandyas, and the Cholas were ruling simultaneously over some parts of Nolambavadi-32000 as contemporaries of the Pandyas.[11] As a matter of fact, the Chalukyas and the Cholas always vied with each other in gaining and retaining control over that region.[12]

Irukkavela or Tribhuvanamalla-Pandya (1080-1126 A.D.) :

Irukkuvela who ascended the Pandya throne in 1083 A.D., was the son and successor of Palamanda or Palatta-Pandya.[13] He is described as 'the staff in Tribhuvanamalla's right hand' (......dakshinahabudanda). The hyperbolic claim made for him that he was the breaker of the Cholas, Andhras, Kalingas, Anga, Vanga, Magadha, Malava and Gurjara kings illustrates the power and influence wielded by him in the Chalukya court.[14] Though much of this description seems to be exaggerated, at the same time, it can be taken as a pointer to the fact that he was a very enterprising war-lord and that he may have fought with at least some of the rulers listed therein. Further he is eulogised as the subjugator of the whole earth for his overlord. A study of several epigraphs of his period undoubtedly reveal the fact that Tribhuvanamalla Pandya had ably assisted his master i.e., Vikramaditya VI in his battles against his enemies. To cite an example, he is stated to have helped his overlord in defeating his vicious brother Somesvara II in about 1076 A.D. as a punishment for dereliction of his royal duties.[15] His participation in this affair appears to have helped him to enter the ranks of the nobility for we find that he was ruling over Nolambavadi-32000 in 1083 A.D.[16] In 1085-86 A.D. he was ruling over Gangavadi-96000 also besides Nolambavadi-32000[17] and in addition, he was in charge of Ballakunde-300 in 1101 A.D.[18] The Kadambalige-1000 province was under his administration in 1111 A.D.[19] He, for the first time, made Beltur (situated near Dharwar) his capital in 1181 A.D. It is interesting to note that he is described as the younger brother of Vira-Nolamba-Pallava-Permanadideva viz., Chalukya Jayasimha, perhaps as a term of endearment.

Achugi II, the Sinda Chief of Yalburga, is known to have defeated the Pandyas along with other chiefs such as the Hoysala, Lakshma, a commender of the Kadamba family and the Malapas when they rebelled against their suzerain and declared their independence, taking advantage of his old age. Achugi II rescued his sovereign by successfully fighting against these chiefs. He is said to have pursued and prevailed against Poysala i.e., Vishnuvardhana, taken Gove, put to flight Lakshma in war, valorously pursued the Pandyas disposed for all times the Malapas and seized the Konkana and brought all of them under the control of his suzerain.[20] In this connection, Desai opines that Tribhuvanamalla Pandya was intoxicated with his early victories against the Cholas and aimed at complete independence.[21] This supposition is only partly true because, more than anything else, the political conditions of this period tempted him to rebel against his overlord; he was probably also influenced by the instigation of other feudatories such as the Hoysalas, and might have felt that the time was ripe for proclaiming himself as an independent chief. He might have realised his mistake after his defeat in this task at the hands of Achugi II and he once again coolly accepted the suzerainty of the Chalukyas.

An inscription dated 1113 A.D. and belonging to Kamadeva furnishes the genealogy of the Pandyas; they were descended from Chandravamsa and were originally the rulers of the Hayve country. Their capital was Sisugali. Kamadeva, who claims to be the Lord of Gokarnapura, is stated to have ruled Konkana-rashtra as a subordinate of Vikramaditya VI.[22] On the strength of this record, the origin of the Pandyas of the present chapter has been elsewhere ascribed to this family.[23] In no way can this Kamadeva be connected with the Pandyas of Uchchangi as his pedigree, the title that he bore, and the family from which he originated according to this inscription, do not agree with the available records of the chiefs of the present chapter. Above all, Tribhuvanamalla-Pandya had firmly established the power of the Pandyas by this time. Quite a few epigraphs of the period record that the Hoysalas were constantly in the habit of attaching the Pandyas and their territories.[24] Hoysala Vishnuvardhana once rebelled, assisted by the Pandyas, against Vikramaditya VI, but his activities no doubt were soon curbed by the Sinda chief Achugi. Vishnuvardhana seems to have subsequently changed his policy towards the Pandyas and began to consider them as his enemies as evidenced by their epigraphs which deal with some encounters between them. Hoysala Vishnuvardhana invaded Uchchangi and Belvola and carried his arms successfully so far to the north as to bathe his horses in the Krishna river.[25] In 1118 A.D. Hoysala Vishnuvardhana, who was ruling from Talakad, was described as the capturer of Uchchangi.[26]

The records pertaining to both the families do not reveal the result of their battles in definite terms. However, the claims of the Hoysalas in their records that they won over the Pandyas is not acceptable for the Pandya chiefs Tribhuvanamalla and his two successors were able to hold their sway over Uchchangi despite the reverses caused by the Hoysalas.

Vikramaditya VI is said to have conquered first the Gangas, then the Cholas and the Lalas, to have levied tribute from the Panchalas and subjugated the rest of his enemies. His subordinate Pandyadeva is also stated to have chased the king of Ratanpur, who was apparently Jajalladeva I, at his master's command in 1122 A.D.[27] He was wielding power over Nolambavadi-32000 from Beluru (obviously a mistake for Belturu) in 1126 A.D.[28]

An inscription of the time of the Hanagal Kadamba chief Taila II states that he married a Pandya princes named Bachaladevi.[29] This lady, according to Desai, was a sister of Tribhuvanamalla Pandya.[30] But it is surprising to note that the available genealogical account of the Pandya chiefs does not say anything about this matrimonial alliance. Hence she may not after all be the sister of Tribhuvanamalla-Pandya.

Tribhuvanamalla-Raya-Pandya (1124-42 A.D.) :

The last record so far known of his predecessor and father is dated in 1126 A.D.[31] and his own earliest available record is dated in 1124 A.D.[32] Therefore it is presumed that Tribhuvanamalla-Raya-Pandya was associated with his father's administration during the last years of the latter's rule. Raya-Pandya bore the title Tribhuvanamalla as he was serving under Vikramaditya VI. A record[33] dated 1124 A.D. refers to his rule over Nolambavadi-32000 and Santalige-1000. Many of his inscriptions ranging in date from 1124 to 1140 A.D. give an idea about the succesful nature of his rule inspite of the disturbances caused by the then prevailing political situation. Like his father he was also a great warrior and a good administrator. That is why, in all probability, he is described in an inscription as "having a fortune four inches higher" *(chatur - angul - onnatasri)*.[34] Further he is described as a confounder of the Chola king, destroyer of Nepala, an invincible barrier to the serpent Kalinga, uprooter of the unsubmissive Simhala, etc.[35] As for as the historical significance of this record is concerned, it reveals that he was able to combat some of the powerful contemporary rulers with much matching vigour and strength.

Sovaladevi is stated to be his wife. She was a daughter of a Billavaraya and younger sister of king Vikramaditya,[36] who has been identified with his namesake, subordinate of the Chalukyas.[37] Sovaḷadevi is highly eulogised in some of the records.[38] Tribhuvanamalla - Raya - Pandya had three sons. They were Pamdita - Pandya, Vira - Pandya and Vijaya - Pandya.

Desai dealt with Pamdita - Pandya in a separate chapter thinking that he may have ruled as a chief though only for a shorter duration[39] inspite of the fact that Rice had doubts about his succession.[40] As Pamdita - Pandya does not possess any records of his own, we know very little about him. However from a later record of their family it is known that he was a disciple of Madhusudana and had a son named Tailapa.[41] On the basis of the non - availability of his records, it is surmised elsewhere that both he and his son did not succeed to the Pandya chieftaincy.[42]

Vira - Pandya (1142 - 62 A.D.) :

Tribhuvanamalla - Raya Pandya was succeeded by his second son Virapandya probably in 1142 A.D.[43] Like his predecessors, he also continued to rule over Nolambavadi and many other countries as the crown prince *(kumara - vrittiyimda)*.[44] On the basis of the availability of two records[45] in Shimoga District, Desai states that the eastern part of this district was included in the domain of Virapandya.[46] A hero - stone[47] dated 1153 A.D. refers to the Hoysala attack on Mahalige. Another epigraph[48] dated 1145 A.D. states that Virapandya subdued Male and offered it as an "ornament of the Chalukyas". Mahalige and Male referred to in these records are one and the same. Desai identifies this Male or Mahalige with Hayve - 500 the province lying on the slopes of the Western ghats.[49] But this identification proves to be incorrect as it can be identified with Mahalige - nadu. Mahalige is the modern village of the same name situated on the right bank of the river Saravati, about 30 miles to the north - west of Humcha in the Shimoga District.[50]

The hostility which prevailed between the Chalukyas and the Cholas seems to have come to a close during this period. A record dated 1143 A.D. describes the Chalukya monarch as Kuntala -raya and as frightening and driving away in alarm the Chola king in battle and to have made the *Cholnela* (the Chola country) to be as if in *Alnela* (slave or servant country).[51]

Virpandya appears to have participated in some of the battles against the enemies of the Chalukyas. It is stated in an inscription that "Virapandya, the favourite of the world, earned the title *Jagadekamalla* by virtue of breaking down the pride and courage of the neighbouring enemies."[52] He made the mighty Ganga, Kalinga, Vanga, Maru, Gurjara, Kerala, Chera, Chola, Gauda, Anga, Varata, Lata, Khasa, Baradara, Kosala, Kuru, Prahara, Andhra, Turushka and Magadha rulers to tremble.[53] From the above narration this much is clear that Chalukya Jagadekamalla II made some of these conquests, though much of it seems to be ficititious.

Uchchangi became the capital of the Pandyas in 1143 A.D. Before this Beltur served as their capital. Many records belonging to his reign state that he was ruling over Nolambavadi from his capital Uchchangi.[54] Uchchangi is called *Rajadhani*[55] and *Jagadekamalla - Pandyanagari*[56] Uchchangidurga now is a village containing a hill - fortress which is reputed to have been a highly impregnable fort, situated in the south - east corner of Harapanahalli Taluk in Bellary District. It is also known as Uchchasringi. Virapandya was also wielding power over the Kadambalige - 1000 province.[57] He had two wives; Gangadevi, also known as Mahadevi, was the daughter of Aditya - Dandanatha and Vijayadevi was the younger sister of a certain Vikramaditya, whose identity is not known.[58] The last available record of Virapandya is dated 1162 A.D. and not 1152 A.D. as believed by Desai.[59]

Permadi (Sivachitta), the Goa Kadamba chief is known to have married a Pandya princess, "born of a king of the race of the moorn".[60] This princess, according to Desai, was the sister of Virapandya. As there is not a single reference in any one of the Pandya records to this princess, the supposition of Desai is highly doubtful.

During the reign of the Gutta chief Vikramaditya I a gift offered by a certain Virapandya is referred to.[61] The Pandya lineage of Virapandya mentioned in this record was doubted earlier.[62] It is evidenced from the above record that Virapandya was the contemporary of Gutta Vikramaditya I whose known date is 1162-63 A.D.[63] Therefore, Virapandya mentioned in the Gutta record can be identified with his namesake, Virapandya whose rule comes to an end in 1162 A.D.[64] and who belonged to the family of the Pandyas of Uchchangi.

Virapandya was ruling over Kadambalige - 1000, Ballakunde - 300 and Kogali - 500 in 1160 A.D.[65] In 1162 A.D. he was administering Kogali - 500 and Kadambalige - 1000 with the title 'Lord of Kanchipura' *(Kanchipuravaradhisvara)*.[66]

Vijayapandya (1161-81 A.D.) :

He succeeded his elder brother Virapandya in about 1162 A.D. He was also known as Kamadeva. *'Nigalamkamalla'* was his title. In the beginning of his reign he refused to acknowledge the supremacy of Bijjala. However, he was brought under his control soon.[67] That Vijayapandya helped his elder brother in political matters is evident from the fact that these two brothers figure as the subordinates of Kalachuri Bijjala in 1161 - 62 A.D.[68] Vijayapandya, however, soon transferred his allegiance in 1165 A.D. to Chalukya Jagadekamalla III, who was only a nominal sovereign in this period.[69]

Vijayapandya, taking advantage of the confusion created by the struggle for supremacy between the Chalukyas and the Kalachuris, declared his independence in about 1166 A.D. and continued in the same position till 1176 A.D.[70]

Hoysala Ballala II, as soon as he ascended the throne, marched against the Changalvas and conquered them. Then he proceeded against the Pandyas of Uchchangi. A record dated 1177 A.D. states that Vira - Ballala II, having made a victorious expedition to all quarters and conquered the Pandya, made Uchchangi as his royal city.[71] The attack on Uchchangi and its capture by Ballala II has been known from some of the epigraphs.[72] Hoysala Ballala, however, restored Uchchangi to Vijayapandya after his submission.[73] Immediately after this event Vijayapandya transferred his allegiance to Chalukya Jagadekamalla III and Somesvara IV in 1181 - 82 A.D. It is evidenced by two epigraphs[74] wherein he is described as *"Jagadekamalladeva - padabjabhringa"* and *"Tribhuvanamalladeva - Padabja - bhringa"*. This attitude of the Pandyas might have enraged Ballala II and forced him to march against them as is testified in one of his records[75] dated 1181 A.D. where in he is described as a wild forest fire to the Pandyakula *(Pandyakuladvanalam)*.

We do not hear much about the Pandya after this incident though we have a record of Tribhuvanamalla-Pandyadeva (?) dated 1199 A.D.[76] Therefore it is clear from the epithet borne by Ballala II as stated above, that he had subdued the Pandyas and had gradually absorbed their kingdom into his empire.[77] However, there is a vague reference to the Pandyas in 1247 A.D. when they are stated to have been defeated by Yadava Krishna.[78]

In the same manner, the members referred to in the genealogical chart such as Palamanda - Pandya, Phondi - Pandya,[79] etc., have not been dealt with in this chapter as Rice himself has expressed the view that these members were of a different branch.[80]

Thus the Pandyas who came to light in the 11th century A.D. as the *mahamandalesvaras* under the patronage of the Chalukyas rose to prominence during the rule of Tribhuvanamalla Pandya under the able guidance of Vikramaditya VI. Vijayapandya was the first and foremost member in this family to rule as an independent chief for some time. The territorial divisions over which the rule of some of the members of this family prevailed were vast and varied from time to time. After the chieftaincy of nearly 200 years ultimately they were defeated by the Hoysalas.

With the help of the epigraphs belonging to this family, the reign - period of the chiefs except the first three can be fixed as follows :

1. Mangaya
|
2. Pandya

3. Chediraja - Pandya — Irukkapala
Irukkapala → Mahadevi

4. Palmanda - Pandya (1070 - 90 A.D.)
|
5. Irukkavela Tribhuvanamalla - Pandya (1080 - 1126 A.D.)
|
6. Tribhuvanamalla - Rayapandya (1124 - 42 A.D.)

Pamdita - Pandya — 7. Virapandya (1142 - 62 A.D.) — 8. Vijayapandya (1161- 81A.D.)

Pamdita - Pandya → Tailapa

The Pandyas of Hayve

While dealing with the Pandyas of Uchchangi we have already stated that Kamadeva, a chief figuring in an inscription dated 1113 A.D., does not belong to that family. He is dealt with here separately as he belongs to a different branch of the Pandyas. His record, mentioned above, furnishes the genealogy of his family. According to this[81] they were said to have originated from the lunar race *(Chamdravamsa)* and originally ruled over the Hayve country which was considered as one of the seven Konkanas. The other six Konkanas were Kirata, Virata, Maratha, Konkana, Ruluva and Kerala.[82] Sisugeli was their capital, the identification of which is uncertain. The place - name Sisugeli is very interesting as it is so called because the childeren *(sisu)* who were born there were knwon for their distiguished courage *(kalitana).* Further it is stated in this record that a certain king named Chandra began to rule after many Pandya kings of that place. His wife was Kammaladevi (obviously Kamaladevi). He was succeeded by his son Kama I. Bhagaladevi, his wife, is describeds as *Rajaputri.* Chandra II succeeded his father Kama I. He is highly eulogised. He had a wife by name Savaladevi.

Mahamandalesvara Kamadeva II was the son and successor of Chandra II. He is described as 'the lord of Gokarnapura' *(Gokarnapuravaradhisvara)*, 'the protector of the Konkana - rashtra' *(Konkanarashtrapala) Nigalamkamalla.* He was ruling over Hayve - nadu in 1113 A.D. as a subordinate of Chalukya Vikramaditya VI. Further information about these Pandyas of Hayve after Kamadeva II is not available from any other record. However, the rule of Jayakesi II, a chief of the Kadamba family of Goa over Hayve - 500 in 1125 A.D.[83] would suggest that the Pandyas of Hayve went into oblivion during his period.

Another family with an appellation, Pandya but different from that of the two branches mentioned above is worthy of note this connection. An epigraph[84] of the reign of Hoysala Narasimha II dated 1220 A.D. contains the genealogy of the members of this family from Palattapandya down to Kamadeva and his son in succession as shown below :

Palattapandya
|
Phondipandya
|
Rayapandya
|
Noleyapandya
|
Kamadeva and his son whose name is lost.

This record at the beginning refers to the rule of the Chalukyas and then to Kalachuri Bijjana (i.e. Bijjala) during which period the Pandyas (apparently the Pandyas of Uchchangi) held their sway over the Nolambavadi. Further it states that Hoysala Ballala II had defeated the Pandyas in a battle and taken possession of Nolambavadi. The beginning of the rule of Palattapandya has been ascribed to 1155 and C. 1160 A.D. respectively by Desai and Rice.[85]

Desai does not seem to have properly understood the text of the record. Hence he thought that Palattapandya had started his rule under the supremacy of Kalachuri Bijjala.[86] Further he went to the extent of stating that he was a rival to Vijayapandya of the Pandyas of Uchchangi.[87] But we should not forget that this record is of the reign of the Hoysala Narasimha II. It states in unequivocal terms that Hoysala Vira Ballala II subdued the Pandyas, a statement borne out by some of his other records wherein he is described as wild forest fire to the Pandyakula *(Pandyakuladavanalam).*[88]

From the above account what we would like to propound here is that Palattapandya had started his chieftaincy immediately after the defeat of the

Pandyas of Uchchangi in 1181 A.D.[89] On these lines, the commencement of his rule can be fixed to C. 1185 A.D. At the time of this record i.e., 1220 A.D. the rule of the sixth chief of this family was in progress. Therefore, it is presumed that within a short span of 40 years all these successors of Palattapandya had ruled. What happened to this family after the rule of Kamadeva's son is not known.

REFERENCES

1. *EC.*, XI (1903), Dg. 41.
2. *Ibid.*, V (1902), Ak. 102. A.
3. *Ibid.*, XI (1903), Dg. 41.
4. Desai : *MUCK.*, p. 224.
5. *EC.*, XI (1903), Dg. 39. This epithet has been wrongly ascribed to Pandya who was treated as the son of Chediraja, whose son was Palants. Cf. KTA., p. 410. Actually Planta or Palmanda Pandya was the son of Chediraja according to the genealogy of the Pandya chiefs.
6. Desai : *op. cit.*, p. 226.
7. *E.C.*, XI (1903), Dg. 5, 39, 40 and 41.
8. *SII.*, IX Pt. I, No. 145.
9. *EC.*, XI (1903), Dg. 39.
10. *SII.*, XVIII, Introduction, p. xxvi.
11. Desai : *op. cit.*, p. 228.
12. *The Struggle for empire*, pp. 174 - 75,
13. *SII.*, IX, Pt. I, No. 153; *EC.*, VII (1902), Ci. 33.
14. *EC.*, XI (1903), Dg. 3; *The Struggle for Empire*, p. 177.
15. The Struggle for Empire, p. 174.
16. *SII.*, IX, Pt. I, No. 153.
17. *Ibid.*, No. 154.
18. *E.C.*, XI (1903), Hk. 25; Dg. 128.
19. *Ibid.*, Jl. 9.
20. Fleet : *JBBRAS.*, XI, p. 269.
21. Desai : *op. cit.*, p. 233.

22. *EC.*, VII (1902), Sk. 99.
23. *KTA.*, p. 410.
24. *EC.*, VI (1901), Cm. 99; *Ibid.*, Kd. 69; *Ibid.*, IV (1898), Ng. 70; *Ibid.*, XII (1904), Ck. 29-30.
25. *IA.*, II, p. 302.
26. *EC.*, IV (1975), Kr. 31.
27. *SII.*, IX, Pt. I, No. 205; *The Struggle for Empire*, p. 177.
28. *SII.*, IX, Pt. I, No. 215.
29. *IA.*, X, p. 254.
30. Desai : *Op. cit.*, p. 235.
31. *SII.*, IX, Pt. I, No. 215.
32. *EC.*, XI (1903), Dg. 2.
33. *Ibid.*,
34. *Ibid.*, Dg. 41.
35. *Ibid.*, Dg. 77.
36. *Ibid.*, Dg. 5, 39, 41 and 76.
37. Rangachar : *IMP.*, I, p. 281.
38. *EC.*, XI (1903), Dg. 39, 41 and 77.
39. Desai : *op. cit.*, p. 243.
40. Rice : *MCI.*, p. 151.
41. *EC.*, XI (1903), Dg. 41.
42. *KTA.*, p. 410/
43. *SII.*, IX, Pt. I, No. 238.
44. *EC.*, XI (1903), Dg. 43; *ARSIE.*, 1918, Nos. 238 and 240.
45. *EC.*, VII (1902), Ci. 39-40.
46. Desai : *op. cit.*, p. 245.
47. *EC.*, VII (1902), Sa. 58.
48. *Ibid.*, XI (1903), Dg. 168.
49. Desai : *op. cit.*, p. 245.

50. *SII.*, XVIII, Introduction, p. xxvi.

51. *EC.*, XI (1903), Dg. 85.

52. *Ibid.*, Dg. 41.

53. *Ibid.*,

54. *Ibid.*, VII (1902), Ci. 38 - 39; *Ibid.*, XI (1903), Dg. 4, 168.

55. *Ibid.*, VII (1902), Ci. 38.

56. *Ibid.*, XI (1903), Dg. 168.

57. Rangachar : *op. cit.*, I, p. 299.

58. *EC.*, XI (1903), Dg. 41.

59. Desai : *op. cit.*, p. 250.

60. Fleet : *JBBRAS.*, IX, p. 274.

61. *SII.*, XVIII, No. 296.

62. *Ibid.*, Introduction, p. xxii.

63. *Ibid.*, No. 296.

64. *Ibid.*, IX, Pt. I, No. 293.

65. *Ibid.*, No. 267.

66. *Ibid.*, No. 293.

67. *The Sturggle for empire*, p. 180.

68. *EC.*, XI (1903), Dg. 84; *SII.*, IX, Pt. I, No. 293.

69. *EC.*, XI (1903), Dg. 77.

70. Desai : *op. cit.*, p. 254.

71. *EC.*, XII (1904), Ck. 36.

72. *Ibid.*, II (1973), 444; *MAR.*, 1926, No. 25.

73. *EC.*, V (1902), Bl. 27; *Ibid.*, VI (1901), Tk. 10.

74. *Ibid.*, XI (1903), Cd. 13 and 33; *The Struggle* for Empire, p. 183.

75. *EC.*, II (1973), No. 571.

76. *Ibid.*, XI (1903), Cd. 36.

77. *KTA.*, p. 411.

78. *The Struggle for Empire*, p. 192.
79. *EC.*, XI (1903), Introduction, p. 18 and Genealogy.
80. *Ibid.*, Introduction, p. 16 and Hk. 56.
81. *Ibid.*, VII (1902), Sk. 99.
82. *Kanara Gazetteer*, Pt. II, p. 75, n. 4.
83. Fleet : *DKD.*, p. 568.
84. *EC.*, XI (1903), Hk. 56.
85. Desai : *op. cit.*, p. 269; *EC.*, XI (1903), Introduction, p. 18.
86. Desai : *op. cit.*, p. 269.
87. *Ibid.*, p. 270.
88. *EC.*, II (1973), No. 571.
89. *Ibid.*,

XIII
THE GUTTAS

Though, at first instance, the claim of the Guttas to have descended from the imperial Gupta dynasty of Magadha (4th - 5th centuries A.D.) appears to be far fetched if not totally unhistorical. The dynastic eulogy of the Guttas as well as the names borne by the members of that family render the claim a distinct possibility.They had such significant titles as *Ujjayini - puravaradhisvara, Patalipuravaradhisvara, Vikramaditya* (i.e. Chandragupta II) - *vamasodbava, Ujjayini - Mahakala - devata - labdha - varaprasada* and *Chandragupta - maharajadhiraja - kula - sampurna* etc. They had the emblem of a lion *(Mriga - raja - lanchchana).*[1]

The rule of the Guttas over the Guttavolal region i.e. the region in and around modern Guttal in Haveri Taluk of Dharwar District commenced from the beginning of the 12th century A.D. under the supremacy of Chalukya Vikramaditya VI (1076 - 1126 A.D.)

Magutta i.e., Mahagupta appears as the earliest member of this family. As much has not been said about him in the genealogical account of this family it is presumed that he was an ordinary local chieftain.

Gutta I (1105 - 12 A.D.) :

Magutta was succeeded by Gutta I who may be considered as the real founder of the family. He is described as *Guptanvaya - vamsagrani, Guttanvaya - rajabhavana - mamgala - kalasa, Guttanvaya - chudamani* and *Guttanvaya tilaka.*[2] He is credited with victory over his enemies whose territories were acquired by him after killing them in the battle field.[3] The enemies with whom he faught are not known. But it is surmised that they were the Kadambas of Hangal, the western neighbours of the Guttas.[4] He seems to have annexed some of the territories belonging to the Kadambas taking advantage of the dispute between the Kadamba princes Santivarman and his nephew Kirtivarman. He is stated to have had a daughter, viz., Bachaladevi who was given in marriage to Biradeva II of the Kadambas of Nurumbada lineage.[5]

Mallideva (1113 - 20 A.D.) :

He was the son and successor of Gutta I. The earliest availabe record[6] of this family, assignable to 1115 A.D. and belonging to the reign of Chalukya Vikramaditya VI, furnishes the genealogy of the Guttas down to Mallideva and of the chiefs of the Jatachola lineage for three generations. He is described in this record as *rajachudamani, tribhuvanatilaka,* etc. It refers to *Mahapradhana* Govindarasa who was administering Banavase - 12000 as subordinate of Chalukya Vikramaditya VI. He had high sounding titles such as *samadhigata - panchamahasabda, Mahasamantadhipati,* etc. The rule of Mallideva over Gutti during this period cannot be ascertained from this record. The non - mention of his rule may be due to the strong administration of Govindarasa referred to above.

In one of his military campaigns Hoysala Vishnuvardhana captured in 1138 A.D.[7] the Banavasi and Hangal provinces which were very close to Guttavolal. The non - inclusion of Guttavolal in this expedition of Hoysala Vishnuvardhana indicates that either Mallideva had successfully defended his territories or that the Hoysala conqueror had, for reasons not known, avoided crossing swords with the Gutta chief. Padmaladevi was his wife. She is stated to have survived her husband by many years.[8] Laliyadevi was his daughter. She was married to Ketarasa III belonging to the family of the Kadambas of Nurumbada.[9]

Joyideva I (Joma I - 1120 - 55 A.D.) :

Mallideva was succeeded by his younger brother Joyideva or Joma I. He was a subordinate of Vikramaditya VI. He is stated to have held the office of the *manneya* of Ponnavartti - 12 (the small circle of villages haveing for its headquarters Ponnavartti modern Honnatti in Haveri Taluk),[10] Beluhuge - 70 (the division which included the villages Guttavolal (Guttal), Nerilage (Niralgi) and Kannavalli (Kanavalli) of the Haveri Taluk) as the chief town[11] and Bennevur - 12 (a circle of 12 villages with Bennevur, i.e. Motebennur in Ranebennur Taulk as its headquarters)[12] from his capital Guttavolal in A.D. 1124 at the same time *mahamandalesvara* Singhanadeva (apparently Yadava Singhana) was administering the Seguna (i.e. Sevuna) country (extending from Nasik to Devagiri, modern Daulatabad),[13] Paliyanda - 4000 (which comprised parts of Osmanabad District of Maharashtra with Poliyanda modern Parenda being its chief town)[14] and the *agrahara* Honnavartti (same as Ponnavartti - 12). Ullaharaja a minister of Mallideva, and Dekanna and Nakanna, his two *pradhanas* are also referred to in this record.[15] The first of a composite record from Chaudadanpur states that Hiriy-Joyideva had, on a former occasion, made a gift of some lands to Sivadeva at the instance of Mananichi Nayaka, the *paramavisvasi* of Tribhuvanamalladeva.[16] Hiriya - Joyidevarasa referred to above may be identified with Joyideva I as the same name appears in another record.[17]

Vikramaditya I (1155 - 70 A.D.) :

He succeeded his uncle Joyideva I. He rose to the status of *mahamandalesvara* in 1162 A.D. and was governing the same places which were earlier under his father.[18] That the status of the Guttas was enhanced during his chieftaincy is borne out by the fact that he was conferred the title of *mahamandalesvara.* It may be remembered here that one of his predecessors held the office of *manneya.* His queen was Siriyadevi. His devotion to the god Ahavamallesvara is referred to in a later record dated 1181 A.D.[19]

Joyideva II (Joma II, 1170 - 90 A.D.) :

He succeeded his father Vikramaditya I. He was ruling over Beluhuge - 70 and Banavasi - 12000 in 1177 A.D. as a *mahamandalesvara.*[20] It is surmised by us that he may have ruled over some parts of Banavasi - 12000 for, being a vast division, it was always placed in charge of the major feudatory power of the day. Ponnavartti - 12 and Bennevur - 12 over which his predecessor had ruled are not mentioned in this record. Whether he lost those two divisions or any other subordinate of the Chalukya monarch was entrusted with their administration it is difficult to know. He is described as *Guptavamsa - varidhi - vardhana - sudhakara.* He is said to have made some gifts to the gods Kesava and Somanatha in 1179 A.D. Further he is also stated to have granted some taxes in Nagarakhanda province over which *mahamandalesvara* Boppadeva was ruling.[21] Whether he was in possession of some territories in Nagarakhanda during this period it is very difficult to ascertain. Boppadeva was forced to accept the overlordship of the Hoysalas in 1182 A.D.[22] while Joyideva continued his subordination to the Kalachuris despite Vira Ballala II depriving them of their hold over the region south of the Tungabhadra.[23] Joyideva II had constructed a temple of Vikramesvara probably in the name of his father at Gottagadi situated on the bank of Tungabhadra and offered some grants jointly with his minister Susanga to this temple in 1181 A.D. during the reign of Kalachuri Ahavamalla.[24] It is said that the lithic record mentioning the above fact is a copy of a copper - plate inscription stated to have been engraved at the instance of Mallugi *Dandanayaka* who was the *desadhikari.*[25] His record[26] dated 1187 A.D. states that *saravapradhana* Tipparasa built a temple of Rajesvara in the premises of the Chamesvara temple of Honnavatti at the instance of *sarvadhikari* Bichisetti.

In the genealogy of the Guttas, Gutta II is known as the younger brother of Joyideva II. Padmaladevi was his wife.[27] No records of his time have been found till now. We shall show below that Joyideva II, his elder brother, and Vikramaditya II his son, had jointly ruled during 1181 - 87 A.D. Under this circumstance, we may conclude that Gutta II did not rule at all and predeceased his elder brother leaving behind an eligible son. Joyideva's last known record is dated in 1187 A.D.[28] The earliest known date of Vikramaditya II is 1181 A.D.[29] Therefore it is obvious that the latter was associated with the former in administration for quite some time.[30]

Vikramaditya II (1180-1235 A.D.)

In 1181 A.D. he is stated to have been administering Beluhuge-70 and Bennevur-12.[31] In the same year Susanga-Dannayaka, his *pradhana*, with the permission of *mahamandalesvara* Vijaya-Pandyarasa had made, in the presence of Bacharasa and the *Mahajanas* of Kuruvatti, a grant of 70 mattars of land for the service of the God Ahavamellesvara. An inscription[32] dated 1182 A.D., belonging to Kalachuri Ahavamalla, refers to Kumara Vira Vikramadeva apparently Vikramaditya II, Susanga-Dandanayaka and other residents of Gudigeri in connection witha a grant of land made for the worship of and offerings to the god Kalideva of Mulasthana. Another record[33] of the same date and the same king contains the genealogy down Vikramaditya II. Sometimes he is called as the son of Joyideva II.[34] He is also referred to as Ahavaditya Vikramaditya.[35] It is interesting to note that Vasudeva-Dandanayaka, who was his subordinate, was the receipient of the grant of Badadaluru in Binnevuru-12. The donors of the said grant were vikramaditya I and Joyideva II, the grand-father and uncle respectively of Vikramaditya II. In 1183 A.D. the aforesaid Vasudeva-Dandanayaka who outlived both the predecessors of his chief, made a gift of land in the village Badadaluru which was granted to him earlier as stated above,[36] for the worship and offerings to the god Mallikerjuna of that village, after effecting repairs etc., to the temple. An epigraph[37] of Vikramaditya II dated 1188 A.D., states that Vira - Pandya, who flourished before 1188 A.D., had made a gift during the rule of Vikramaditya I. It is not possible to indentify this Vira-Pandya at present.

Another inscription[38] dated 1186 A.D. of the reign of Somesvara IV (1184-1200 A.D.) furnishes the genealogy of the Gutta chiefs. In this record Sovaladevi, the wife of Vikramaditya II, is described as belonging to the family of Vijaya - Pandya. Further Vikramaditya II is reported to have routed the armies of Hoysalesa and Pandya who were apparently allies. Vijaya - Pandya has been connected with Vikramaditya II's fight against the Hoysalas and the Pandyas referred to above whose army attacked the territory of Bhujabala - Pandya, a subordinate of Hoysala Vira Ballala II in 1185 - 86 A.D.[39] An allusion to Somesvara's overcoming the Kalachuris made in the above record evidently shows the hostility that existed between the two major dynasties of the period. Vikramaditya II himself offered some grants in 1188 A.D. for the merit of his mother Padmaladevi, besides other gifts given by his *mahapradhana* Desiraja.[40] He was wielding his power over Banavasinadu from his capital Guttavolal in the same year.[41] The identity of Jagadeva - Pandya and Vijaya - Pandya, son of Odeyarasa referred to in the same year is not known. In the next year he got constructed a temple called Padmesvara for the merit of Padmaladevi who was his mother *(dhatri)*.[42] His inscription[43] dated 1191 - 92 A.D. seems to refer to the death of Bamaya - Nayaka in a fight. Unfortunately the details about this fight are not known. However, this period is known for its political confusion.

Yadava Bhillama, towards the end of his rule, engaged himself with the Hoysalas in a terrible struggle. Ballala II launched an aggressive campign against the Yadavas and captured Hanagal, Rattapalli, etc.[44] In brief, both the major parties were busy in trying to thrust their sway one upon the other.

In this background, if we consider the incident that took place in 1191 - 92 A.D., it becomes a possibility that there were some skirmishes between the feudals on acount of their attempts to gain independence availing the opportunity of political disturbance caused during this period. However, the above fight did not have any adverse effect on the Guttas for we hear that Vikramaditya II was holding sway over Banavasi-nadu in 1192 A.D.[45] His record[46] dated 1213 A.D. gives an interesting account of his family. It states that Vijayamahadevi was his sister. She was given in marriage to Singinripala who is said to have belonged to Santali - mandala. Singinripala is identical with Singi, brother of Jagadeva whose three records are dated in 1165 A.D.[47] Santali - mandala is the same as Santalige - 1000. Then it continues to state that Vikramaditya II had a daughter by name Tuluvaladevi from his queen Pattamahadevi whom he gave away in marriage to Ballala, his nephew whose record is dated in 1195 A.D.[48] Some time later Tuluvaladevi passed away after giving birth to a son called Bamma. In her memory he got constructed tha temple of Tuluvalesvara in the vicinity of the temple of Svayambhu Somanathadeva at Gottagadi on the western bank of the Tungabhadra.

The epigraphs belonging to Vikramaditya II, bearing dates from 1188 to 1213 A.D., do not mention any overlord. On the basis of this it is presumed that he ruled independently during this period.[49] However, there is a reference to transfer of his allegiance to Yadava Singhana in 1211 A.D.[50] Desai doubtfully felt that Vikramaditya II died in about 1225 A.D.[51] This surmise was based probably on the non - availability of his records of a later date at that time. As known at present, however, his last record[52] is dated 1233 A.D. It is of great political significance as it is dated in the year 1155 (apparently of the Saka era) in the reign of Chalukya Chakravarti Soyideva i.e., Somesvara IV (1184 - 1200 A.D.). We know that in 1233 A.D. the Chalukyas were not in effective possession of the Karnataka empiere. Could the evidence of the above inscription be taken to indicate that Somesvara IV was alive in 1233 A.D. and that he continued to enjoy the allegiance to some of the traditional feudatory families? This period really was one of confusion and the erstwhile Chalukya kingdom had been divided between the Yadavas and the Hoysalas fighting against each other for supremacy. Under these circumstances, Vikramaditya II was ruling over Banavasi - nadu[53] without any hindrence. On the basis of the title of *Ujjayinipuravaradhisvara* attributed to Vikramaditya II, Desai thought that he (Vikramaditya II) had extended the boundaries of his ancestral kingdom beyond Guttavolal, and held territories both to the north and to the south of the Tungabhadra.[54] This view cannot be accepted in the absence of more reliable corroborative evidence. Vikramaditya had three sons viz., Gutta III, Joyideva III and Vikramaditya III.[55]

Joyideva III (1235 - 40 A.D.)

He is the son and successor of Vikramaditya II. According to his own copper - plate grant,[56] he was a subordinate of Yadava Singhana II.

Vikramaditya III (1240 - 52 A.D.)

There is a reference to two grants, each made in the year 1242 and 1242 - 43 A.D. respectively during the rule of Yadava Singhana.[57] The details of these two grants are not clear. At this juncture if we presume that these two grants were made during the rule of Vikramaditya III, then the commencement of the rule of Vikramaditya III, the younger brother of Joyideva III, may be fixed to c. 1240 A.D. It is known from a record[52] that he was a *mandalesvara* of Yadava Kannara i.e., Krishna (1246 - 60 A.D.). There is reference to a fight in which Masanabove a hero fought courageously under the orders of the local officers of Hebballi which was a *kumara - vritti* of *mandalesvara* Vikramaditya III.

A badly mutilated inscription[59] from Havanur, the date of which is lost, refers to one Vikramaditya and to a Yadava king (whose name is lost). It appears to record a grant made by a certain Mailaladevi for offerings to the god Bhillesvara and for a charity - water - shed. From the records of this family we know that Mailaladevi was the wife of Vikramaditya III. Therefore, we can identify Mailaladevi as well as Vikramadity of the damaged epigraph from Havanur with their namesakes belonging to the Gutta lineage. Vikramaditya III had four sons viz., Vikramaidtya IV, Gutta IV, Hiriyadeva and Joyideva IV.[60]

Gutta IV (1250 - 70 A.D.)

He succeeded his father. He made some gifts in 1259 A.D. as a subordinate of Kannaradeva (i.e. Krishna 1246 - 60 A.D. of the Yadava family).[61] Further, he offered some gifts in 1262 A.D. during the reign of Yadava Mahadeva (1260 - 70 A.D.). Bamma-gavaunda, son of Rama - gavunda of Bevolal (Obviously Beluvolal), made a gift of land to Sivadeva of Muktikshetra in 1262 A.D. under the orders of Gutta IV who was ruling at Guttavolal. The genealogy of the Gutta chiefs down to Gutta IV is given in this record.[62] *Mahapradhana sarvadhikari* Devarasa of Toragale is said to have made a gift of land and house sites to Sivadeva who is referred to as *Guttanavaya - Rajaguru* under orders from king Mahadevaraya. The gift land was obtained from Mailadevi (evidently Mailaladevi), the mother of the Gutta chiefs Guttarasa, Hiriyadeva and Joyideva, in 1265 A.D.[63] From this account we can presume that Mailaldevi was still alive and living with her three sons. The non - mention of the name of her first son viz., Vikramaditya IV in this connection tempts us to surmise that he had predeceased his brother.

Vikramaditya V (1270 - 80 A.D.)

An inscription[64] from Hirebidri dated 1283 A.D. of the reign of Yadava Ramachandra (1271 - 1311 A.D.) contains a short pedigree of Vikramaditya V. It is stated in this record that grants were made by Padmaladevi wife of *mahamandalesvara* Vikramadityadeva (i.e., Vikramaditya V) son of Joyideva IV for the worship of and offerings to the god Svayambhu Kalinathadeva of Bidirahalli. The manner in which Vikramaditya's valiant character has been described in this record makes it certain that he had died before the date of the record, i.e., 1283 A.D., June 26. It may not be out of place if we refer here to two more records belonging to the Guttas out of which the former, being undaed mentions the rule of *mahamandalesvara* Joyidevarasa,[65] who of course cannot be identified so easily at present as we do not get other details about him. Due to the fragmentary nature of the other inscription[66] the date as well as the name of a Gutta chief and his subordinate who also seems to have been referred to in this inscription are lost.

Thus the Guttas who came into existence in the beginning of the 12th century survived till the end of the 13th century thereby serving for nearly 200 years as powerful chieftains under the Chalukyas, Kalachuris and Yadavas. It is interesting to note in this connection from their records that they never became feudatories of the Hoysalas who, however, are stated to have retained their hold over Banavase-nad in 1276 A.D. which was earlier in the hands of the Guttas. A careful study of some of the records belonging to this dynasty shows that some of the chiefs like Vikramaditya I, Vikramaditya II who wielded power continuously for nearly 55 years and Joyideva II had enjoyed independent status at least for a few years.

We do not hear much about Vikramaditya V except the rhetorical descriptions narrated at the time of offering of some grants to Svayambhu Kalinathadeva of Bidirahalli[67] by his wife Padmaladevi during 1282 A.D. It is well - known that he was no more by the time of this record. This leads us to surmise that he may have not left behind any heirapparent to rule over Guttavolal as his successor. Therefore, it appears that Vikramaditya V was the last chief of this family after whose death the chiefdom of Guttavolal may have passed into the hands of his Yadava suzerain.

The genealogy of the Guttas[68]

Magutta

Gutta I (1105 - 12 A.D.)

Mallideva (1113 - 20) Joyideva (Joma) I (1120 - 55)

Vikramaditya I *m.* Siriyadevi (1155 - 70)

Joyideva (Joma) II (1170 - 90) Gutta II *m.* Padmaladeve

Vikramaditya II Vijayamahadevi *m.* Singideva

m. Pattamahadevi and Sovaladevi

Tulualadevi Gutta III Joyideva III Vikramaditya III

m. Ballala (1235-40) (1240 - 52) *m.* Mailaladevi

Vikramaditya IV Gutta IV (1250-70) Hiriyadeva Joyideva IV

Vikramaditya V (1270 - 80) *m.* Padmaladevi

REFERENCES

1. *SII.*, XVIII, Nos. 112 and 299.
2. *Ibid.*, No. 112.
3. *Ibid.*,
4. Mores : *Kadambakuls*, p. 108.
5. B.R. Gopal : *MDSIK.*, I, p. 69.
6. *SII.*, XVIII, No. 112; Fleet : *DKD.*, p. 581.
7. *EC.*, V (1902), Cn. 912.
8. *Ibid.*, VIII (1904), Sb. 412.
9. B.R. Golpal : *op. cit.*, p. 69.
10. *SII.*, XVIII, Introduction, p. xxvii.
11. *Ibid.*, p. xxiv.
12. *Ibid.*,
13. *Ibid.*, p. xxvii.
14. *Ibid.*, p. xxvi.
15. *Ibid.*, p. xxvi.
16. *Ibid.*, No. 244.
17. *Ibid.*, No. 302.
18. *Ibid.*, No. 293.
19. *Ibid.*, IX, Pt. I, No. 389.
20. *Ibid.*, XVIII, No. 294.
21. *EC.*, VII (1902), Sk. 123.
22. *Ibid.*, Sk. 197.
23. Desai : *MUCK.*, p. 291.
24. *SII.*, XVIII, No. 296.
25. *Ibid.*,
26. *Ibid.*, No. 302.

27. *Ibid.*, No. 297.

28. *Ibid.*, No. 302.

29. *Ibid.*, No. IX, Pt. I, No. 389. It is wrongly stated that 1182 A.D. is the earliest known date of Vikramaditya II instead of 1181 A.D. according to this epigraph. Cf. *Ibid.*, XVIII, Introduction, p. xx.

30. *SII.*, XVIII, Introduction, p. xx.

31. *Ibid.*, IX, Pt. I, No. 389.

32. *Ibid.*, XVIII, Nos. 190 and 192.

33. *Ibid.*, No. 191.

34. *Ibid.*, Nos. 191 - 92. Desai is of the opinion that Vikramaditya II was an adopted son of Joyideva II. Desai : *op. cit.*, p. 292.

35. *SII.*, XVIII, Nos. 244 and 299.

36. *Ibid.*, No. 192.

37. *Ibid.*, No. 296.

38. *Ibid.*, No. 163.

39. *Ibid.*, No. 368; *Ibid.*, Introduction, p. xxii.

40. *Ibid.*, No. 296; Desai wrongly calls Dasiraja as Basiraja. Cf. Desai : *op. cit*, p. 294.

41. *SII.*, XVIII, No. 295.

42. *Ibid.*, No. 297.

43. *Ibid.*, No. 298.

44. *The Struggle for Empire*, p. 186.

45. *SII.*, XVIII, No. 299.

46. *Ibid.*, No. 300.

47. *EC.*, VIII (1904), Sa. 112 - 14.

48. *SII.*, IX, Pt. I, No. 390.

49. Fleet : *op. cit.*, p. 579.

50. *The Struggle for Empire*, p. 188.

51. Desai : *op. cit.*, p. 296.

52. *SII.*, XVIII, o. 301.

53. *Ibid.*,
54. Desai : *op. cit.*, p. 293.
55. *SII.*, XVIII, No. 244.
56. *BBRAS.*, XV, p. 384.
57. *SII.*, XVIII, Nos. 246 and 244.
58. *Ibid.*, No. 231.
59. *Ibid.*, No. 244.
60. *Ibid.*, No. 244.
61. *Ibid.*,
62. *Ibid.*, No. 246.
63. *Ibid.*, No. 247.
64. *Ibid.*, XX, No. 221.
65. *Ibid.*, XVIII, No. 304.
66. *Ibid.*, No. 243.
67. *Ibid.*, No. 221.
68. Genealogy as given in *Ibid.*, Introduction, p. xxi.

BIBLIOGRAPHY

Epigraphical Publications :

Annual Reports on Indian Epigraphy

Annual Reports on South Indian Epigraphy

Coorg Inscriptions

Corpus Inscriptionum Indicarum

Epigraphic Carnatica

Epigraphic Indica

Hyderabad Archaeological Series

Inscriptions from Madras Presidency

Karnatak Inscriptions

Mysore Archaeological Reports

Mysore Inscriptions

Mysore and Coorg From Inscriptions.

Select Inscriptions

South Indian Inscriptions

Books :

Balambal, V., 1978

Feudatories of South India Chugh Publication, Allahabad

Coelho, 1950

The Hoysalavamsa, Indian Historical Research Institute, St., Xavier's College, Bombay.

Desai, Dinakara, 1951

Mahamandalesvaras under the Chalukyas of Kalyani, Indian Historical research Institute, St. Xavier's College, Bombay.

Desai, P.B., and others 1970

A History of Karnataka Kannada Research Institute, Karnatak University, Dharwar.

Derrett, D.M., 1957

The Hoysalas, Oxford University Press, Madras.

Diwakar, R.R., 1968

Karnataka Through the Ages, Government of Mysore, Bangalore.

Gopal, B.R., 1981

The Chalukyas of Kalyana and the Kalachuris, Prasaranga, Karnatak University, Dharwar.

Gopal, B.R., 1982

Minor Dynasties of South India : Karnataka - Volume I, New Era Publications, Madras.

Govindasamy, M.S., 1965

The Role of Feudatories in Pallava History, Annamalai University Annamalainagar.

Krishnamurthy, M.S., 1980

The Nolambas, Prasaranga, University of Mysore, Mysore.

Krishnaswamy Aiyangar, S., 1923

Some Contributions of South India to Indian Culture, University of Calcutta, Calcutta.

Majumdar, R.C., 1954

The Classical Age, Bharatiya Vidya Bhavana's History and Culture of the Indian People Volume III, Bombay.

Majumdar, R.C., 1955

The Age of Imperial Kanauj, Bharatiya Vidya Bhavan's History and Culture of the Indian People, volume IV, Bombay.

Majumdar, R.C., 1966

The Struggle for Empire, Bharatiya Vidya Bhavan's History and Culture of the Indian People Volume V, Bombay.

Moraes, G., 1931

Kadambakula, Indian Historical Research Institute, St. Xavier's College, Bombay.

Narasimha Murthy, A.V., 1971

The Sevunas of Devagiri, Rao and Raghavan, Mysore.

Narasimha Murthy, A.V., 1975

Coins of Karnataka, Geetha Book House, Mysore.

Nilakanthasastry, K.A., 1966

History of South India (Third Edition), Oxford University Press, Madras.

Pathak, K.B., 1898

Kavirajamarga, Bangalore.

Ramesh, K.V., 1970

A History of South Kanara, Karnatak University, Dharwad.

Ritti, S.H., 1973

The Sevunas, Department of Ancient Indian History and Epigraphy, Karnatak University, Dharwar.

Saletore, B.A., 1936

"History of Tuluva" in *Ancient Karnataka,* Volume I, Oriental Book Agency, Poona.

Sampath, M.D., 1980

Chittoor Through the Ages, B.R. Publishing Corporation, Delhi.

Sewell, R., 1932

The Historical Inscriptions of Southern India, University of Madras, Madras. (Sewell's List).

Srinivasan, C.R., 1979

Kanchipuram through the Ages, Ages Kala Prakashan, Delhi.

Vaidya, C.V., 1926

History of Mediaeval Hindu India, Volume III, Poona.

Vasantaraj, M.D., 1971

Sanmatisrivihara (Kannada), Jaihind Press, Mysore.

Felicitation Volumes :

Gopal, B.R., 1973

"Gudnapur inscription of Kadamba Ravivarma" in *Srikanthika,* Dr. S. Srikantha Sastri Felicitation Volume, Geetha book House, Mysore p. 61 ff.

Krishnan, K.G., 1971

"Rattapadi Seven and a half lakhs" in *Studies in Indiun History and Culture,* Prof. P.B. Desai Felicitation Volume, Dharwar, pp. 270 - 71.

Journals :

Altekar, A.S., 1935

"The Silaharas of Western India" in *Indian Culture* Volume II, Calcutta, pp. 393 ff.

Desai, P.B., 1953

"The Banas of Khandavamandala" in the *Journal of Oriental Research* Volume XXI, Kuppuswamy Sastri Research Institute, Madras, p. 98 ff.

Desai, P.B., 1958

"A New Kadamba Family" in the *Indian Historical Quarterly,* Volume XXXIV, Calcutta, pp. 167 ff.

Fleet, J.F., 1973

"Notes on Inscriptions at Gaddak, in the Dambal Taluka of Dharwad District" in *Indian Antiquary,* Volume II, Education society's Press,. Bombay, p. 296 ff.

Fleet, J.F., 1975

"A series of Sanskrit and old Canarese Inscriptions Relating to the Ratta Chieftains of Saundatti and Belgaum" in the *Journal of the Bombay Branch of the Royal Asiatic Society*, Volume X, Society's Library, Bombay, pp. 167 ff.

Fleet, J.F., 1882

'Sanskrit and Old Canarese Inscriptions" in *Indian Antiquary*, Volume XI, Education Society's Press, Bombay, 1244 ff.

Fleet, J.F., 1883

"A copper - plate grant of the Devagiri - Yadava king of Singhana II" in the *Journal of the Bombay Branch of the Royal Asiatic Society*, Volume XV, Society's Library, Bombay, pp. 383 ff.

Fleet, J.F., 1884

"Five Copper plate grants of the Western Chalukya dynasty, from the Kurnul District" in the *Journal of the Bombay Branch of the Royal Asiatic Society*, Volume XVI, Society's Library, Bombay, p. 223 ff.

Fleet, J.F., 1890

"Sanskrit and old Kanarese inscriptions" in *Indian Antiquary*, Volume, XIX, Education Society's Press, Bombay, p. 242 ff.

Fleet, J.F., 1900

"Notes on Indian History and geography" in *Indian Antiquary*, Volume XXIX, Education Society's Press, Bombay, p. 280.

Fleet, J.F., 1903

"Notes on Indian History and Geography" in *Indian Antiquary*, Volume XXXII, Education Society's Press, Bombay, p. 213 ff.

Foulkes, T., 1884

"Grant of the Bana king Vikramaditya II" in *Indian Antiquary*, Volume XIII, Education Society's Press, Bombay, p. 6 ff.

Mahalingam T.V., 1952

"Banas in South Indian History" in the *Journal of Indian History*, Volume XXIX, University of Travacore, Triveandrum, p. 281.

Nagaraja Rao, H.M., 1973

"Kongalvas" in *Manavika Karnataka* (Kannada), Volume III, No. 2, University of Mysore, Mysore, p. 7 ff.

Narasimha Murthy, P.N., 1980

"Inscriptions of Lokanathadevarasa" in the *Journal of the Epigraphical Society of India*, Volume VII, Epigraphical Society of India, Dharwar, p. 112 ff.

Pathak, K.B., 1885

"An old Kanarese inscription at Terdal" in *Indian Antiquary*, Volume XIV, Education Society's Press, Bombay, p. 14 ff.

Ramachandran, T.N., 1931

"The Banas" in the *Journal of Oriental Research*, Volume V, Oriental Research Institute, Madras, p. 299 ff.

Ramesh, K.V. and Madhav, N. Katti, 1966 – 67

"The Origion and the Early History of the Santaras of Santalige - 1000" in the *Quarterly Journal of the Mythic Society*, Volume LVII, Mythic Society, Bangalore, pp. 25 ff.

Rice, B.L., 1886

"Mudayanur Plates of Saka 261 of the Bana king Malladeva - Nandivarman" in *Indian Antiquary*, Volume XV, Education Society's Press, Bombay, p. 172 ff.

Gazetteers :

Abhisankar, K., 1975

Shimoga District Gazetteer, Government of Karnataka, Bangalore, pp. 126 - 28

Bhandarakar, R.G., 1895

"Early History of the Dekkan" on *Bombay Gazetteer volume* I, Part II, Bombay Government, Bombay.

Fleet, J.F., 1896

"Dynasties of Kanarese Districts" in *Bombay Gazetteer*, volume I, Part II, Bombay Government, Bombay.

Fleet, J.F., 1896

"Great Feudatory Families" in *Bombay Gazetteer*, Volume I, Part II, Bombay Government, Bombay.

Hayavadena, Rao, C. 1930

Mysore Gazetteer (New edition) Volume II, Part II, Government of Mysore, Bangalore, p. 859.

Hayavadena, Rao, C. 1883

"Kanara" in *Bombay Gazetteer* Volume XV, Part II, Bombay Government, Bombay.

Research Report :

Hiriyanniah, K.N., 1964 – 66

Report on *Minor Dynasties of Karnataka* (1000 - 1300 A.D.) submitted to the University of Mysore, Mysore.

INDEX